The Battle for
LONDON

The Battle for
LONDON

Stephen Porter &
Simon Marsh

AMBERLEY

First published 2010

Amberley Publishing
Cirencester Road, Chalford,
Stroud, Gloucestershire, GL6 8PE

www.amberleybooks.com

British Library Cataloguing in Publication Data.
A catalogue record for this book is available from the British Library.

ISBN 978 1 84868 847 6

Typesetting and origination by Fonthill.
Printed in Great Britain

Contents

Acknowledgements

We are very grateful to Malcolm Wanklyn and Richard Holmes for reading the manuscript and making helpful comments, and to John Tincey, Keith Roberts and Glenn Foard for discussions about the Edgehill part of the campaign and the deployment of seventeenth-century armies. James Wisdom, Val Bott, Jonathan Smith, Peter Norton, Janet McNamara, Sam Hearn and Howard Simmons of the Brentford and Turnham Green battlefield interpretation project helped to raise awareness in this important phase of the Civil War. We have conducted annual walks of the two battlefields for several years on behalf of the Battlefields Trust and have received helpful information and pertinent questions from those who have attended, for which we are also grateful. Jonathan Reeve of Amberley has provided much support during the publication process. Over a far longer period, our families have given boundless help and encouragement in what has been a lengthier project than either of us anticipated.

1

The Crown & the Capital

When contemporaries came to reflect on the outcome of the civil wars in the 1640s, they accepted that London's role had been of crucial importance. As the national capital and by far the largest city and seaport, it had resources of manpower, money, arms and equipment unmatched by any other city or region. London remained aligned with parliament throughout the period, but its allegiance was not predetermined and the city had to be secured, both politically and militarily. This was achieved at the outset, initially when parliament's supporters in the City secured control of its administration through a reversal of political fortunes at Guildhall, and subsequently by halting the king's army that was intent on military capture, rather than a negotiated settlement.

By the middle of the seventeenth century, London had a population of roughly 400,000 and was continuing to grow prodigiously. Like all early modern cities, its death rate exceeded the birth rate, and its growth was fuelled by migration from the provinces and, to a much lesser extent, from abroad. From the late sixteenth century successive governments had been concerned that it was draining wealth and vitality from the rest of the country and tried to check its seemingly inexorable expansion. From 1580 they imposed controls on building, but none of them were successful. Neither government policy nor the high death rates, exacerbated by severe plague epidemics in 1603, 1625 and 1636, deterred those who were drawn to the capital by the economic opportunities which it offered.[1]

On the north bank of the Thames, between the Tower and the Temple, was the City, the area of over a hundred parishes that was the home of the mercantile and business community, governed by the corporation. Along the river downstream from London Bridge were the many wharves that handled overseas trade, as well as the coastal vessels which brought in food and the colliers that carried coal from north-east England. But the built-up area grew ever outwards from this historic core and by the middle of the seventeenth century the population of the City was outnumbered by that of the suburbs. To the west, a ribbon of development that included aristocratic mansions and bishops' palaces led to Westminster, which contained the principal royal palace, the court and the meeting place of parliament, with all the trappings of government and the courts of law. The development of the Covent Garden district in the 1630s marked the beginning of the West End, which was to become the focus for the aristocracy and gentry. Around the northern and eastern fringes of the City were steadily growing suburbs, less prosperous and salubrious than the central parishes, and, it was feared, with less effective local government. On the south bank, across the only bridge, was the substantial but somewhat disreputable suburb of Southwark, which contained inns catering for travellers coming to the city from the south, but also alehouses and brothels, theatres and the bear-baiting arena. These disparate elements combined to form a metropolis that was economically vigorous, with an important manufacturing sector, and handling roughly 80 per cent of the country's overseas trade.

London was also a significant military resource, through its militia soldiers, or trained bands, who were householders, and two military societies of citizens, one at the Artillery Garden outside Bishopsgate and the other at St Martin's-in-the-Fields. In 1614 the City's trained bands were limited to 6,000 soldiers. The two societies were described by a contemporary as 'great nurseries or academies of military discipline' and they provided well-trained officers for the trained bands. In 1639 the king recommended Philip Skippon to the Society of the Artillery Garden and it appointed him as its Captain-Leader. Skippon was an experienced professional soldier who had served on the continent for many years, under Sir Horace Vere and in the Dutch armies, and had recently returned to England.[2] He was a competent and popular officer, and events were to show that, from the king's point of view, this was an unfortunate recommendation.

Throughout the growing crisis that followed the calling of the Long Parliament in 1640, Londoners had been restive. They were worried by the economic downturn and the adverse effects of the court's policies, including the two Bishops' Wars against the Scots, in 1639 and 1640, and unhappy with the religious changes introduced during William Laud's time as Archbishop of Canterbury, since 1633. Their anger and frustration led many thousands of them to subscribe to petitions pleading for change and it boiled over from time to time into large demonstrations. Tens of thousands of people took part, especially at moments of heightened tension, such as May Day 1641, during the trial of the Earl of Strafford, formerly the king's leading, and immensely unpopular, minister. Some saw these as orderly and organized protests by a sober citizenry and others regarded them as the clamours of an uncontrollable mob.[3]

Sections of the mercantile élite participating in the government of the City had also become disenchanted with the court's actions during the period of the personal rule since 1629, during which Charles I had ruled through the Privy Council, without calling parliament. They were especially offended by its attacks on their management of the Londonderry plantation and sales of crown lands; its support for trades separating from the existing livery companies to create their own organizations; the creation, in 1636, of the Corporation of the Suburbs, a potential rival administration; the granting of exemptions for new buildings as a way of raising money, which undermined the avowed policy of restricting the city's growth; and policies which threatened the economic interests of some of them as privileged concessionaires of patents and licences.[4]

On the other hand, strong financial ties bound the wealthy citizens to the crown, and they were apprehensive of the effects of political breakdown and popular disorders. And the court contented itself with the belief that the disturbances involved 'the meaner sort of people and that the affections of the better and main part of the City' favoured the king. The criticisms of his policies could thus be blamed on 'factious persons'. Such complacent views were reinforced by the inability of the puritan element in the City to wrest control from its established, pro-royalist, rulers who held the reins of power at Guildhall. Most members of the Court of Aldermen, the City's executive body, were loyal to the king. The Court was a self-perpetuating oligarchy of twenty-four members, who served as lord mayor in rotation, according to seniority. Common Council, the legislative body, was much larger, with 237 members by 1640, but could not take the initiative in City affairs because it was called and dissolved by the lord mayor, and its agenda was provided by the aldermen, who also exercised the right of veto over its proceedings. The third body in the City's government was the Court of Common Hall, which acted only in an electoral capacity, with the right to vote restricted to the 4,000 or so freemen of the City.[5]

Despite the control of the City's government by pro-royalists, at the elections to the Long Parliament in October 1640 four Members were returned who were opposed to the court, which provided a significant indication of where the City's sympathies lay. And the establishment's candidates were challenged at the election of the lord mayor in September 1640 and that for the two sheriffs in the following summer (which was settled only with the arbitration of the House of Lords). But in neither case were the popular candidates returned and in September 1641 Alderman Richard Gurney was elected lord mayor, despite opposition from within Common Hall. Gurney was a committed royalist and at that stage it seemed that the challenge from those who were sympathetic to the policies that John Pym, John Hampden and their supporters were pursuing in the Commons had been defeated.[6]

The alliance of City and court was conspicuously displayed in the entertainment laid on for the king when he entered London on his return from Scotland on 25 November 1641. The City fathers agreed to provide 'as great shew of glory as at any time heretofore hath been performed to any prince' and they certainly welcomed him in an extravagant fashion, providing a great feast, with the conduits flowing with wine.[7] The king responded by promising some concessions to ease their concerns on issues which had antagonized them over the previous decade, such as the Londonderry plantation. He graciously knighted Gurney and the Recorder, Thomas Gardiner, and all seemed well.

Indeed, continued loyalty to the king in the City was matched by a wider growth in support for his cause. At the opening of the Long Parliament, in November 1640, almost the entire political nation had been opposed to the policies followed during the eleven years of the personal rule. But the fall and execution of Strafford, the imprisonment of Archbishop Laud, and the success of Pym and his group in tackling the grievances of the 1630s satisfied many members of both Houses, who were wary of further encroachment on the royal prerogative. A growing opinion that reform had gone far enough and that allegiance was owed firstly to the king produced a gradual shift in his favour, both within parliament and in the country generally.

Yet this did not bring a settlement nearer; the mutual mistrust which existed between the king and his opponents remained a stumbling block preventing a satisfactory agreement. That suspicion might have continued simmering, without provoking a crisis, but for the eruption of a major, widespread and bloody rebellion in Ireland towards the end of October 1641. News of the outbreak reached London at the beginning of November and reports on its progress were accompanied by lurid accounts of horrible brutalities committed by the rebels. Clearly, an army had to be assembled urgently to suppress the revolt, but could the king be trusted not to use it first to restore his position in England? Many thought not and the problem of Ireland made the possibility of a political solution even more remote and gaining control of London an urgent issue for the king's opponents in parliament.

During the weeks following the Guildhall feast, a major shift in the City's political make-up took place. On 21 December the elections to Common Council saw a further challenge to the City's rulers, and this one was successful. Its old leadership was defeated and many new men were elected, and they acted quickly to alter the balance of power. The elections were held against the background of growing popular agitation, creating a quite different mood from that which the king had experienced towards the end of November. The last few weeks of the year were marked by frequent demonstrations, involving thousands of Londoners, who swarmed around Whitehall Palace, intimidating those who they regarded as politically repugnant and clashing violently with the king's supporters.[8]

They were anxious about the safety of parliament, with Whitehall pestered by groups of royalist officers, in London to demand their pay arrears, and the threat from the Tower. The fortress had a dominating presence at the east end of the city and a visitor to London in 1600 had no doubt that one of its functions was to intimidate the citizens, noting that on the top of the White Tower, 'there are 16 cannon which are trained upon the City'.[9] An inventory of 1635 recorded on that tower 'Brasse ordnance mounted uppon field carriages'; these were fourteen demi-culverins – heavy guns firing shot of between nine and twelve pounds – and one saker, a much lighter piece.[10] Work carried out on the Tower during the 1630s, under the direction of Inigo Jones, included the strengthening of the roof of the White Tower so that up to twenty-one pieces could be mounted there. When Lord Cottington was appointed Constable of the Tower in May 1640 he set about strengthening its defences, bringing in a garrison of 200 men and building up stocks of ammunition and provisions. He also had the guns trained on the City. Much of it was within range of these demi-culverins and the cannon on the outer works, so it was small wonder that, in the words of the Royalist statesman and historian Edward Hyde, later Earl of Clarendon, the Tower 'was looked upon as a bridle upon the city'.[11]

The first Army Plot in the spring of 1641 highlighted the danger of it being seized in a coup, by a handful of conspirators with a modest force of 100 men. As well as taking control of the fortress and its magazine, the plotters would have released the Earl of Strafford, now under sentence of death following an Act of Attainder passed by parliament. They had gone about their arrangements in a clumsy way, making hardly any effort to disguise their intentions, and had been thwarted by the stark refusal of the Lieutenant of the Tower, Sir William Balfour, to admit them. But the failed plot showed how real the danger of a royalist coup was, and so helped to seal Strafford's fate. He was executed on 12 May on Tower Hill, before an enormous crowd.

In December attention was again focused on the Tower, when the king removed Balfour from his post and attempted to install Thomas Lunsford, whose conduct and reputation made him manifestly unsuitable for such a sensitive position. This was enough to provoke howls of protest, led by the City and the two Houses of Parliament, who perceived it as a prelude to a coup by the royalists. The king gave way to their urgent objections and appointed instead the more acceptable Sir John Byron as Lieutenant, compensating Lunsford with a knighthood.[12]

The appointment of Lunsford had been a serious mistake, increasing the citizens' fears of an attack on the city by the king's ill-disciplined supporters. In this atmosphere of growing crisis the king began the process of impeaching five Members of Parliament and one peer, Lord Mandeville, on a charge of treason. On 4 January he made a catastrophic error of political judgement by going to the House of Commons with a body of about 400 armed men to attempt to arrest the five members, and actually entered the chamber hoping to apprehend them. The five, who included Pym and Hampden, had already made a well-timed withdrawal by water to the City and they then skilfully exploited the propaganda opportunity which the king had handed them. When Charles went to Guildhall on the following day to demand that they should be handed over, he met with another rebuff, and experienced at first hand the animosity of the Londoners, who lined the streets and heckled him as he passed. This was a far cry from the feasting and mutual admiration of late November and removed any lingering doubts which he may have had about the citizens' resentment.

On the day that the king went to the Commons, the new Common Council took the unprecedented step of creating a Committee of Safety, with a membership predominantly parliamentarian in sympathy. Then, on the night of 6 January, a panic swept the City, caused by an urgent rumour that royalist soldiers were on their way, to attack the City and set it on fire. To deal with this emergency, and to reassure the citizens, the trained bands were called out, but without the lord mayor's authority, as was required. The impact of that dreadful night, with the citizens so fearful of being attacked, was so much to the advantage of the pro-parliamentarian elements in the City's government that the royalists later claimed that the false alarm had been a deliberate ploy. This was denied, but in its aftermath the opportunity was taken to obtain control of the trained bands.[13]

When the Privy Council authorized the lord mayor to discover who had in fact called out the trained bands on that night, parliament immediately and decisively intervened, declaring the king's Commissions of Lieutenancy to be illegal, which effectively nullified the lord mayor's authority over the militia. Skippon, who had been made a freeman only four days earlier, was appointed its commander as Sergeant Major General, a post which, according to Hyde, was 'never before heard of', and, crucially, he was not to be subject to the lord mayor, but to a majority of the lord mayor, aldermen and Common Council.[14]

The crisis deepened and the king's nerve cracked first. On 10 January he abruptly left Whitehall, unable to face up to the political effects of his failed coup and fearful for the safety of his family because of the demonstrations around Whitehall Palace. The next day, the five members took boat in the City and returned in triumph to Westminster, where they were received by a parade of the City trained bands under Skippon.

Those dramatic days were marked not only by the king's futile attempt to improve his political position, but also by further changes in the City's government, which saw the authority of the lord mayor severely curtailed. On 13 January the House of Commons gave the Committee of Safety the right to order the lord mayor to call the Common Council meetings and, on 22 January, it removed control over the trained bands and entrusted it to that committee, henceforth known as the Militia Committee. Thus, the City's actions, political and military, could be driven by the Committee's members, not by the lord mayor and aldermen, and they could act in conjunction with the elements in parliament hostile to the court. Some royalist aldermen reacted to this undermining of the previous arrangements by petitioning the House of Lords in protest, on 16 February. When the petition, which had 351 signatures, including those of 'divers of the very wealthy citizens', was seen by the Commons, it responded by treating it as a potential counter-revolutionary move and ordered that two of the aldermen who were deemed to be its authors should be imprisoned.[15]

By that time the position of the new administration of the City had been further secured when control of the Tower of London was obtained. Despite the king's climb-down over Lunsford, a royalist remained in command of the fortress, despite an attempt to oust him. On 12 January the Commons ordered the trained bands under Skippon's command to keep guard around the Tower, effectively blockading it. But this was a slow method of testing Byron's resolve and Skippon hoped to take advantage of his temporary absence, when he answered a summons by the House of Lords, by bringing a force of up to 500 men to the Tower 'very privately when it was dark'.

His ploy to get them inside failed, but Byron's position was now so difficult that he pleaded with the king to be released 'from the vexation and agony of that place', and on 11 February Charles agreed to the appointment of Sir John Conyers as his replacement.[16] Conyers had been the Commons' choice as Lieutenant when it campaigned against Lunsford, and was seen by Pym and those around him as a safe pair of hands.

Control of the Tower gave parliament its military resources. Byron claimed that they were now small and declining, for almost all of the arms had been sent to the armies deployed against the Scots, and more recently to Ireland, the gunpowder supply was being reduced and would be further diminished to supply the navy in the spring.[17] No doubt his assessment was partly motivated by a wish to play down the scale of the loss to the king's cause following his departure from the Tower. But the citizens could not know how many arms it contained and they were relieved of the anxiety engendered by its continued occupation by potentially hostile forces. The merchant community, in particular, was reassured, which was essential, for:

> the Tower of London is the great Magazine of the Kingdom, and the Place where the Bullion of the Kingdom is kept and coined; and, if a Person be there, in whom they may not confide, it would put a Stop to Trade.[18]

Within less than two months, London had been secured for parliament, with very little bloodshed.

Parliament also set about enhancing the military value of the London militia. On 12 February an Ordinance increased its size, from 6,000 to 8,000 men in 40 companies, which required an increase in the number of regiments, from four to six, each commanded by a colonel, with a total of thirty-four captains. Of the six colonels appointed, four – Isaac Pennington, Thomas Atkins, John Towse and John Warner – were to emerge as political radicals, only Thomas Adams became a moderate, or political presbyterian, while Sir John Wollaston has been described as a 'trimmer'.[19] On 4 April the London Militia Ordinance allowed the trained bands to operate beyond London, at parliament's direction, and they were brought under a single command when Skippon's authority was extended to those of Westminster, Southwark and the suburbs. With parliament's consent, on 10 May the first general muster of the newly reorganized trained bands took place in Finsbury Fields, as a grand and expensively staged event, doubtless to impress royalist onlookers and to reassure parliament's anxious supporters.[20]

The citizens' fears of a royalist coup in the City receded, for although the royalist lord mayor remained in office, he had been politically emasculated. His final attempt to revive his authority came with the king's order to issue his Commission of Array, which instructed the Lords Lieutenant to raise and train troops (see page 17). In London this right had already been lost in the changes made in January. Nevertheless, Gurney courageously acted as the king had instructed him and proclaimed the Commission in London on 10 June, thereby giving parliament a pretext for his impeachment. Some Common Councilmen took the opportunity to present two petitions drawing attention to other actions of his which they regarded as obstructive, and a number of them testified at his trial. On 12 August he was found guilty and the House of Lords ordered that he should be imprisoned in the Tower, where he died in 1647.[21] It also directed that he be removed from office and a replacement chosen.

Gurney's successor was Isaac Pennington, even though five aldermen were senior to him. He was blamed by the royalists for organizing the Root and Branch petition from the City to parliament calling for radical overhaul of the church, was one of the City's Members of Parliament, a member of the Militia Committee and colonel of a regiment of the trained bands. A key figure in the political transformation at Guildhall, he served the balance of the term of office for the mayoral year 1641–2 and also the full year following. And so the overthrow of the established order in the City's government had been completed.

Parliament had been able to consolidate its control of London during the winter and spring of 1642, without direct interference from the king. He did not return to his capital, or attempt to gather military support in south-east England. After he left Whitehall on 10 January he first travelled to Hampton Court, before moving to what he perceived to be the greater security of Windsor Castle. The shock of the events in early January – his failed coup against parliament, the unrest in the City, the reduced size of his retinue and its inability to provide his accustomed comforts ('at Windsor none of the bedding [was] made ready') – must have sapped his confidence, albeit briefly.[22]

From Windsor the king reopened discussions with parliament on control of the armed forces. While this was played out against the backdrop of the revolt in Ireland and the need for an English army to restore order there, a more fundamental principle was at stake for Charles – his God-given kingly rights and the royal prerogative. By the beginning of February he had concluded that no deal could be struck which maintained those privileges and decided to send the queen and Princess Mary to Holland, ostensibly for Mary to join her husband, the Prince of Orange, but also for the queen to raise money, arms and political support.

On 23 February the queen took leave of her husband at Dover and sailed for Holland; he then returned to Greenwich. By now he was planning to go to York as a 'place of receipt and conveniency for those who were willing to attend him'.[23] As he began his journey north, parliament continued to press him to agree to its control of the defence of the kingdom, but Charles remained resolute in his opposition. Following the king's rejection of its submission at Theobalds on 1 March, parliament passed the legislation allowing it to control the military power of the state as an ordinance, rather than an act, negating the need for the royal assent. The Militia Ordinance, passed by both

Houses on 5 March, gave parliament legal control over the county trained bands, magazines, fortifications – including the Tower of London – and the navy, and in effect marked its break with the king. Even so, this was not yet regarded as irrevocable and the king continued to be urged by representatives of the House of Lords to accept parliamentary control, as he continued his journey north through Newmarket on 9 March, though to no effect.[24]

Travelling via Cambridge and Huntingdon, the king reached York on 19 March, with only thirty-nine gentlemen and seventeen guards but, according to Hyde, 'found his reception there to be equal to his expectation, the gentry, and men of ability of that great and populous county, some very few excepted, expressing great alacrity for his majesty's being with them, and no less sense of the insolent proceedings of the Parliament'.[25] But support for the crown in Yorkshire was not as universal as Hyde implied. Ferdinando Lord Fairfax and his son Sir Thomas, magnates of the West Riding, were staunch supporters of parliament, as were the citizens of the cloth-making towns.

The king attempted to strengthen his position by taking control of the military supplies in the north. By the middle of April arms and ammunition had been taken to the Tower of London from Berwick-upon-Tweed, where they were no longer needed, now that the war with Scotland was at an end. The larger stock at Hull was the next objective. These could be diverted to Ireland, by sending them first to the Tower. At least that was the argument which parliament deployed when it made this point to the king and requested his permission to transfer them there. But its main aim was to deny him the magazine there and take control of the largest stock of arms remaining in England at the time because, by February 1642, the Tower had shipped almost all its stores of muskets, pikes, pistols, carbines and swords to Ireland and some supply warrants for such weapons remained outstanding.[26] His refusal was greeted with alarm by the Commons, but they need not have worried. When the king arrived at Hull with a few hundred armed men on 23 April he was refused admission by the governor, Sir John Hotham. Mightily relieved at Hotham's firm stand, parliament proceeded to transfer many of the munitions to London, without the king's agreement, entrusting some of the arms to the Militia Committee for storage at the Guildhall, and in Leadenhall, Blackwell Hall and the halls of the apothecaries' and leathersellers' companies. The lord mayor also asked the livery companies to report the contents of their own armouries.[27]

The events at Hull showed that both sides already attached great importance to securing military resources, even though there was no armed conflict and no armies had yet been enlisted. A political solution to the crisis was impossible while the king rejected offers to negotiate and an impasse seemed to have been reached. As the political process faltered, the rival factions began to prepare for the military alternative and in the summer of 1642 the country steadily drifted towards civil war.

2

Raising the Armies

Charles's failure to curb the opposition in parliament by political means encouraged him to mount a military challenge. This was possible because of the growth of a royalist party, willing to wage war for the king. Parliament had to respond, and so both sides gradually began to recruit troops. They could be confident of raising an army; enough trained men were available, as were willing recruits who were prepared to fight, out of a sense of duty, to uphold their principles, or for the prospect of pay and provisions. The two Bishops' Wars, in 1639 and 1640, had provided recent experiences of the process for raising armies and the lessons that could be drawn.

The militia were the trained forces for the defence of the realm. Their organization had been revitalized during the early years of Charles I's reign, with the appointment of experienced soldiers to oversee their training, and in some areas gentlemen and yeomen were organized for military training in 'freeholder bands'. There were, too, those soldiers who had served in the continental wars and had returned, or could be recalled when the political crisis seemed likely to develop into war. The Tudors had employed mercenaries from abroad when necessary, to provide a core of professional soldiers. If the forces available were inadequate, men could be forcibly impressed for the armies, although such recruits were untrained, would, understandably, have lower morale and a greater tendency to desert than those who had agreed or volunteered to serve.

These sources of men had been tapped under Elizabeth and the early Stuarts. Between 1585 and 1602 the government impressed at least 105,810 men in England and Wales for service overseas. And in the 1620s roughly 50,000 were enlisted for the armies raised to pursue the Duke of Buckingham's foreign policy and other campaigns on the continent. Far fewer men were needed for such purposes during the 1630s, although the government was prepared to listen to requests by other states to raise levies in Britain.[1]

In 1638 England and Wales had almost 100,000 men trained in arms, who could be drawn upon to serve the crown.[2] Some of them were called out for the first of Charles I's domestic wars, the First Bishops' War in 1639. The king hoped that the raising of an army would be enough to cow the recalcitrant Scots into submission, but the size and quality of his forces were matched by the Scots and he did not achieve his objective. In the following year the second campaign against them required the raising of another army, which was outmanoeuvred by the Scots and defeated in a skirmish at Newburn. The Scots then occupied Newcastle-upon-Tyne.

In both wars the crown managed to raise an army of between 15,000 and 20,000 men. The militia provided a disappointing and ill-disciplined force, largely because the government allowed the practice of substitution, whereby a trained man could avoid serving by paying for an untrained man to go to the army in his place. In the Second Bishops' War the crown also used the expedient of Commissions of Array. The Privy Council was satisfied that the impressment of men on this authority was justified by a statute of Henry IV's reign, which had been accepted at the time for use if the country was threatened by invasion, which could be construed as being the case in 1640.

The king also negotiated for foreign troops. In 1639 he pursued negotiations for a force of 6,000 foot and 400 horse from the Spanish Army of Flanders, to be shipped to Scotland to capture Edinburgh and defeat the Covenanters' army. The political damage to the king of employing Catholic troops, and Spanish troops at that, to enforce his church policy can only be guessed at, for the plans were abandoned. In 1640 he investigated the possibility of using a force of a similar size to be provided by the Danish government. Had Charles defaulted on the payment for that army, the Orkney Islands would have passed to the Danish crown.[3] That scheme, too, come to nothing, but the king fostered similar plans to bring over foreign armies to fight for him against his own subjects throughout the civil wars.

The experience of the Bishops' Wars no doubt influenced the way in which the king's entourage approached the problem of raising an army in 1642. But only after his rebuff by Sir John Hotham at Hull, on 22 April, did the king begin to convert the potential support he had into a military force. This was possible because of the growing numbers of the nobility and gentry that had come to York. But the king's actions at this stage were partly a defensive response to Hotham's forces in Hull, which were also increasing. Hyde later wrote that Hotham was 'more likely to be able to take York, than his majesty to recover Hull'.[4]

The king issued individual commissions to local gentry to either take control of the trained band units in the county or begin to raise soldiers independently. By mid-May he had formed a troop of horse consisting of gentlemen volunteers, known as the Prince of Wales's troop or, more commonly, the Prince's troop, with Sir Thomas Byron as its captain. At the same time he took Sir Robert Strickland's regiment of the Yorkshire trained bands, consisting of about 575 men, to guard his person. These soldiers were paid weekly at his own expense.[5]

Commissions to command other Yorkshire trained band regiments of foot were also issued in May. That to Sir Henry Slingsby for York's trained band was dated 11 May.[6] But the funding for those regiments does not seem to have been forthcoming from the royal purse until early to mid-July, when the regiments of Sir Henry Belasyse, Sir Henry Griffiths and Sir Thomas Metham (estimated at 400, 575 and 600 men respectively) began to receive payments from the king.[7] It is unclear whether Slingsby received royal pay for his regiment at this time.

The appointment by the king of loyal gentry to command the trained band regiments seems to have angered the rank and file; Slingsby's attempts to execute an order to provide guards for the king's residence in York resulted in few soldiers reporting for duty. Hyde's comment that the king, after three or four weeks at Beverley, 'dismissed the train-bands, weary of their service' might reflect the initial grudging reaction of the trained band soldiers to royal service. Lack of funds also appeared to be a factor, as the king was:

> so far from having money to levy or pay soldiers, that he was... compelled, for very real want, to let fall all the tables kept by his officers of state in Court, by which so many of all qualities subsisted.[8]

In addition to the shortage of money to raise and pay his soldiers, the king lacked arms and ammunition. With the help of his nephew, Prince Rupert, the queen continued her efforts to obtain military supplies in the Low Countries and by early July had managed to put together a consignment of 200 barrels of powder, 800 muskets, 500 pairs of pistols, 200 swords and seven or eight field pieces, which was despatched in the *Providence*. The vessel successfully evaded the parliamentary blockade off the Yorkshire coast and grounded in Kenningham creek, a tributary of the Humber that was too shallow for the parliamentary vessels blockading the river. Here it was unloaded and also stripped of its own ordnance, providing the king with a small initial store of arms and ammunition.[9]

Other attempts were made by the queen in July to provide the king with supplies. Muskets, gunpowder and other arms were delivered to the northeast and a separate consignment consisting of several thousand firearms, pikes and saddles as well as gunpowder, mortars, field pieces and petards appears to have been seized by parliament. Supplies that did get through to the north east from the continent were forwarded to the king, reaching him in September at Nottingham.[10]

With the supplies from the *Providence* and the soldiers from the trained band regiments the king was strong enough to attempt to make another attempt on Hull, blockading the town from mid-July into August 1642. As originally conceived, this strategy depended in part on Sir John Pennington, whom the king had named as his admiral, being able to take command of at least some of the navy. But it had come under the Earl of Warwick's control before the king's advance to Beverley and parliament was able to re-supply Hull by sea, negating the effect of the royalist blockade. The king's second attempt to gain control of Hull therefore ended in failure.

From June, with the growing likelihood of war, both sides set out to create an army. The king chose his general officers on 3 July, with Robert Bertie, Earl of Lindsey, appointed Lord General of the army and Sir Jacob

Astley granted a commission as Sergeant Major General, the senior infantry officer. Prince Rupert was appointed Lieutenant General of the horse when he joined the king at Nottingham in August, and he was given the further honour of membership of the Order of the Garter.[11] Other appointments created the necessary command and administrative structures for the army, but it was still under-provided with soldiers.

Without the option of parliamentary approval for raising troops, Charles again used the Commission of Array – now of even more doubtful legality than in 1640, as the country was not threatened by a foreign invasion. Commissions were issued for each county and major city, naming prominent men who might be expected to support the royal cause. They were to take charge of military affairs in their locality and consolidate the militia and magazines. This could be construed as raising troops; the letter to the commissioners for Leicestershire authorized them 'to array and train our people'.[12] The commissions effectively prompted individuals to decide whether they were prepared to act on this authority, and so declare their loyalty to the king. Some were not ready to commit themselves and their counties at this stage and adopted a neutral stance, replying that such steps were unnecessary, while those opposed to the king attempted to obstruct the implementation of the commissions. In Warwickshire a summary of the gentry's reaction to the Commission of Array estimated that ninety-two supported its implementation, thirty-six were opposed and fifty were neutral. The first Commission for Worcestershire was issued on 24 June, but an attempt to hold a muster outside Worcester on 13 July had to be abandoned because too few gentry appeared, under pressure from the local MPs, who had acted to obstruct it. A second, revised, Commission was issued on 18 July and a muster was successfully held on 12 August, seven weeks after the first Commission was issued. Because the Commissions of Array were in Latin, their contents could be misrepresented to those unfamiliar with the language. And there were many doubts about the legality of the process and the 'unlimited power' that it gave to the commissioners, overriding the familiar authority of the lords lieutenant and the justices of the peace.[13]

The Commissions of Array were executed in only eleven counties: Yorkshire and Lancashire; those along the Welsh border (Cheshire, Shropshire, Herefordshire and Monmouthshire); Worcestershire, Warwickshire and Leicestershire in the Midlands; and Cornwall and Somerset in the south-west. This did not indicate effective royalist control throughout those counties, for in a number of them parliamentarian magnates were able to mobilize support and raise troops, and some towns successfully resisted royalist attempts to capture them, such as Manchester, Coventry and Warwick.[14]

Following the disappointing response to the Commissions of Array, from the second half of July Charles adopted the approach that he had used in Yorkshire in May, issuing commissions to individuals to raise soldiers, but now at their own expense, presumably with some expectation of repayment in the future. Sir Ralph Dutton was commissioned to raise a regiment by late July; his Lieutenant Colonel, Stephen Hawkins, received his commission at Beverley on 25 July.[15] Sir William Pennyman, who had commanded one of the Yorkshire trained band regiments in 1639, apparently had received his commission earlier, as Richard Symonds described his regiment, partly raised in Yorkshire, as the oldest in the army.[16] The Yorkshire trained band regiment commanded by Sir Henry Belasyse was paid out of royal funds from at least 14 July and could therefore claim to have been equally early. The regiment, or elements of it, may have been transferred to his younger brother, John Belasyse, in August. John's Yorkshire soldiers were subsequently augmented with men raised in Nottinghamshire to a total of around 1,000 men. Sir Thomas Lunsford also had a commission to raise a regiment of foot in Somerset by late July and within a week had around 240 men under command, probably recruited from the county trained bands or soldiers who had served with him in the north in 1640.[17]

Other commissions were issued in early August. At least one of the officers in Sir Lewis Dyve's regiment of foot received his commission around 13 August. The Earl of Northampton received his for a foot regiment on 8 August and, in Staffordshire, Lord Paget was similarly commissioned on 16 August and turned to Richard Bolle, a professional soldier with continental experience, to train and lead his men.[18] Charles persisted with this approach throughout August and September, issuing commissions for foot soldiers in Cheshire, Staffordshire and Wales.[19] In Lancashire, Lord Strange, who became the seventh Earl of Derby upon his father's death in September, enjoyed more success executing the Commission of Array than some commissioners elsewhere. By early July he had taken control of the magazines at Lancaster, Preston and Liverpool, which provided over forty-three barrels of powder and allowed him to arm at least 700 men. Some of these soldiers appear to have formed the nucleus of the foot regiments raised by Sir Gilbert Gerard and Lord Molyneux.[20]

Commissions were also issued to individuals to raise regiments of horse. Members of the court had already agreed in late June to subscribe individually to pay for a total of around 2,000 horse for a three-month period, with most commissions apparently issued in early July. Lord Grandison had two troops of horse in his regiment by late July, Lord Wilmot was recruiting troopers for his regiment by 5 August and Sir Thomas Aston seems to have started recruiting his regiment in September. Sir John Byron was raising troopers from late July, after receiving £5,000 'mounting money' from the Marquess of Worcester. Elements of Prince Rupert's, Prince Maurice's, Lord Digby's and the Earl of Carnarvon's regiments of horse are likely to have formed part of the 800 or so horse under Rupert's command at Leicester in late August, implying that the commissions for these forces were issued sometime earlier.[21]

Some commissions must also have been issued for the raising of dragoons, as the king had 800 of them at Uttoxeter on 14 September. Sir Edward

Duncombe, one of his dragoon colonels, had been the lieutenant colonel of Sir Robert Strickland's trained band regiment which had attended the king at York, and is therefore likely to have been one of the first officers commissioned to raise such troops.[22]

By mid-August the king was frustrated by the slow progress of recruitment, in part caused by the patchy response to the Commissions of Array. Aware of the growing restlessness of his supporters in York and the fact that George Goring, governor of Portsmouth, had declared for him, Charles resolved to raise the royal standard at Nottingham by 25 August. He required all who could bear arms to rendezvous there. This was the way that medieval kings had called together an army and, in the context of the summer of 1642, was essentially a declaration of war on parliament. According to Hyde, Nottingham was preferred to York for this purpose as the king wanted to be nearer to London and Portsmouth, and had expectations of support from the west, which was more accessible from Nottingham than York. Given the commissions for the raising of troops issued to members of the gentry in Wales and Cheshire, such expectations were not unreasonable.[23]

The king went first to Lincoln, where arms were taken from the militia to augment the meagre royal arsenal. Distracted by a futile attempt to take Coventry, the king eventually arrived in Nottingham on 16 August and raised the royal standard at Castle Hill on the 22nd. But despite his issuing of commissions, in Hyde's words, 'there was not one regiment of foot yet levied and brought thither; so that the trained bands, which the sheriff had drawn thither, was all the strength the king had for his person, and the guard of the standard'. The parliamentarian army was forming at Northampton, just 60 miles away, and so the royalists' weakness caused concern for the king's security. Astley commented that 'he could not give any assurances against his majesty's being taken out of his bed, if the rebels should make a brisk attempt to that purpose'.[24] With recruitment continuing, the principal military force available to the king was the horse under Rupert at Leicester.

From this unpromising position, the king's military situation improved dramatically while he remained at Nottingham. Roughly 2,000 arms were brought into the city from Nottinghamshire and 'adjacent counties', and when he left, on 13 September, five regiments of foot, 500 horse, 800 dragoons and a train of twelve pieces of artillery were reported to have assembled there.[25] It is likely that the lifeguard, under the command of Lindsey's son, Lord Willoughby d'Eresby, was also recruited at this stage. In late August the king had offered to exempt Derbyshire miners who joined his army from duties of lot and cope and in response a group of them offered to form a lifeguard for him. In early September, parliamentary newsbooks reported that 400 miners had mustered at Derby, presumably to augment the soldiers already raised for the lifeguard by Lord Willoughby in Lincolnshire. The army was joined outside Nottingham by the county trained bands; 500 of them were enlisted while the remainder were disarmed and their weapons incorporated into the king's arsenal.[26] He now had an army in being, although one that was as yet too weak to challenge that being raised by parliament.

The royal army therefore marched west, with the aim of joining the 5,000 foot and 400 horse which were said to have been recruited in Wales and the borders. At Derby a decision to march to Shrewsbury was made following receipt of information that that town was 'at [the king's] devotion'. It also had the practical advantage, in terms of clothing the troops, that most cloth produced in north Wales was marketed by the Shrewsbury drapers. Charles was at Uttoxeter on 16 September and Stafford the day after. On the 19th the army was ordered to rendezvous at Wellington, a day's march from Shrewsbury, where the king gave 'his military orders for the discipline and government of the army to be read at the head of each regiment'. The following day he entered Shrewsbury with the banner royal at the head of the Lord General's regiment, followed by the train of artillery, three foot companies of the Shropshire trained bands, which had met the king outside the town, and six foot regiments. A seventh regiment under Sir William Pennyman had probably been detached to Bridgnorth. This implies that the army had been joined by a further regiment of foot since leaving Nottingham, probably the Staffordshire men under Bolle.[27]

Meanwhile, Sir John Byron's regiment of around 200 troopers had been despatched at the end of August from Leicester to Oxford, to take charge of money which had been secretly sent from London for the king. Byron's force had skirmished with parliamentary dragoons at Brackley in Northamptonshire, suffering losses of around fifty men, before reaching Oxford. His force was too insubstantial to hold the city and on 10 September he withdrew, to go to Worcester, taking new recruits with him, as well as the money from London and plate from the university.[28]

Having learned that the parliamentarian army was heading for Worcester, on 21 or 22 September the king ordered Rupert to go there, with what Hyde described as 'the greatest part of the horse', numbering around 700 troopers. Rupert's task was to secure the plate and money in Byron's care and protect efforts to recruit the royal army around the city. On the 23rd his troopers encountered advance elements of parliament's army at Powick Bridge, south-west of the city. In a confused skirmish, the royalist cavalry defeated around 500 parliamentary horse and dragoons before withdrawing, first into Worcester and then to Shrewsbury.[29]

On the same day the king travelled to Chester, according to Hyde 'to assure that city to his service, which was the key to Ireland, and to countenance Lord Strange... against some opposition he met with on behalf of the parliament'.[30] Charles's visit to Cheshire was also an attempt to strengthen his army further; Lord Strange, who he met in Chester, had been recruiting in Lancashire and Sir Edward Fitton, Earl Rivers and Sir Thomas Aston had been similarly active in Cheshire. In addition, Chester put the king close to the gentry in north Wales who were raising troops for his cause, and he took the opportunity in the four days he spent there to despatch 'letters and agents into Wales, Cheshire and Lancashire, to quicken the levies of men which were making there'. Chester was the port of departure for troops going to Ireland and the king may have anticipated finding stockpiles of arms and ammunition. He certainly found horses and wagons, which were taken to Shrewsbury to be incorporated in the royal train. Even if these supplies were limited, there was always the possibility of making use of the Cheshire militia or, at the very least, its weapons, powder and match. This was achieved in some degree when Lord Grandison's regiment of horse and some dragoons were despatched by the king from Chester to Nantwich. The arms and ammunition they captured there were sent to Shrewsbury.[31]

Fitton's and Rivers's regiments were with the royal army by 12 October. But the Lancashire regiments were not ready to join the army for some time. As well as the full regiments, a number of companies of Cheshire foot appear to have been added to the king's lifeguard. Recruiting for the royal army also took place in Shropshire; the regiment under Thomas Blagge, officered by men from parliamentary controlled Suffolk, probably recruited some of its strength in the county. At the end of the seventeenth century Richard Gough, the local historian of Myddle, wrote that the king was not disappointed with the response from Shropshire, for 'multitudes came to him dayly. And out of these three townes, Myddle, Newton and Marton, there went noe lesse than twenty men, of which number thirteen were kill'd in the warrs.'[32]

The Shropshire iron industry and its gun founders helped to increase the royalists' stock of artillery. By 4 October the train of twelve cannon with which the king had departed from Nottingham had been doubled and now consisted of two demi-cannon, four culverin and demi-culverin, a minion, a saker and sixteen smaller pieces. Its ammunition consisted of over 1,500 cannon rounds, including case shot, along with 7 tons 9 cwt of powder, 2 tons 13 cwt of match and 8 tons of musket shot.[33]

Although the numbers of men and horses, and the amount of munitions, had greatly increased, money was still a problem. Despite the addition to the royal coffers of the plate and money brought from Oxford by Byron, there was '[no] hope that [the royal army] could march, till a good sum of money were assigned to it'.[34] The king asked Roman Catholics in Shropshire and Staffordshire to pay their recusancy fines two or three years in advance and collected between £4,000 and £5,000 by this means in less than a fortnight. A further £6,000 was obtained through the sale of a baronetcy to Sir Richard Newport and smaller sums were given by the local gentry. Silver plate made up a large proportion of these contributions and a mint was established at Shrewsbury, apparently at the beginning of October, to coin the plate to supply and pay the army, using staff and equipment from the royal mint at Aberystwyth. Around £2,000 seems to have been distributed to the army from the mint while it was at Shrewsbury or during the march into Warwickshire.[35]

By 12 October the king was ready to march. At Shrewsbury he had
gathered six additional foot regiments; those of Sir Edward Fitton and Earl
Rivers from Cheshire; Sir Thomas Salusbury's from north Wales; Colonel
Richard Fielding's raised in Herefordshire; the Earl of Northampton's
regiment; and that of Colonel Thomas Blagge. The army now consisted
of thirteen foot regiments, ten of horse, three of dragoons and a train of
artillery, with expectations of further regiments from Lancashire and Wales.
The foot were organized initially into three brigades under Sir Nicholas
Byron, Colonel Henry Wentworth and Colonel Richard Fielding. All three
were professional soldiers who had fought in the Thirty Years War and had
seen service against the Scots during the Bishops' Wars.[36]

Patrick Ruthven joined the king's army at Shrewsbury and was appointed
Field Marshal (Marshall General). He was a sixty-nine-year-old officer, with
long military experience in Swedish service. He had served in the Second
Bishop's War and in March 1642 the king created him Earl of Forth.[37] David
Lloyd, in his hagiographic 'Memoirs', described him as a:

> stout... hail man made for the hardship of soldiers, being able to digest
> anything, but injuries; the weight of his mean birth depressed not the wings
> of his great mind, which by valour mediated advancement.[38]

Hyde was more circumspect. While acknowledging that Ruthven 'had
been a very good officer, and had great experience and was still a man of
unquestionable courage and integrity', he noted, with reference to 1644, that
he was:

> now much decayed in his parts, and, with long continued custom of
> immoderate drinking, dozed in his understanding, which had been never
> quick and vigorous; he having been always illiterate to the greatest degree
> that can be imagined.

Hyde also commented on Ruthven's taciturn nature, deafness – which
caused him to claim 'not to have heard what he did not then contradict, and
thought fit afterwards to disclaim' – and his tendency to tell the king what
he wanted to hear.[39]

In the seven months since his arrival at York the king's military fortunes
had improved dramatically. From having fewer than twenty guards, and being
without military materials or finance, he had raised an army of 12,000 men,
with an artillery train. Meanwhile, the Duke of Newcastle was assembling a
royalist army of 8,000 men in the north-east that was ready for action by the
beginning of November.[40] The king could now begin a campaign with some
confidence, facing parliament's army, which had also been newly formed.

That army was nominally raised for the king's safety, as well as the defence
of parliament and the preservation of the true religion, the laws, liberties,

and peace of the kingdom. This was based upon the notion that his safety was threatened by those malign advisors who surrounded him, and the army's role was to rescue him and bring him back to his loyal parliament. But in a petition prepared for presentation to the king, parliament stressed that it was he who:

> incensed by many false Calumnies and Slanders, doth continue to raise Forces against us and Your other peaceable and loyal Subjects, and to make great Preparations for War, both in the Kingdom and from beyond the Seas.[41]

In other words, the raising of parliament's army was justified by the king's military activity.

Parliament's own preparations had begun following the adoption of the Militia Ordinance in March and the king's attempt to seize the magazine in Hull in April. It ordered the sheriffs and justices of the peace in Yorkshire and Lincolnshire to suppress any forces raised in their counties, particularly those that might threaten to attack or blockade Hull.[42]

The problem of suppressing the rebellion in Ireland remained and parliament began to raise funds for an army of 6,000 to 8,000 men to serve there under Lord Wharton. The king refused permission for its creation, for allowing parliament to assemble and command an army would encroach on the royal prerogative and create a precedent for further challenges to kingly authority. His refusal did prevent the creation of the army, for parliament was unwilling to execute the Militia Ordinance and so create a possibly irrevocable breach with the king. He issued a proclamation on 27 May that forbade any trained bands to obey the ordinance and warned that those who did so would be treated as 'violators of the laws and disturbers of the peace of this kingdom'.[43] But the funding, identification of officers and locations of volunteers at that time probably helped when the decision to form an army was finally taken.[44] For example, when Wharton's regiment was established in the summer, at least three of the senior officers that had been due to serve in Ireland were listed in it.[45]

Subscriptions of money and horses were being accepted for what appears to have been military purposes as early as 10 June, but on 6 July the House of Lords effectively embarked upon the creation of the parliamentary army when it resolved to raise a force of 10,000 foot, 5,000 of whom were to be recruited in London and the remainder in adjoining counties. On 12 July parliament appointed the Earl of Essex as its general. Three days later it extended his responsibilities to include command of 'all the Forces, Train Bands, Forts, and Castles, fortified, and to be fortified, within the Kingdom of England, and Dominion of Wales' and conferred upon him the rank of Captain-General.[46]

Following Essex's appointment and the votes of both Houses on 12 July that an army should be raised, other senior officers were given commands and its structure was put in place. William Russell, Earl of Bedford, was appointed General of the Horse on 14 July and on 7 August Sir William Balfour was appointed as his Lieutenant-General. Sir John Meyrick was listed as the army's Sergeant Major General, the senior infantry officer, and received pay in this post from 27 July.[47] The administrative organization was created with the appointment of other officers during July and August. Sir Gilbert Gerard was appointed as Treasurer for the Army on 28 July. John Dalbier was appointed Quartermaster General, James Ramsay Commissary General, John Ward and Lionel Copley were made Commissary General for Provisions for the Horse and Foot respectively, Richard Band was Commissary General for the Victuals for the Army, Thomas Richardson was Waggonmaster General, James Seymour was Provost Marshall General and Anthony Asten was Scoutmaster General.[48]

The reluctance to defy the king's proclamation of 27 May caused some delay before parliament attempted to implement the Militia Ordinance, but when it did so it had far more success than the royalists achieved with the Commissions of Array. Between late May and mid-July musters were held in fourteen counties, including four where the Commissions of Array had been executed (Lancashire, Cheshire, Worcestershire and Leicestershire), and in nine more counties by the end of October. Although its legality could be questioned, the procedure employed was a familiar one, initiated by the lords lieutenant, and so not as contentious or as threatening to existing local authority as were the Commissions of Array. Many of the counties were in East Anglia and the south-east, which became parliament's core area in the first Civil War, despite active support for the king in some areas, such as Kent. During the summer, volunteers also enlisted for parliament in towns outside those counties, such as Shrewsbury and Taunton.[49]

Following the first implementation of the ordinance, on 9 June parliament ordered payment of 2s 6d per day to those providing horses and horsemen and on 20 June a committee was established at Guildhall to enrol volunteers who wished to serve in the cavalry.[50] Once sixty volunteers were available a troop could be formed and officers appointed to command and train them.

By 8 August over 750 horsemen were formed into individual troops.[51] Most were harquebusiers, light cavalry armed with one or two pistols, a sword and a carbine, though the three troops under Sir Philip Stapleton, commander of Essex's lifeguard, Bedford and Balfour, were more heavily armoured cuirassiers. These troops were also larger, consisting of 100 men for Stapleton's and Bedford's troops and 80 men for Balfour's. Although no effort to form these troops into regiments appears to have been made in August, colonels of horse regiments were appointed from 15 August onwards, with a sergeant major under each colonel. But the first consistent evidence of individual troops being placed under the command of regimental colonels is not until 6 September, when Captain Thomas Jackson was paid as an officer in Sir William Waller's regiment. The colonels included Essex, Bedford, Balfour, Basil Lord Feilding,

Lord Willoughby of Parham, Arthur Goodwin, Edwin Sandys and Sir William Waller. Sir Philip Stapleton commanded Essex's lifeguard of cuirassiers and also acted as regimental colonel for his regiment of horse.[52]

With the command structure in place and recruitment under way, parliament became impatient at the sluggishness with which the army was being formed and on 23 July Essex was urged to make haste. He attended a general muster in the Artillery Garden in London three days later, where 4,000 volunteers were listed.[53] By late July commissions were being granted to individuals to raise infantry regiments.[54] Both Lord Wharton's and John Hampden's commissions to raise a regiment of 1,200 foot were issued on 30 July.[55] From the beginning of August money was issued for the levying and payment of officers and men, and to cover the costs of purchasing colours, partisans, halberds, drums and a surgeon's chest. The largest sum was for Essex's regiment of 1,500 men; the others were originally proposed with establishments of 1,200 men, though by 30 August, when the Earl of Peterborough received money to recruit a regiment, experience had tempered expectations and the proposed establishment for his regiment was 800 men.[56] Indeed, individual colonels had different experiences in recruiting and by September most foot regiments were being recruited against a more realistic figure of 800 men. This did not entail a reduction in the overall number of ten companies in a regiment, but was achieved by reducing the number of soldiers in each company.

Some foot regiments were raised relatively early. By 8 August Denzil Holles's regiment consisted of at least six companies, recruited from among the butchers' and dyers' apprentices, according to a royalist source.[57] John Hampden's regiment was recruited in Buckinghamshire and on 20 August he was assigned £1,500 for pay.[58] Hampden's and Holles's regiments were among the first to be recruited and so presumably had the pick of willing volunteers and achieved their intended numbers, as did those of Essex, Meyrick and Sir Henry Cholmley.[59]

The initial payments to regimental colonels were subsequently augmented with the issue of coats, shirts, shoes and knap (or snap) sacks for the infantry. Most were authorized between 20 August and 6 September, with that for the Earl of Peterborough's regiment issued on 22 September.[60] The recruiting sergeants for the Earl of Peterborough's regiment were still busy in Smithfield in the middle of September.[61] Holles's regiment was equipped with red coats and Henry Cholmley's regiment with blue ones by 3 September, and payments were made on 10 September and 12 October for grey coats trimmed with orange for Essex's personal guard of thirty halberdiers.[62]

Two regiments of dragoons were also established, under Colonel John Browne and Colonel James Wardlawe. Brown received £3,792 to pay and equip his regiment of 600 men in six companies, excluding officers, on 19 August. Wardlawe's regiment was established by 1 September, also with six companies, each of 100 men.[63]

The artillery train was formed around the beginning of September, with the Earl of Peterborough appointed General of the Ordnance and Philippe Emmanuel du Bois as his Lieutenant General. Warrants to equip the train were issued throughout August and September. Cannon, mortars and related equipment were supplied from the Tower, which on 2 September delivered four cannon firing a 12lb ball, a demi-culverin, four cannon firing a 6lb ball and eleven three-pounder drakes, as well as a six-inch 'English' and a seven-inch 'Dutch' mortar. Ladles, sponges and wadhooks were supplied, with over 4,000 round shot and over 1,000 case shot for the cannon, two petards, 900 calthrops and a range of associated equipment. Powder, match and musket, carbine and pistol shot were also issued for the whole army. This train of twenty-two pieces of ordnance was augmented with a further eighteen pieces once the army had begun its march.[64]

While much of the army was still forming, the foot regiments of Denzil Holles, Henry Cholmley and John Hampden, and some troops of horse, rendezvoused in Buckinghamshire under the command of Thomas Ballard. This brigade then advanced to relieve Warwick, under siege by the Earl of Northampton's troops since 4 August. At Southam on 22 August, having been reinforced by troops of horse under Lord Brooke, the parliamentarian force barricaded the town to defend it from attack, acting on intelligence of a royalist advance. Although there was no attack that day, early the following morning the parliamentarians were alerted to a royalist force of around 1,000 horse and 300 foot, mainly musketeers, approaching from the north.

The parliamentarians attempted to draw out into battle array, marching through the corn fields to reach the higher ground of either Bascote or Snowford Hill. But the royalists were already drawn up for battle in the Itchen valley by the time that one of the parliamentary infantry regiments had deployed with some horse and six pieces of artillery. In Southam field the royalists had set ten rudimentary mines, which were 'underminings, and therein great store of powder layd under faggots and billets, with great wedges of iron'. They opened fire with their two cannon, but the shot fell short and the parliamentarians returned artillery fire. This cannonade caused only a small number of casualties among the royalists, but resulted in their foot fleeing from the battlefield and their horse retreating. The parliamentarians pursued them towards Long Itchington, through Bascote and Marton. The mines were not detonated during the action and were later dismantled. Captured royalist soldiers were imprisoned in Warwick Castle and others attempted to sell their weapons in neighbouring villages. Cannon balls and skeletons discovered at Bascote in 1815 and bullets embedded in the stonework of Marton church are testimony to the skirmishing which occurred during the pursuit.[65] Ballard's brigade then continued its march to Coventry, where it rested until 31 August before pressing on to Northampton, where the remainder of the army was forming.

At Northampton, parliamentary regiments practised their drills and probably had the Lord General's 'Laws and Ordinances of Warre' read to them. The soldiers also listened to sermons from the chaplains of Holles's, Stamford's, the Earl of Essex's and Mandeville's regiments. Essex's preparations were much more advanced than those of the king, but all was not well. The soldiers were ill-disciplined and poorly paid, and desertion was rife. On 15 September Essex appealed to the City of London for pay and expressed his concern that, without it, the army might disband. The City responded positively and, on 17 September, provided him with funds.[66]

Essex attended a general muster on 14 September, but not all of the army's regiments were there. Those of colonels Ballard, Charles Essex, Fairfax and Constable were still in London a week later; the former two because they were behind with their recruiting, the latter two because they had been earmarked for service in the north and were only ordered to march to join Essex on 24 September. Wharton's regiment was near Coventry on the 19th and Lord Saye and Sele's regiment, presumably raised in his own county of Oxfordshire, was in Oxford on the 14th. The city was used as a staging post for other parliamentarian regiments en-route to Worcester in late September and early October; on 27–28 September there were roughly 3,000 soldiers in the city. The regiments included those of Thomas Grantham, companies in Lord Brooke's regiment raised in London, and probably William Fairfax's and Constable's. It seems likely that none of these regiments had been at Northampton and travelled to Worcester through Oxford. William Bampfield's regiment never joined the army, having been despatched to the West Country.[67]

Despite the problems and delays, by mid-September Essex had an army that was large enough and well enough equipped to take the field. At that time the king had a much smaller army and was moving from Nottingham into Shropshire and Cheshire, to add to its strength. He was not yet in a position to march on London and so Essex had the initiative and could choose what course of action to follow.

3

The Opening Campaign

Essex's main concern when he began the campaign was to place his army where it could obstruct any royalist movement towards London. He did not set out to pursue the king's army with a view to bringing it to battle, perhaps because he felt that his army was not ready for action and required more preparation. Although Essex's force was considerably larger than that of the king, it is unlikely that he and his officers had more than a general idea of the royalists' strength.

Essex could have had no doubts about his objectives, which had been set out by parliament. He had been ordered to:

> march with such forces as you think fit, towards the Army raised in his Majesties Name against the Parliament and Kingdom. And you shall use your utmost Endeavours, by Battle or otherwise, to rescue his Majesty's Person, and the Persons of the Prince and Duke of York, out of the hands of those desperate persons who are now about them.[1]

This was a clear instruction, although Essex was free to decide how best parliament's aims could be achieved.

Essex was fifty-one years old. His father had been executed as a traitor by Elizabeth I, for attempting to raise a rebellion, but his birthright, titles and inheritance were restored by James I soon after his succession to the throne in 1603. Between 1620 and 1625 Essex served with the armies of the Palatinate and the United Provinces against the Spanish, seeing action at the siege of Breda in 1625. Later that year Charles I appointed him vice-admiral in the expedition against Cadiz. Despite this early sign of favour, the king had subsequently snubbed him and Essex became increasingly associated with the opposition to the court in the Lords. Brought out of military retirement as deputy commander during the ill-fated expedition against the Scots in 1639, Essex was dismissed from his command by the king in a particularly public manner when the war was over. He naturally resented this blow to his prestige and dignity.[2]

His combination of military experience and opposition to the king made Essex the natural choice to lead parliament's army. As a senior member of the aristocracy he would have felt it his right to do so and would certainly have resented the appointment of anyone else. But he was a cautious commander, who, as future engagements would show, preferred to be reactive rather than proactive and was at his best fighting a defensive battle.

On 19 September Essex's army left Northampton and marched towards Worcester, where it was to rendezvous with those regiments coming from London through Oxford. Marching via Rugby, the army rendezvoused on Dunsmore Heath in Warwickshire on 20 September, where it was joined by the additional artillery train and Lord Brooke from Warwick. It then proceeded along a broad front, quartering in villages as far north as Brinklow and as far south as Southam, as it advanced on Warwick. There the army paused again to allow the train of artillery, now consisting of forty guns, to catch up. From Warwick some units marched south to Stratford-upon-Avon before turning west, while others took a westward route through Barford, Aston Cantlow and Alcester. The army appears to have been short of provisions on this section of the march and, to make matters worse, on 23 September the weather broke and it trudged through the rain on its final advance towards Worcester. The advance guard of horse was badly mauled in the engagement at Powick Bridge that day, by royalist cavalry under Rupert, and the army was forced to spend the night outdoors in the pouring rain. Sergeant Nehemiah Wharton, of Denzil Holles's regiment, described the experience:

> we has small comfort, for it rained hard. Our food was fruit, for those who could get it, our drink, water, our beds, the earth; our canopy, the clouds, but we pulled up the hedges, pales and gates, and made good fires.[3]

Before entering Worcester the next day, Essex made his army stand in the rain while he delivered a speech – his longest recorded – to his subordinate officers, setting out his objectives as the advancement of the protestant religion, securing the king's person and maintaining parliament's privileges. Before re-reading his 'Lawes and Ordinances' to the assembled soldiery, Essex made it clear to his officers that military discipline applied to all and that he expected them to exercise their men carefully and 'bring them to use their arms readily and expertly, and not to busy them in practising ceremonious forms of military discipline'.[4]

When Essex reached Worcester his army consisted of nineteen regiments of foot, two of dragoons and up to sixty-six troops of horse. It strength was just under 15,000 foot, about 3,000 cavalry and around 1,500 dragoons, including the firelocks of the Lord General's regiment. Even with his increased strength, Essex did not march on the king at Shrewsbury, but chose instead to consolidate his position at Worcester. The city's strategic position on the Severn and its size and prosperity made it a suitable base for the army.

The parliamentarians consolidated their position politically by arresting the mayor and sending him as a prisoner to London, and by purging the corporation of royalist sympathizers. Militarily, work was needed to strengthen the defences, which consisted of the medieval walls and gates, which had not been maintained. The parliamentarians built fortifications around the city, spending £600 in early October.[5] They imposed a levy of £5,000 on the citizens and received £20,000 from London. The army's presence placed such a strain on the existing administration that the corporation ordered a doubling of the numbers of parish constables, because of the 'extraordinarie providing of souldiers and other great services concerning the great army now abiding in this cittie'. The citizens not only needed to provide accommodation and supplies for the troops, but also had to endure their outrageous conduct. Nehemiah Wharton admitted that they plundered the people and ransacked the cathedral, smashing its stained-glass windows, wrecking monuments, tearing up bibles and service books, and breaking up the organ.[6]

Essex did not keep all of his army together, ready to pursue the king when he made a move towards London. At the end of September, at the request of parliament's leading supporters in Herefordshire, he despatched a force of around 900 foot and 180 horse to Hereford, in rain and unseasonable snow, to take the city for parliament. This was achieved without opposition and the city was subsequently garrisoned by the Earl of Stamford's regiment.[7]

Occupying Hereford protected Worcester from the west, and Essex also placed garrisons in towns north of the city. He first established one at Bewdley, with its important bridge over the River Severn, on 3 October using Sir Henry Cholmley's regiment. On the 11th, as concerns about the movement of the king's army rose, he placed forces in and around Kidderminster, deploying a brigade of four foot regiments, including those of Cholmley and Lord Wharton, with ten troops of horse and a small by-train of five pieces of artillery. Droitwich was also fortified on the 11th. In addition, Essex left a brigade consisting of Sir William Constable's and Lord Peterborough's regiments, Browne's dragoons and some troops of horse at Warwick, to cover any attempt by the king to take Coventry.[8]

These were essentially precautionary measures and Essex's relative inaction needs explanation. Politically moderate, he was reluctant to strike the first blow against his king and still hoped for a political settlement. Parliament was allowing Essex to make his own military decisions based on local circumstances and was placing no pressure on him to take precipitate action against the king. The Commons decided on 3 October:

> The Lord General shall be desired to proceed according to his former instructions, in such manner as in his own judgment he shall think fittest, and most advantageous for the service.[9]

These factors, combined with Essex's uncertainty about the king's plans, and the poor weather, undoubtedly contributed to his decision to wait at Worcester. But he had covered the various options open to the king and his dispositions were sound. With a brigade at Kidderminster and another at

Warwick he had forces which could warn of, or possibly delay, moves by the king towards Worcester or London.

The royalists themselves were uncertain of their best course of action. A council of war held before the departure from Shrewsbury was divided; some of its members advised a march on Worcester to confront Essex, on the basis that the parliamentary army there grew stronger each day with supplies from London. But the king was persuaded by others that it would be better to march on London and force Essex to interpose himself between the capital and the royal army. The fact that the topography on the march to London was much more suited to cavalry action than the enclosures around Worcester, and so favoured the royalists, was an important factor. The strategic aim was to bring Essex's army to a decisive battle on terrain of the king's own choosing before pressing on to make a triumphant entry into London. Intelligence from London which suggested that many of Essex's senior officers were prepared to switch sides in return for a pardon may have convinced Charles that, at such an encounter and with some encouragement from him personally, the parliamentarian army might simply fall apart, negating the need to fight a battle at all.[10]

On 12 October the royal army marched from Shrewsbury to Bridgnorth, where it mustered together for the first time. The three Lancashire foot regiments of Sir Gilbert Gerard, Charles Gerrard and Lord Molyneux, promised by Lord Derby, probably rendezvoused with the king around 15–17 October in the Wolverhampton and Birmingham area, while those under Sir Thomas Lunsford, Sir John Beaumont and Sir Edward Stradling appear to have joined the army on 19 October at Kenilworth. These additions increased the number of brigades from three to five and its strength to roughly 15,000 men. After a two-day rest, the army marched from Kenilworth via Southam towards Banbury, arriving at Edgcote, north of Banbury, on the 22nd, having covered the 100 miles from Shrewsbury in ten days. A council of war was held at Edgcote.[11]

Thus far the royalists had stuck to their purpose of marching towards London and had not allowed themselves to be tempted into laying siege to the parliamentarian strongholds at Warwick and Coventry. That may have enticed Essex to come to their relief and so brought on the battle that the royalist commanders wished for. But it would have taken time and resources to engage in such operations, and those garrisons could be bypassed. Banbury, however, lay in the army's path. It was a market town and was indefensible against a force of even a moderate size, but its castle provided a citadel for the garrison that would offer greater resistance. And so while the bulk of the army took a rest, orders were given for a force of 4,000 foot with four pieces of ordnance to capture Banbury.[12] Essex's whereabouts were as yet unknown and probably unsuspected, for it is reasonable to assume that the detachment would not have been separated from the army had there been any suspicion that the enemy was only a few miles away.

Essex had reported to parliament on 12 October that Rupert was raiding Birmingham and that royalist horse and ordnance were at Wolverhampton, and so he was aware that elements of the royal army had left Shropshire.[13] But he was still unsure about the king's intentions – whether he planned to march on Worcester or not – and had been ordered by parliament to present a joint petition from both Houses to the king. This he attempted to do on the 15th, but was rebuffed by the king, who stated that he would not receive any communications from those he had proclaimed traitors. Writing to the Committee of Safety three days later, Essex indicated that the response was not unexpected, although his anger and resolve were clear:

> And for my Head, that is so much sought after, (and please God) I intend to sell it at such a Rate, the Buyers shall be no great Purchasers. My Lords and Gentlemen, I shall not in this Letter presume further upon your Patience, acknowledging the great Affairs you have.[14]

But he cannot have been surprised by the royalist movement. The parliamentarian brigade from Kidderminster had been following the royal army since 12–13 October and presumably intelligence that the king had marched almost 10 miles east from Birmingham and was at Packington on the 18th must have convinced Essex that the royalists' march was towards London through the Midlands, and not down the Severn valley and across the Cotswolds to the Thames. He realized that he needed to move his army to remain in contact with them and prevent them making an uninterrupted approach to the capital.[15]

Leaving garrisons in Worcester and Hereford, with a combined strength of 2,400 men, he advanced his army on a fifteen-mile front, between Studley in the north and Ilmington in the south, towards the king, who appeared to have designs on Banbury. Stratford-upon-Avon and the neighbouring villages again played host to Essex's soldiers. The army was due to rendezvous at Alcester on the night of 19 October, but it is unclear whether this was achieved. Progress was slowed by the poor state of the roads, made worse by the heavy rains which continued to fall and by the large artillery train that included a number of heavy siege pieces. Essex was forced to detach a cavalry regiment, a dragoon regiment and two of infantry to guard the train as the main body pressed on.[16]

By 22 October Essex's army was around Kineton, almost equidistant from Stratford-upon-Avon and Banbury, where it was detected by one of Rupert's patrols that evening. The king then wheeled his army around and ordered it to draw up on Edgehill, 2 miles from the village, ready for battle the next morning. Although taken by surprise, the royalist commanders had achieved their objective of drawing Essex into a position where they could fight the decisive battle they sought, on ground of their own choosing. They had the added advantage of being aware of the enemy's presence before he was alive to the situation, for Essex's quartermasters in Wormleighton had been surprised and captured, none of them getting away to warn the army.[17] Essex had also accomplished his aim, of intercepting the king's army, although he did not become aware of that until he was on his way to church in Kineton on the morning of 23 October, when he was surprised to learn of the approach of the royal army. The stage was set for the first major battle of the war.

The royalist army gathered on Edgehill throughout that morning, the order for the detachment to march to Banbury having being countermanded. The royalists' preparation for fighting a battle had involved a dispute over the way in which the army was to be deployed. Rupert and Forth argued for using the Swedish system that had been favoured by Gustavus Adolphus in the early 1630s, while Lindsey preferred the much simpler Dutch formation of deploying units along a straight front, more suitable for inexperienced troops. With the Swedish system each brigade was divided into four battalions in a diamond formation, the centre one pushed forward, with two others placed on either side of it and to its rear, and the fourth further back, behind the forward battalion. This was an aggressive arrangement, with the pikemen deployed in front of the musketeers in the forward battalion and in the centre of the flanking ones, able to spearhead a charge.

Forth had joined the royal army at Shrewsbury and it seems likely that the discussions about the best formation to use would have started there. On leaving Shrewsbury the army was in a three brigade structure, which suggests a Dutch approach to fighting. The army did not move to the five-brigade structure until it reached the area around Wolverhampton and Birmingham, because that is where Charles Gerrard, one of the additional brigade commanders, joined the army. The five-brigade structure can be seen as indicative of an intention to fight in the Swedish formation. The final decision to fight this way could therefore have come at any time thereafter, though some of the ground must have been prepared at Shrewsbury and the influx of additional foot soldiers improved the option of adopting that deployment. The army spent four days in the Wolverhampton and Birmingham area and another two at Kenilworth, so these are the most likely places for the army to have trained for this change.

The choice of tactics rested with the king and he decided in favour of Rupert and Forth, perhaps because he was persuaded that the more aggressive formation would bring him an outright victory. Lindsey was so displeased at having been overruled, and at the way in which the army was to be deployed, that he announced that he would fight on foot with his own regiment raised in Lincolnshire. It is surprising that the king did not order Lindsey, his most senior officer, to remain with the other general officers, so that he could give advice during the battle, rather than let him risk his life fighting, at the age of sixty, with the infantry. The dispute highlights the divisions within the royalists' high command and the way in which its military decisions were made.[18]

While the royalists were assembling their army, Essex marched his troops along the old road from Kineton towards Banbury and wheeled them to the left.[19] Around midday the royalists moved off the hill and deployed beyond the village of Radway, facing Essex's army. There was an exchange of artillery fire and royalist dragoons attempted to clear their parliamentarian counterparts and commanded musketeers from the hedgerows on the right and left of Essex's position respectively. Then, shortly after two o'clock, the royalist cavalry charged the flanks of the parliamentarian army. Prince Rupert led the cavalry on the right wing and Lord Wilmot those on the left. Rupert routed most of the parliamentarian horse opposing him and caused some of Essex's infantry regiments to break and flee, while Wilmot may have routed the cavalry regiment under Lord Feilding. The royalist horse pursued the fleeing parliamentarians as far as Kineton, where they set upon Essex's baggage train. Back on the battlefield, both sets of infantry came up and a general melee developed. Parliamentarian cavalry, under Sir William Balfour and Sir Philip Stapleton, which had remained on the battlefield, joined their infantry to defeat two of the five royalist brigades of foot. Balfour also succeeded in driving off the soldiers manning the king's artillery. By evening the parliamentarians had forced the royalists back behind a stream near their start position, but both armies were exhausted after several hours of fighting. Though 1,500 men lay dead, the battle had been a stalemate.[20]

The following morning neither the king nor Essex was willing to recommence the fight. The king had pulled his army back on to Edgehill during the night, with Sir Edward Fitton's regiment reportedly the last to leave the field,[21] while Essex had been reinforced by Lord Willoughby's horse regiment and Hampden's and Grantham's foot regiments as the battle was drawing to a close. Lord Rochford's foot regiment joined Essex's army the following day.

Neither army was in a good state to fight. Many of the royalist troops of horse remained disorganized and large numbers on both sides had fled and not yet returned to the colours. The soldiers had suffered a cold night in the open with little food and water, and exhaustion undoubtedly pervaded the ranks following the adrenalin of close combat the day before. Both commanders may also have been numbed by the experience; Essex, who at heart probably favoured a negotiated settlement to the political crisis, because he had fought, treasonously, against his king, reducing the chance of a peaceful resolution; and the king because he had failed to secure the decisive victory he craved and had seen many of his subjects, particularly those of noble blood, killed and wounded. The Earl of Lindsey was among those who died of their wounds. A professed desire to avoid an 'effusion of blood' was to become a characteristic of the king's military decision making as the war progressed.[22]

Throughout 24 October both armies watched each other across the battlefield, neither willing to attack. In the afternoon and evening Essex began to withdraw his army to Warwick and Coventry. This recovery operation was harried by Rupert on the following morning, resulting in the loss of twenty-five parliamentarian wagons laden with ammunition, medicine and other baggage, including Essex's plate and letters. The parliamentarians also left on the field seven pieces of artillery, probably two guns firing 12lb shot, one firing 6lb shot, two firing 3lb shot, a Falconet (1¼lb shot) and Robinet (¾lb shot), that were subsequently captured by the royalists. Three broken parliamentarian cannon may also have been left behind.[23] The overall mishandling of the parliamentarian artillery train was to cost the Earl of Peterborough and du Bois their posts, and they were replaced by Sir John Meyrick and Sir Edward Peyto respectively. Officially, this occurred in mid-November, but in practice it appears that they had adopted these roles following the battle and, in Peyto's case, possibly just before. Lord Feilding's cavalry regiment was taken over by John Middleton, the reformado who had joined Essex's army in Worcester and had commanded a hastily assembled regiment of dragoons during the battle. Feilding's loss of command may have reflected the poor performance of his regiment during the battle and doubts about his political loyalty.[24]

Although most of Essex's cavalry had been routed, it was those of his foot regiments that had also fled which suffered most during the battle. Returns to the parliamentarian exchequer for wounded soldiers treated at Warwick and Coventry show that the foot regiments that were routed had a higher proportion of wounded soldiers than those that stayed to fight. This presumably reflects the damage the royalist cavalry was able to inflict on the fleeing parliamentary foot, as well as the sprains and broken limbs sustained as a result of panicked running across open countryside. Essex's dragoons under Colonel John Browne also had a high proportion of wounded soldiers, indicating the hard nature of the battle they fought in the hedgerows on the parliamentarian right. Of Essex's regiments which were undefeated, the Lord General's and Sir William Constable's seem to have had the hardest battle. The number of wounded treated in the makeshift hospitals at Warwick, Coventry and Stratford-upon-Avon was at least 475; others would have been less badly wounded and so did not require treatment there.[25] The parliamentarian dead and wounded probably numbered no more than 1,100, with the wounded slightly outnumbering those who died. Others were taken prisoner or fled from their colours.

The number of casualties in the royalist army is more difficult to estimate. A figure circulating in the army after the battle was that 2,500 men had been lost, which included dead, wounded and renegades. But some of those who fled from their colours or had been lightly wounded slowly returned to the army over the following days. On 28 October Sir Edward Sydenham wrote that 'our armie dayly increases'.[26]

As the parliamentarians had withdrawn, the royalists were free to resume the campaign, after a delay of a few days while the army reassembled.

The road to London was open, but uncertainty regarding the location and condition of Essex's army produced indecision and, according to Hyde, the king 'knew not how to direct his march'.[27] Probably on 26 October, when the army again rendezvoused, a proposal was made that Rupert should command a 'flying column' of 3,000 horse and foot, with the infantry 'doubling up' by riding as pillions, to ride on ahead of the main army and occupy Westminster, before Essex could recover. This would have divided the army and created the possibility that the two sections would be defeated separately. That part remaining with the king probably would have been too small to avoid defeat should a resurgent Essex bring it to battle. Nor would the detachment under Rupert's command be assured of success. Had it succeeded in riding the 80 miles without being attacked by parliamentarian forces and suffering casualties, and had then captured Westminster, despite not having artillery, it would have been besieged there by the trained bands and a newly recruited army under the Earl of Warwick, and been bombarded by the parliamentarian vessels on the river. The scheme, perhaps suggested by Rupert himself, was based on the mistaken notion that the capital was badly prepared and weakly defended.

Wiser counsels prevailed and a more conventional approach was adopted, with the army kept together. The earlier plan of capturing Banbury was revived and on 27 October a detachment of foot, with artillery, was sent to take the town and its castle.[28] Without the prospect of being relieved by Essex, the garrison of approximately 1,000 men surrendered and roughly a half of them joined the royalist army.[29] Broughton Castle nearby was also surrendered. Nestling among the low hills of north Oxfordshire, it was indefensible against artillery. It may have given the king some satisfaction to have seized the castle, which was the seat of Lord Saye and Sele, one of his most prominent opponents in the House of Lords.

Essex did not follow the royalists as they marched towards Banbury. He maintained his army in and around the Warwickshire towns until probably the morning of 29 October. Royalist prisoners were housed in the Leather Hall in Coventry and horses were collected, no doubt to replace those lost in the royalist attacks on the baggage train during the battle and on the artillery train two days later. Colonel John Browne was buried at Coventry and Mr Baxter, Christopher Mills and Jonathan Benion were all compensated for the costs they incurred in burying soldiers who had died of wounds received in the battle. Humphrey Elcox, a soldier in Lord Brooke's regiment of foot, who had been wounded at Edgehill and taken to Warwick, died there and was buried along, no doubt, with others who succumbed to their wounds.[30]

Assuming that the location of the majority of wounded soldiers is indicative of where their parent formation was based after Edgehill, most units were at Warwick, with only Browne's dragoons, Holles's and possibly Cholmley's foot and Waller's horse at Coventry. As these two foot regiments were in separate brigades at Edgehill, it is possible that the organization within the army had either been changed or, more likely, had frayed during the retreat from Kineton.[31]

Even after three or so days rest, the army was unlikely to be ready to fight again in the immediate future and so Essex took the decision to retreat along his line of communication back to London. It is likely that he reassembled his army on Dunsmore Heath, just outside Coventry, and then proceeded along the London Road – the modern A45 – to the army's base at Northampton, a distance of about 28 miles. He reached Northampton by 31 October and remained there until 2 November for reasons that are unclear, but probably related to keeping the army together and ensuring it moved as a coherent body. Shortages of wagons, carriages and teams of horses to pull them may also have been a factor in this temporary halt. Sir Edward Peyto had been purchasing carriages on behalf of the army in Warwickshire in the three days before the battle at Edgehill and the loss of wagons to Rupert on the 25 October, with others from the baggage train during the battle, would probably have reduced the transport available. The inhabitants of Harpole, east of Northampton, were forced to provide a team of horses for Essex's retreating army, which were returned after ten days, presumably because the horses were accompanied by their owner to London, and it is likely that other villages around the town were required to provide similar support.[32]

It is clear that Essex was aware that the royalists had reached Oxford by this time, but the intentions of the royal army remained uncertain. Colonel John Hampden wrote to parliament's Buckinghamshire committee asking for news of royalist movements, because 'I believe your intelligence is better from Oxford and those parts than ours'.[33] Both Essex and Hampden were also concerned about how the events at Edgehill were being interpreted among parliament's supporters in London and elsewhere. Essex wrote to the Committee of Safety on 1 November asking to be consulted before a parliamentary petition was sent to the king, trying to begin the process towards a settlement that would avoid further bloodshed. Hampden wrote similarly to his contacts requesting that they hold their nerve while the army returned.[34]

Perhaps spurred by concerns of failing political will in London, Essex resumed his march on 2 November. He appears to have marched south-east from Northampton along the Bedford Road before turning south through Olney and Woburn to join Watling Street – the modern A5. From here the army continued through Dunstable and reached St Albans by 5 November. Essex had managed to cover the 47 miles from Northampton in three days; the decision to call a halt there to refresh and no doubt replenish his soldiers had been vindicated by the relatively rapid rate of march achieved on the return to London. At St Albans the army again halted and Sir James Ramsay, who had commanded the cavalry on the left wing at Edgehill, was court-martialed for his conduct during the battle, by the senior officers of the army, except Essex, and acquitted.[35]

Parts of Essex's army appear to have taken a more westerly route on the return to London. While parliamentarian newsbook claims of a battle fought at Aylesbury on 1 November appear to be far-fetched, skirmishing between parliamentarian forces and, probably, royalist cavalry, took place as the armies neared London. According to the Visitation of Buckinghamshire, John Hampden's eldest son, also John, was killed fighting at Chenies on the Buckinghamshire-Hertfordshire border in 1642, probably on or around 4 November. Separately, one parliamentarian newsbook claimed that on the same date twelve 'cavaliers', with 400 or 500 more close by, fired upon its soldiers somewhere between Dunstable and Watford. In the ensuing skirmish, four royalists were said to have been killed, three wounded and the rest taken prisoner. While parliamentarian casualties are unrecorded, this could conceivably have been the fight at Chenies. At around the same time newsbook reports were placing royalist forces at Colnbrook, Wycombe and Marlow, suggesting that the opportunities for engagements to take place between detachments from the armies as they closed on the capital were growing.[36]

As Essex was reaching St Albans, parliament was sending out wagons laden with supplies of powder, shot and match to meet the army at Barnet. But these were not required, as his men pressed on through the town on 6 November towards London. Some took the opportunity of being so close to home to slip away from their units and enter the city, necessitating parliament to issue the first of a number of orders requiring troops to return to their colours. The main body of the army stayed at Highgate overnight before entering the capital on the 7th. On arrival, Essex and members of the Houses of Parliament who were serving in the army were thanked by the Lords and Commons for their 'worthy service' at Edgehill.[37] Essex had indeed brought his army back to London in good time and relatively good order, considering its condition on the day after the battle.

4

Preparations in London

During the autumn campaign, both parliament and the City had been active in tightening their control of London. When Essex went from the capital on 9 September to take up his command he left behind a city that was seemingly secure, politically and militarily. He would have had complete confidence in Philip Skippon's loyalty and ability to organize its defence. Even so, there was no room for complacency and further measures were taken to ensure that it remained safely allied to parliament.

With the coming of war, attention had again been focused on the Tower. Conyers continued as Lieutenant, but its security could not be taken for granted, and with the needs of Essex's new army being added to those of the forces sent to Ireland, its resources were again low, even with the inflow of weapons from the houses of royalist suspects. By August it contained very little gunpowder and ordnance was removed to form the artillery train for Essex's new army. One payment in the accounts for the establishment of the train was to a haulier, for 'drawing of 20 peeces of ordnance, & 126 loade powder match shott & other materialls from the Tower to the new Artillery Gardens'.[1]

The quickly growing provincial forces were also acquiring arms in London. On 1 November the Commons approved the purchase of 100 muskets 'out of the public magazine in London' for use in Derbyshire.[2] The House must have been confident that there were enough in the capital for immediate needs, and it could not discourage its supporters in the counties by refusing their requests, even at the risk of depleting the city's stock of arms and equipment. The myriad requirements of the armies were partly supplied by the London manufacturers, but at this stage they were not geared up to meet the high level of demand and could not provide for all of the military needs. The shortfall was supplied from imports by City merchants from Holland and France. By 4 October these included 5,580 pikes, 2,690 muskets, 980 pairs of pistols and 246 carbines. In the first year of the war London armourers provided 275 sets of armour, but 3,788 sets were imported from Amsterdam.[3]

Following the news of Edgehill, the Commons appointed a committee to check on the Tower's security. The committee's members were anxious about the loyalties of the warders, sixteen of whom lodged in the buildings, and the numbers of servants attending the prisoners, who were accommodated in the warders' houses. This arrangement was seen to be a security risk, for each house was large enough to hide as many as twenty men, who could be infiltrated into the Tower and then co-ordinate an attack to overthrow the garrison. Such a coup could have been organized by the prisoners and their contacts outside. Although the Tower held just fourteen prisoners at this time, they were thought to be a danger. To prevent them plotting among themselves, they were forbidden to dine communally, to speak or write to each other, or to talk to visitors, except in the presence of the Lieutenant. They could keep only two servants each, who were not free to come and go from the Tower, and two women were expelled, suspect because members of their families were serving with the king. Nor could anyone keep horses or vehicles there, except the Lieutenant. These were strict measures, reflecting the concerns for the Tower's safety. An earlier order had required that the maypole in East Smithfield, close to the Tower, be pulled down, because the 'tumultuous assemblies' around it were seen as compromising the Tower's security.[4]

The number of soldiers in its garrison was thought to be adequate, for it was guarded by 200 members of the trained bands. But there were no gunners, so its artillery was useless. This was an oversight which required a swift remedy and prompted the Commons to order that ten gunners should be sent there.[5] Perhaps London was short of gunners, many of them having gone with Essex's artillery train. And other gun batteries had to be served, at the barricades and on the new emplacements that were being constructed to defend the main roads into the city, at Skippon's direction. A list compiled on 9 September itemized twenty-eight pieces of artillery, four sakers and two 'small peeces' that had been supplied to the Militia Committee. This appears to have been a partial response to a warrant issued by Essex the day before, ordering that a total of sixty-one cannon be delivered to the Committee 'for the safety of the City'. At the end of October these were supplemented by twenty demi-culverins and two mortars, with ammunition and other supplies.[6]

By the end of October great efforts were being made to complete the fortifications; many citizens, including women and children, were 'working incessantly with a great number of pioneers'.[7] By the first week of November there were 'watches and guards at the out works and trenches' in a wide arc that included St James's, Hyde Park, Piccadilly, St Giles-in-the-Fields, St Pancras, Gray's Inn Lane, Holloway Road and, south of the Thames, at Newington. The new forts were in Hyde Park, at Bermondsey Street in Southwark, which mounted artillery by 12 November, and St Thomas Waterings, on the Kent Road, also completed by 12 November.[8] In the following spring the forts around London were connected by a continuous line of earthwork ramparts and ditches, when, once again, thousands of Londoners willingly joined in the work.

The forts constructed in the autumn of 1642 were only the outer line of a series of improvised works which provided defence in depth. Although weak, the medieval city walls were still intact enough to be defensible.

This is implied by an order of the Commons on 28 October, that 'all and every the Sheds, on the Outside of the Walls... be speedily pulled down and demolished', which the Lords repeated shortly afterwards.[9] Removal of the structures from around the wall provided a clear field of fire for its defenders and allowed the ditch to be renovated. At this stage it seems not to have been thought necessary to pull down properties within the wall, so that it could be packed with earth as a reinforcement against artillery fire, and to provide a clear passage for defenders. This may have been because of the number of properties that would have been involved and the potentially hostile reactions of their owners.

At a local level, the streets were blocked by chains and posts, and guard-houses (courts of guard) were built, so that the trained band soldiers could mount guard around the clock. Authority for these works was given by the House of Lords on 20 August and the City's Common Council ordered the setting up of such defences in late October.[10] On 10 October the Venetian ambassador, Giovannie Giustinian, reported that the 'most notable highways are blockaded with timber and thick chains of iron'. This was before parliament issued an order for this work in those parishes around the edge of the built-up area, which it did on 15 October. Posts and chains were also set up in Southwark and Rotherhithe. The chains were to prevent horsemen riding along the streets, and could be supplemented by barricades, as obstructions to hinder attackers and to provide cover for defenders. A sutler's bill from December 1642 for the court of guard in New Palace, Westminster reveals repairs to the house, work on the windows and the hearth and 'for putting up boards to avoid the annoyance of the Lordships by pissing' to make it fit for purpose. Other courts of guard were set up at Charing Cross, Tyburn, Lord Goring's House (the site of modern Buckingham Palace), Old Ducathouse, the Military Yard, the Malting Yard and James Street, while three were constructed at Hyde Park Corner.[11]

The costs were to be paid by the local officials of the wards and parishes, by levying a special rate. The churchwardens at St Margaret's, Westminster did not delay while the rate was being collected, but borrowed the money to cover the costs, the loan to be repaid from the levy.[12]

On 24 October parliament ordered that the shops in London, Westminster and Southwark should be closed, so that the citizens could help in preparing the defences, and even absolved them from observing the fast two days later. Their efforts impressed Giustinian, for towards the end of October he could tell his government: 'There is no street, however little frequented, that is not barricaded with heavy chains, and every post is guarded by numerous squadrons.' A fortnight later, on 11 November, he reported that artillery had been placed in the principal streets, constantly attended by gunners with lighted match; small wonder that there was a shortage of artillerymen elsewhere.[13]

These defences were no doubt aimed at containing an insurrection mounted by royalists within the city, as well as hindering an attack by the king's army. And the medieval walls could serve as a barrier or cordon between the wealthy City parishes and the populous suburbs, which perhaps were less politically secure. Sir Henry Mildmay, MP for Maldon in Essex, expressed concern in the Commons about 'delinquents in the suburbs'.[14] Four pinnaces and eight shallops (each crewed by twenty-five men and so probably sloops) were kept on the Thames to intercept boats transporting men or arms and a hulk called *Marin[e] Protection*, crewed by forty men, was moored upstream from Whitehall. The hulk's captain was ordered to seize horses at the ferry across the Thames to Lambeth and all boats carrying ammunition or arms.[15]

The trained bands were put in a state of preparedness, but their role was to defend the city and they could not be expected, at this stage, to serve away from London. And so on 1 September Common Council ordered that two regiments of foot, both 1,200 men strong, should be raised. They were commanded by John Venn and Randall Mainwaring, both of whom were members of the Honourable Artillery Company and were involved in City politics as members of Common Council (Venn had been elected one of the City's MPs in June 1641). Venn's regiment was guarding Windsor Castle by late October.[16]

In addition to the extra regiments, the Commons decided that another army was needed, specifically to protect parliament and London. The Lords approved the proposal on 21 October and instructions were sent to the Lords Lieutenant of fifteen counties in south-east England and East Anglia to raise troops from their militia soldiers and volunteers. This force was to consist of 14,700 foot and 1,418 horse. The fleet had declared for parliament, almost unanimously, and its Admiral, the Earl of Warwick, could therefore be spared to serve as Captain General of the new army and of all forts and castles. His naval command was to pass to his Vice Admiral, William Batten. A greater potential problem arose with regard to Essex's sensitivity to an encroachment on his authority, and so parliament was careful to rule that Warwick's command was not to detract from that of the Lord General.[17]

The new force could not be assembled, organized and trained quickly. Giustinian reported that some doubted if it could be effective against the king's army, which comprised members of the aristocracy and 'substantial persons'.[18] The county authorities would not have been encouraged by parliament's frank admission that it was unable to provide funds to pay the troops, instructing them to raise the money, on promise of future repayment. Nor would the more distant counties have been keen to assemble a force and then send it away to London, leaving their own area exposed to royalist incursions. The capital could rely chiefly on the forces raised in and close to London. The quotas allotted to Middlesex, Essex, Kent, Surrey and Hertfordshire provided for 5,400 foot and 460 horse. London again had a considerable input. Among the regimental commanders, Skippon and George Langham were members of the Honourable Artillery Company and were serving in the London trained bands at the outbreak of war. Skippon appointed three officers from the trained bands as captains to his regiment, raised in the City. At least twelve other trained band officers were assigned to the new force. The volunteers who enlisted included London apprentices and considerable numbers from Essex (the Earl of Warwick was Lord Lieutenant of that county).[19]

This potentially weakened the trained bands themselves, and caused other problems, for the gentry who had raised troops in Essex had expected to officer the force, and the recruits, too, preferred those officers with whom they had enlisted. This became such a serious concern that Warwick had to issue a reply, stressing that, in the circumstances, experienced military men who had seen active service were required, and that the good of the Commonwealth must come first. Two of the regimental commanders (Henry Barclay and James Holborn) were Scottish professional soldiers, appointed for their military experience, and that may also have been the case with William Ogleby. Whatever the difficulties of recruiting and keeping volunteers, the regiments began to be formed in late October and mid-November.[20]

The regiments commanded by Langham, Holborn and Barclay seem to have been the most complete at the time of the royalist advance on London. Barclay's had absorbed the companies initially raised for a planned regiment under Warwick and was said to be 1,120 men strong on 18 November. Langham's was deployed in defending Hammersmith on 27 October and was 688 men strong by 22 November. Holborn's was at least seven companies strong by mid-November and it was deployed at Acton and Kingston on 27 October. Henry Bulstrode's regiment, apparently raised in Buckinghamshire, was probably four companies strong by mid-November and may have been in and around London until it was sent to be the Aylesbury garrison in early December, when it contained 717 men.[21]

In addition to the two infantry regiments, the Common Council resolution of 1 September called for the raising of four troops of horse.[22] By 11 October subscriptions were being accepted for six troops of horse to be raised 'chiefly' for the defence of the City under Sergeant-Major-General Skippon and captains Buller, Richard Browne, Robert Mainwaring, Heriot Washbourne and Edmund Harvey. But, other than those troops, there is little evidence of cavalry being recruited, apart from the mention of some under Sergeant-Major George Barnes and Colonel Henry Morley in early and late November respectively.[23] The dragoons recruited by the City and for the reserve army in the autumn of 1642 were also small in number, and did not appear on the order of battle until the end of November and December. They seem to have been commanded by Sir John Seaton and were deployed in no more than eight companies.[24] Seaton was despatched to Lancashire in late December with one of his troop commanders, John Sparrow, but until then most of the companies appear to have been kept in London because of the imminent royalist threat.[25]

The reserve army under the Earl of Warwick, therefore, consisted mainly of infantry. By 12 November it was said to consist of 6,000 men, although the pay warrants suggest that its true strength was roughly 3,000.[26] The army's primary purpose was as an insurance policy if Essex failed to check the royal army. While the availability of equipment, the cost of the soldiers – infantry were, in all respects, cheaper than cavalry – and the time available to train the new recruits may have been contributory factors in the army's composition, its defensive purpose probably was the decisive consideration. Infantry were the best sort of troops to deploy in the enclosures that surrounded the suburbs of London and in the new fortifications that were being built to protect both the City and surrounding area from royalist attack.

Recruitment to the London trained bands themselves had become more flexible, with the acceptance of the principle of substitution, whereby householders who could afford to pay but were reluctant to serve could hire men in their place who could not afford to maintain themselves. This breached the rule that only householders could serve, but clearly allowed for much wider recruitment. And the preparations and training of the militia were so thorough and effective that the royalist historian Thomas Hobbes later acknowledged that when Essex returned to London 'a most complete and numerous army' was waiting to serve under him.[27]

Giustinian's reports vividly convey the citizens' involvement and degree of commitment to the parliamentary cause, yet he was a grudging admirer of their efforts, for his sympathies lay with the king, not his rebellious subjects. (The king's goldsmith was making a gold chain and medal as his gift to Giustinian, who left England in December.[28] One of his concerns during these increasingly tense weeks was to stress that Charles had good and growing support within London. Giustinian had the impression that some of those who had been prepared to go along with the parliamentarians were having second thoughts, now that the king was at the head of an army that could advance on the capital. His supporters there had become bold enough to wear rose-coloured bands on their hats, to display their loyalty. According to Giustinian, by the middle of October 'a goodly number of men' were doing so, and a dozen captains of the trained bands had decided to resign, fearful of a royalist victory. If his information was accurate, and not exaggerated for partisan purposes, then this was a serious loss of many of the militia's captains. He also reported 'a riot of some importance' in St Paul's Cathedral on a Sunday early in October, when some puritans who were planning to wreck the organ were successfully resisted by royalists.[29]

Parliament reacted to the riot by ordering the lord mayor to close the cathedral, which he did, taking the keys into his own custody. When the Dean and Chapter petitioned the Lords to have it reopened, they were refused.[30] It also responded to those publicly identifying themselves as royalists by ordering:

All those who, in the City of London, or any other Place, shall wear any Colours, or other Marks of Division, whereby they may be distinguished from others, and known to be of the malignant Party, shall be examined, searched, and disarmed.

By an order of 18 October this also applied to those citizens who, by refusing to pay taxes or loans, made themselves suspect as royalist delinquents.[31]

Other measures were taken to reduce the effectiveness of any royalist revival in the capital. Houses and stables were searched, horses were confiscated, suspect householders were disarmed, anyone thought to be sympathetic to the king was arrested, and newcomers to the city were listed, in case they were infiltrators. Roman Catholics were given twelve hours to leave and, if they did not go, or subsequently came within 20 miles of London, they risked imprisonment. The stop and search policy was carried out a little too thoroughly in some cases. Rings and plate were taken from Lady Vere's coach at Mile End by the trained band soldiers, which was 'very uncivil, and of ill Consequence'; Lady Grey's coach was stopped at one of the gates, where the guards threatened to confiscate the horses; and the Duc de Vendome's house was searched, despite his safeguard from the House of Lords. In at least one case the search was justified, for the householder, near Gray's Inn, was found to have a considerable private armoury on his premises.[32]

Nothing concerning parliament could be printed without its consent and those pirated pamphlets that reached the streets were confiscated and burnt, and their printers arrested, if they could be traced. Not all passively accepted this restraint on the press's freedom, newly gained by the lifting of censorship as the authority of the Archbishop of Canterbury and Bishop of London collapsed. Gregory Dexter left before he could be questioned, but his wife Abigail remained behind and not only printed a book which gave offence, but when questioned by the Lords admitted the fact and defiantly refused to disclose the author's identity. She was committed to the King's Bench prison.[33]

Many Londoners were imprisoned as parliament's orders were implemented and by mid-November they included seventy 'substantial merchants', many of whom had been active in opposing the changes in the City's government earlier in the year.[34] Richard Walcott paid the £100 demanded and Thomas Smyth double that sum, and both were released, but the numbers in custody were such that new prisons were required. With no other prison-like building available, the ecclesiastical palaces were considered. The Commons disliked the suggestion that Lambeth Palace should be used and preferred Winchester House in Southwark. Concerns were raised that not all of the prisons were secure, because of the doubtful loyalties of those in charge of them. The keeper of the Gatehouse was impeached for high treason, for conniving at the escape of a royalist prisoner, and the keeper of the Clink was reputed to be a papist. Some prisoners were moved to Colchester Castle to reduce overcrowding and the danger of intrigues.[35]

Suspect clergymen were removed from their livings and parliament, acutely aware of the power of the pulpit, ordered the arrest of some who overstepped the mark in their sermons. Mr Cheslyn, parson of St Matthew, Friday Street, was given a hearing by the Commons, accused of including 'scandalous words' in his sermons, which he did not 'absolutely deny', and he was imprisoned. So was John Gifford, rector of St Michael Bassishaw; Mr Jackson of St Giles, Cripplegate; Thomas Swadlin, curate of St Botolph, Aldgate; and Mr Hughes of Shepperton, who had touched a raw nerve by saying that, 'if he were King, he would take the Tower, and beat down the City about the Inhabitants Ears'. Roman Catholic priests were dealt with more brutally and the year was punctuated by the execution of some of those who were detained. Parliament appointed James Wadesworth to search for Catholic clergymen, who included Thomas Sanderson, 'a Rhomish priest', ordered to be kept 'in strict Imprisonment'.[36]

In removing so many suspect clergy and citizens from circulation, parliament and the City deprived the royalists in London of leadership. They may have been numerous enough to impress Giustinian, but without direction they were not capable of mounting an organized uprising. Parliament's seemingly heavy-handed tactic of imprisoning not just known royalists, but others, who were merely lukewarm in demonstrating their support for its own cause, was successful. Similarly, confiscating horses and arms throughout the city for its urgent needs also deprived royalists of their use. Yet parliament's control could not be total, for spontaneous, small-scale, riots were difficult to prevent, and groups of royalists could still triumph in the occasional skirmish with parliament's supporters.

As well as tirelessly suppressing royalist propaganda, parliament was assiduous in proclaiming its own views of the growing conflict. Giustinian reported:

> In the churches the preachers here do not cease to urge the people strongly to resist His Majesty. They falsely induce the most simple to believe that he intends to suppress by force the religion and liberty of the country.

Such arguments, he thought, could delude the 'common people', but not those of 'good sense'.[37]

The predominant issues among the current political controversies were only a part of the propaganda campaign, with the conduct of the royalist troops also a target for the parliamentarian writers. They took especial aim at the king's nephews, Princes Rupert and Maurice, sons of Frederick V, Elector Palatine, and Charles's sister Elizabeth. Frederick's acceptance of the throne of Bohemia had precipitated the Thirty Years War and he and his family were expelled by Imperial troops and the Palatinate was occupied, first by

Spanish soldiers and later by French forces. These vicissitudes had brought
them much sympathy in England. The puritan element in parliament and
the writers of pamphlets had been vociferous in pressing James I to launch
a campaign to recover the Palatinate. He refused, but Charles did make an
attempt, although the expedition, under the protestant commander Count
Ernst von Mansfeld, fizzled out without achieving anything. This had been
an issue of the 1620s rather than the 1630s, but Elizabeth, the 'winter queen',
had remained an extremely popular figure, as a Calvinist who symbolized
the sufferings inflicted by Catholic aggression.[38]

The princes' choice of sides in the Civil War was therefore seen as a betrayal,
especially by the puritans, who had faithfully supported their family's cause.
And their elder brother Charles Louis – Elector Palatine after Frederick's
death in 1632 – had drawn back from supporting their uncle, had returned
to The Hague and successfully applied to parliament for financial support.
The pamphleteers had to overcome lingering sympathy for the princes and
their family's predicament, hence the degree of vitriolic criticism directed
at them and the conduct of their troops. Both had fought in the wars in
Germany and so could be accused of bringing the cruel practices employed
there to England. Any remaining doubts about the princes' commitment
to the royalist cause were removed by their involvement in the skirmish at
Powick Bridge on 23 September. News of their role in that action helped to
intensify the feeling of 'utmost indignation' against them.[39]

Rupert, in particular, was a target for the parliamentarian writers virtually
from the moment he set foot in England in August. He was commonly
referred to as Prince Robert, easily transposed into Prince Robber. Rupert
could be attacked in a way that the king could not at this stage, and so was
held responsible for the unrestrained behaviour of the swaggering cavaliers,
terrifying the country people who were innocent of war and its effects.[40]
The king's army was said to consist of 'Papists, and all Sorts of Malignants',
who were depicted as having an especial malice towards London. They
planned to plunder its citizens of their wealth, take down the signs at the
doors and hang the householders in their place, ravish the women, beat the
elderly, decapitate the citizens and build a tennis court where they could
play tennis with their heads, and to burn the city 'like a sodom in her own
flames'.[41] By portraying the king's army as being composed of Catholics, the
parliamentarian propagandists implicitly equated it with the Imperial armies
that were widely known to have ravaged much of protestant Germany. The
plundering papist soldier and an underground Catholic conspiracy were
long-standing fears, all that the writers needed to do was to prompt their
readers to recognize the connection.

Rupert's own conduct was depicted as especially reprehensible. Allegedly
he had ordered a soldier to be disguised as himself, and the soldier had been
attacked and killed by parliamentarian forces as a result. This sacrifice of a
common soldier for his own safety showed him to be a 'pale coward'. Even

worse was his use of disguises so that he could act as a spy, 'to be an Eye witnesse, and to know his Excellencies strength'. He was a cross-dresser, too, coming to London in a woman's clothes, to examine the new fortifications. His disguises were so good that he travelled widely incognito and an old widow in Worcester not only failed to recognize him but told him 'a pox choake Prince Robert... he might have kept him where he was borne, in his own Country, this kingdome has beene the worse ever since he landed'. This imagined anecdote neatly not only described the brash young warrior deservedly being put down by an elderly woman, but appealed to English prejudice against foreigners. The campaign against him was so sustained that by mid-November one writer was confident enough to report that Rupert was so loathed that he 'is dayly slayne with wishes; and whose death is the expectation of the Kingdomes happ[i]nesse'.[42]

This was strong stuff, designed to convert those who might still have some respect for members of the Palatine family. Nehemiah Wallington, a London wood-turner, was convinced by what he read and heard, confiding in his journal that he trusted that God would comfort the poor people in places where:

> that bloody prince Rober & those cruel cavilers doe so plonder & pillage
> & commit Rapin & use such cruelty that the poore people are caused to fly
> from house and home to save their children.[43]

Nor were the wealthy spared by the royalist troops, and their complaints added substance to the generalizations. On 4 November an outraged Bulstrode Whitelocke told the Commons that royalist troops under Sir John Byron's command had ransacked his house at Fawley Court near Henley-on-Thames, where they had killed his deer, taken his horses, robbed his tenants, rifled his papers and looted his library. By early November the Commons had gathered evidence of 'the Mischiefs they do by Plunderings', which they sent to Essex, with other intelligence. Such testimony from such a senior source gave credibility to the allegations of the parliamentarian writers.[44]

Their objective was not only to cause the citizens to fear for their own safety, but was directed at the merchant community, in pointing out the economic damage that the royalists were causing without even reaching London. And so confiscation of shipments of cloth from the West Country to London was eagerly reported. The royalists had, according to one pamphlet, 'seized upon whole cart-loads and waggons full of cloth coming to the city out of Glocestershire', and other publications carried similar items.[45] They would have caused widespread dismay in London, for clothing was the capital's largest single industry, occupying roughly one-fifth of its workforce, and cloth was by far the biggest item of London's exports.[46]

Manipulation of the news was more difficult when reports of Edgehill reached London. Those who arrived first had left the battlefield early, fearing a royalist victory, and so they gave gloomy accounts of the outcome, to justify fleeing from the scene. These could be countered by the despatch to parliament from members of both Houses with the army. They were far more positive, presenting the battle as a parliamentarian victory. Isaac Pennington's chaplain Thomas Case was delivering a sermon to the Commons three days after the battle, when Lord Wharton sent to him in the pulpit an account of 'a wonderfull and stupendious Deliverance and Victorie' at Edgehill. Wharton had been sent to London by Essex to give a report of the battle. According to his relation the royalists had lost 3,000 dead and the parliamentarian army no more than 300. Case's congregation was so relieved at the news that they could not contain their emotions; 'abundance of teares being shed for joy'.[47]

In the following days more and more eye-witnesses, both royalists and parliamentarians, straggled into London, putting quite contrary views. Judgements and reactions became more considered and attempts to describe the battle as an unqualified victory for Essex were no longer credible.[48] Nor were they desirable, for the belief that the king had been defeated could have lulled the citizens into a false state of security, at a time when their active support was needed to defend the city. The demonization of the royalist army had been designed to stiffen the Londoners' resolve and it would have been disastrous to have allowed that to be weakened by over-optimism, as it became clear that it had recovered from the battle and was free to continue its march towards the capital.

The loss of London at the beginning of the year had been a serious blow to the king's prospects, but his cause had revived and the royalists had come to pose a real threat. The response of parliament and the new regime at Guildhall, aimed at securing the city from attack or insurrection, showed that they were keenly aware that what the king had lost by electoral defeat, political procedures and popular demonstrations he could regain by military action. Essex's timely appearance resolved doubts about the outcome of the Edgehill campaign and his army's strength. It was now on the spot, to confront any threat, but the initiative lay with the royalists.

5

The Royalist Advance on London

From Banbury the royalist army set off southwards along the Cherwell valley towards Oxford, 23 miles away. The king went to the royal manor of Woodstock and the next day, 29 October, he and his army entered Oxford. Although the war was still in its early stages, the city had already been occupied by both royalist and parliamentarian forces. At the end of August a troop of royalist horse commanded by Sir John Byron had arrived, a little the worse for wear after a skirmish at Brackley. His force was too insubstantial to hold the city and on 10 September he withdrew it, to join the main army. During Byron's stay of two weeks earthwork fortifications were begun and hundreds of members of the university volunteered for military service and began training. Roughly a hundred of them left with him, to fight for the king.[1]

The beginning of the war had sharpened the differences between the university, which was predominantly royalist in sympathy, and the city, and also among the citizens themselves, who were divided in their loyalties. In July the university had responded to an appeal from the king for assistance by swiftly raising £10,667, which had been safely conveyed to him, attracting his grateful thanks and parliament's angry resentment. Its troops now occupied the city and the new Lord Lieutenant of Oxfordshire, Viscount Saye and Sele, took charge. Those parliamentarians who had fled during the period of royalist occupation returned, but they were unable to consolidate their control. They hoped that Saye would garrison the city and favoured the appointment of Bulstrode Whitelocke, MP for Marlow, as governor. Saye regarded him as unacceptable, yet did not produce a candidate of his own. Nor was he able to persuade the city council to elect his nominee John Nixon as mayor. His awareness of the vulnerability of his position, militarily and politically, was reflected in his order to destroy the new defences, rather than strengthen them. He then withdrew, as did the parliamentarian troops, leaving the city undefended.[2]

The arrival of the royal army triumphantly carrying sixty or seventy colours captured at Edgehill put an end to this period of rapidly changing fortunes, for Oxford was to serve as the king's headquarters and principal military base until the end of the war. This, of course, could not be foreseen, either by the citizens – who were to play host to the court, royalist administration and army for almost four years – or the royalists, who at this stage were concerned to regroup after the march from Shrewsbury and battle at Edgehill.

Their immediate concern was to enlist new recruits and replenish their arms and supplies. Both Byron and Saye had implemented searches of the colleges and the citizens' houses, for weapons, money and valuables. But evidently many weapons remained, for when the royalists ordered that householders who still had arms should bring them to the guildhall, some 265 of them did so, depositing a motley collection of weapons, including more than 100 muskets, a fowling piece and a battleaxe. More formally, and correctly, the city council presented the king with a gift of £250, and the Prince of Wales, the Duke of York and Prince Rupert with a pair of gloves each, the traditional gift to distinguished visitors to Oxford. The university also paid formal homage to the king, and many of its members joined his army, swelling the ranks depleted by the losses at Edgehill and the need to leave garrisons at both Banbury and Oxford when it resumed its advance. Presumably the volunteers included many of those who had been undertaking military training since the summer and so were not simply raw recruits.[3]

The royalists' sick and wounded were also cared for and some were able to rejoin the army. They included Lieutenant William Holles, who 'Whilst the army quarter'd about Oxford was thoroughly recovered' from an injury sustained at Edgehill. But not all of them recovered, or indeed survived; thirty-one were buried in St Aldate's parish alone.[4] On the other hand, the battle at Edgehill had not diminished support for the cause; more recruits arrived to join the army and morale was high. According to one royalist in the city, writing on 30 October, the king's forces 'increase daylie and the harts of his souldiers more resolute to live and die in the Kinges quarrell'. By the middle of November the army was said to be larger than it had been on the eve of Edgehill, both in horse and foot.[5] But it still had shortages, including draught animals, and so the countryside around was scoured: 'They pillage extremely about Oxon. Whole teams taken away.'[6]

The formalities of the king's reception, the practical arrangements for the occupation of the city and the recruitment and re-equipping of the army all took time, but the view in Oxford was that, 'The Kinge intends for London with all speede.'[7] This was, after all, the purpose of the campaign. Yet, according to Hyde, the members of the king's council held differing opinions regarding the best course of action to follow; a continuation of the march on London was not the only option. He, Viscount Falkland – who had been appointed as one of the two Secretaries of State in January – and Sir John Colepeper, Chancellor of the Exchequer, had argued the king's case in parliament before the war began and shared a similar view of affairs, despite their personal differences. Hyde's opinion was that a military victory would not produce a satisfactory outcome to the crisis, and throughout the war Colepeper, too, supported negotiations. All three probably agreed that a negotiated settlement should be the priority and so favoured ending the campaign at this point, with Oxford secured as a base, where Charles 'found himself in good ease', and could remain for the winter, with the senior members of the royal entourage comfortably accommodated in the colleges.[8] The area under royalist control which could provide resources could be enlarged by garrisoning the towns around the city, which would also relieve pressure on the accommodation and food supplies in Oxford itself. The season for military operations was well advanced; wet and cold weather, muddy roads and shorter days combined to make campaigning increasingly difficult for a large army.

Good political arguments could also be adduced for not advancing further. Essex's failure to achieve a victory with a knockout blow at Edgehill was likely to deepen the divisions within parliament, between those who saw the need to defeat the royalist army and those who preferred negotiations. The members who argued for a military solution were now in a weaker position, as the campaign had illustrated the difficulties of achieving an outright victory. Similar divisions in London could also widen, as the detrimental consequences of a prolonged war began to prey on the minds and diminish the finances of the merchant community. Such factional divisions in parliament and London could be exploited by the king, by not posing a further military threat and magnanimously offering to negotiate, which parliament could hardly refuse to do without losing much support. Fear of a royalist attack was one of the factors that united many Londoners behind the popular party in parliament. If that was removed, for the time being, that cement would weaken and the rifts between those supporting the war out of conviction and those who did so more out of a concern for their own safety would intensify.

Had the king abandoned the march on London before Edgehill it would have been seen as a tacit admission of his military weakness, but in the aftermath of the battle it could be presented as a statesmanlike gesture, displaying unequivocally a preference for negotiations over fighting and a genuine care for the lives and welfare of his subjects. The argument put forward in the immediate aftermath of the battle, that the king should re-enter his capital as a magnanimous and forgiving statesman, rather than as a conqueror, still applied. According to Hyde, he possessed two further advantages; his army was thought to be much larger than it actually was, and he received daily intelligence of what had been discussed by both Houses of Parliament and their committees. All of this persuaded some of his council that the army should winter in Oxford and they should pursue a political solution. Hyde's account, written with the benefit of hindsight, implies that Charles himself had agreed to that course of action: 'It had been very happy, if the king had continued his resolution of sitting still during the winter, without making farther attempts.' But several voices were busy presenting persuasive arguments to the king.[9]

One of the arguments that the swordsmen could advance in response was that the army had recovered its strength after Edgehill, but would be

numerically weaker by the spring, as men slipped away over the winter
and more places required garrisons. The queen was still buying arms on
the continent, but getting them to Oxford would be hazardous. The ships
in which they were freighted would be at risk of capture by the navy and,
even if the arms were landed safely, they would then require a strong convoy
from the coast. Meanwhile, parliament would be able to strengthen its
arsenal more easily from imports, especially from the Netherlands, which
was the hub of the arms trade in northern Europe. Military reasoning would
point to a continuation of the campaign, while the army was still relatively
strong and its reputation and morale were high. Nor did negotiations have
to be refused if the advance on London was continued, for there was an
advantage in bargaining from a position of strength, sword in hand, rather
than from the relative remoteness of Oxford. A further point was the belief
among many royalists that the divisions within London were so great that,
if the king advanced to the city, resistance would crumble and he would
be welcomed back. Charles was prepared to give credence to this notion
that support in London for his political opponents was fragile and ready to
disintegrate. But that opinion was later condemned as being 'the advice from
unskilful persons'.[10]

Rupert and the other soldiers could rightly point out that negotiations had
failed so far, and there was no reason to think that the king could achieve his
aims by political bargaining now any more than he had been able to in the
past; in other words, that the military advantage should not be abandoned
in favour of talks which would most likely fail. Whether Forth took a part
in trying to influence the king is not clear, but Rupert and some of his fellow
cavalry officers, such as Henry Wilmot, the Commissary-General of horse,
were impatient to press on with the army. Rupert and Wilmot developed
an irreconcilable mutual antipathy during this campaign and became bitter
rivals, but they were likely to have shared the same opinion of the conduct
of military operations and already were hostile to the politicians around the
king.[11] They may have been supported by George Digby, a man who played
several roles but at this point was a soldier; having convinced Rupert of
his ability and been appointed as Wilmot's second-in-command he fought
at Edgehill. Before the war he had been an ally of Falkland, Hyde and
Colepeper, and after his appointment as Secretary of State in October 1643,
having given up his regiment and reverted to being a politician, he became
anathema to the military commanders.[12] His influence on this campaign
was limited by the fact that he remained in Oxford as commander of the
garrison, although he may have left with reinforcements to join the army
on 9 November.[13] Rupert, Wilmot and Digby actively participated in the
labyrinthine intrigues that were a perpetual feature of life at Charles's court,
albeit as rivals.

Rupert had refused to receive orders from the king through Falkland and
had been strengthening his position by awarding military appointments

to professional soldiers, such as Sir Arthur Aston, appointed just before Edgehill as Sergeant Major General of dragoons.[14] But policy making was complicated by the fact that courtiers held military posts. Edward Walker, Chester Herald since 1638, was made Secretary at War by the king, a position he had held in the First Bishops' War; John Ashburnham, a Groom of the Bedchamber, became treasurer and paymaster of the army; and Endymion Porter, also a Groom of the Bedchamber, was colonel of a regiment, although this was purely nominal and he later declared that he had never been in arms against parliament. Porter was something of an intriguer and had been employed to carry out diplomatic missions and, like Ashburnham, was one of the king's trusted companions. A simple division between those who made policy and the military commanders who executed their orders does not reflect the complexities within the royalist leadership, either in the autumn of 1642 or later.

These rivalries and factional feuds were to bedevil the royalist cause throughout the war and played a part in the conduct of the campaign after Edgehill, although the absence for the time being of the queen and Henry Jermyn may have made policy making a little less complex than it became later. The statesmen had some other advantages, in their ability to present a cogent argument and to deconstruct those put by others, which Colepeper, in particular, was good at. They had the further asset that Colepeper was a friend of Ashburnham, of whom the king was extremely fond and 'trusted very much', and he often put Colepeper's viewpoint to Charles. Both Colepeper and Falkland had fought at Edgehill and Colepeper had some earlier military experience and, in Hyde's view, 'might have made a very good officer', so they could not be dismissed by their opponents as being completely ignorant of military matters.[15] But although Forth was, according to Hyde, willing to listen to arguments and displayed good judgement when choosing between them, Prince Rupert 'loved not debate' and he 'liked what was proposed as he liked the persons who proposed it'.[16] The circumstances were not conducive to the making of a clear decision in favour of one course of action, to be pursued vigorously.

The weather improved around the turn of the month, which raised the possibility that the campaign could be renewed. The royalist horse, quartered at Abingdon, was probing the parliamentary outposts in Buckinghamshire and the Chilterns, and along the Thames valley. According to Hyde, a detachment went further than its orders had allowed and discovered that Reading had been abandoned by the parliamentarians, and so it occupied the town and sent word back to Oxford. The royalists believed that Essex was still at Warwick 'having no army to march' and so the king and his whole army moved up and occupied the town, effectively resuming the advance on London.[17] Hyde's account implies that no clear choice had been made between the military and diplomatic options and that the king was uncertain which course to follow, until the soldiers' actions presented a possibility, to which he responded. The inference is that the army advanced more in response to circumstances than because of a clear decision. This does seem to be unlikely; the military preparations at Oxford would not have been carried out had the intention been to wind down operations for the winter, and a detachment of foot would have been enough to garrison Reading. The movement of the whole army along the Thames valley and across the Chilterns indicates a readiness to resume the march on London.

The king dined in Christ Church Hall on 2 November and on the following day he, the princes and his guards left Oxford. They arrived in Reading on the 4th, where the king was welcomed by the leading citizens, who gave him a sum of money – said to have been £2,000 – to prevent his army from plundering the town, an arrangement that was becoming customary, and asked him for a pardon. The church bells were rung and local royalists took the opportunity to plunder known supporters of parliament, according to a jaundiced account in the London press.[18] Rupert with the bulk of the horse had already crossed the Chilterns, by-passing Reading and entering Henley on 2 November and Maidenhead two days later.[19] The royalists had broken through into the lower Thames valley without difficulty and now threatened to continue their march on London. On 5 November John Pym told the Commons that the king had spent the previous night at Reading and that he 'is coming hither' and on the same day the writer of a letter, in London, thought that he was within 15 or 20 miles of the city.[20] On 4 November Essex's army was roughly the same distance from London as the royalists were at Reading.[21]

The loss of Reading was indeed seen by parliament as a serious development, for it lay at the confluence of the Thames and the Kennet and the royalists were now able to stop trade with the west of England, including consignments of cloth coming from the manufacturing towns to London. Its strategic position had been recognized by the parliamentarians, who had ordered a detachment with five light cannon to occupy the town, with Henry Marten appointed governor. He was an obvious choice, as one of the MPs for Berkshire in both the Short and the Long Parliaments, but was not a military man, and he had judged that his small force of 200 dragoons and 800 foot was unable to hold the unfortified town against the royalist army. After his retreat parliament ordered that 3,000 or 4,000 dragoons should be despatched to Berkshire and that the bridges at Henley and Marlow should be broken down, to try to slow Rupert's further advance.[22] This seems to have been done, for the bridges were repaired three weeks later, but it is not clear that so many dragoons were available to oppose the royalist cavalry, which now ranged around the Thames valley without encountering serious resistance.[23]

Despite the absence of an enemy force, the royalists did not energetically pursue their advantage after the capture of Reading, Henley and Maidenhead. Rupert and the horse were busy plundering and terrorizing the people along the Thames valley, according to the London pamphlet writers. One of them reported that Rupert's soldiers had hanged a man at Henley, for being a roundhead and for warning the town that they were coming.[24] It was at this point in the campaign, while Rupert was at Henley, that Whitelocke's property at Fawley Court was ransacked by Sir John Byron's troopers. Royalist soldiers also burned part of Sir Thomas Hampson's house at Taplow, near Maidenhead. More alarming for Londoners was the realization that their trade with the West Country could now be cut.[25]

Parliament's next defensible point towards London was Windsor Castle. On 23 October twelve companies of the London trained bands had been sent there, but they returned to London two days later, when the local militia forces took over. Another change followed on the 28th with the arrival of Colonel John Venn's regiment of foot, newly raised in London. Although Sir Philip Warwick described the castle as 'no more than a house magnificence, being no little strength, tho' it was called a castle', Wenceslaus Hollar's perspective drawing, taken at about this time, shows that the walls, towers and the central keep on the motte had been maintained, so that it remained a powerful fortress.[26] Its weakness was that the masonry walls were vulnerable to the heavy artillery pieces in a siege train, and at this stage outer protective earthworks had not been added.

Marten had returned to Westminster and there was no sizeable force which could seriously delay the royalist army, other than the Berkshire and Surrey trained bands, and Venn's regiment. Yet it still advanced only slowly, rather than marching purposefully forward with the objective of getting as close to London as possible before being checked. Hyde's explanation was that the king 'could not overtake his horse, which was still before'.[27] This, however, was the conventional arrangement for an army on the march, with the horse leading the advance. In a curious and almost self-contradictory phrase, Sir Philip Warwick described the king as having 'hasted to be there by such marches as might not wear out his soldiers'.[28] His statement suggests a retrospective justification for the sluggishness of the royalists' progress.

Unlike the royalists, Essex had pushed on and his army arrived in London on 7 November, the day on which Rupert's troops occupied Windsor, just 6 miles along the Thames from Maidenhead, and still 23 miles from the capital.[29] It had not really been a race for the city by the two armies, for the royalists had moved only slowly. The king had remained in Reading, where he spent four nights, the same time that he had spent at Oxford. Not until 8 November did he move forward with his entourage, to Maidenhead, where he spent two nights. At Reading the Council of War had taken the opportunity to equip some of the troops, ordering 1,000 suits of clothes from the town's tailors. But it is unlikely that the army's advance would have been delayed while they were delivered, and the warrants were not issued until the 8th and 9th of November.[30] The royalist advance may have been hampered by a shortage of vehicles. Warrants to the local parish constables to provide fifty carts for the royalist army ordered that they should be brought to Maidenhead by 10 November and royalist troopers who rode into Cobham were looking 'for carriages'.[31] These were the same difficulties that Essex's army was experiencing.

The king may have been reluctant to move forward because of the possibility that Oxford, with those courtiers who had remained there, could be captured by Essex. Although the royalists had left a small garrison in the city, the destruction of the defences had left it pretty much defenceless against an army and some senior royalists with the king perhaps were looking over their shoulders with apprehension, as much as forwards with intent. Sober consideration should have produced the realization that parliament would not regard the capture of Oxford as a priority while London was in danger of attack, but the nervous anxiety of the courtiers and citizens probably prevailed over such a rational assessment. On 4 November there was 'a false alarum' in Oxford on the news that Essex's army was just 4 miles away. It was soon realized that the report was false, but the threat remained so long as his whereabouts were unknown, and that may have kept the royalists lingering at Reading, from where they could return to defend Oxford if needed.[32]

In Windsor Castle, Venn could have felt similarly exposed, with more reason, having only an untried regiment and knowing that the remainder of the royalist army was following the horse. Yet he proved to be resolute when summoned by Rupert to surrender the castle, refusing to either capitulate or negotiate. A cavalry and dragoon force was unable to tackle a fortified stronghold and, after a skirmish, the prince continued to advance along the Thames valley.[33] The castle was not the objective of the campaign and when the remainder of the army came up it could advance beyond it towards London, leaving a detachment to prevent Venn from sallying out to threaten its communications. Yet a substantial force did halt there. On the morning of 10 November three foot regiments under Wentworth's command, with at least one and possibly up to a further five under Fielding, perhaps 4,100 men in all, were at Old Windsor. On that day Forth ordered Sir John Heydon to supply Wentworth's tertia of approximately 1,600 men with gunpowder, musket balls and match.[34] Fielding's tertia was not included in this warrant and one of his regiments, Sir Edward Fitton's Cheshire infantry, marched from Windsor to the royal palace at Oatlands, near Weybridge.[35] It may be that all five regiments in that tertia, approximately 2,500 men, made the same march. The remainder of the foot, perhaps a further 5,700 men, were still at Maidenhead, with the king. At this point the army was strung out along a front more than 10 miles long.

Rupert and his troops had kept ahead of the foot and the king's entourage. From Maidenhead he 'struck Staines ward, destroying all before him' and on 9 November he was at Egham, from where he requested to be supplied with ammunition, perhaps for dragoons. A possible objective was the gunpowder mills at Chilworth, beyond Guildford, and 15 miles from Egham; their capture would have done much to ease the royalists' shortage of powder, but they had already been damaged by the parliamentarians as a precaution.[36] Perhaps learning of this, he then pressed on to Oatlands, where he was well positioned to attack Kingston and capture its strategically important bridge over the Thames.[37]

The movement of Fitton's regiment, and perhaps the other regiments of Fielding's tertia, to Oatlands implies that an attack on the town was considered, or perhaps a march across Surrey to attack London through Southwark, which is less likely as it would have meant leaving the Kingston garrison in its rear. Kingston's capture would have cleared the way for the royalist forces to operate freely on the river's south bank, co-ordinating with the main army to protect its flank and using artillery to enfilade any defences on the north bank, for instance at Brentford or Hammersmith. Control of Kingston Bridge would allow the royalists to move their troops from one side of the river to the other.

The town probably was defended by detachments from the Surrey and Berkshire trained bands, with a stiffening of other troops, apparently including part of Warwick's new army. The parliamentarian force numbered approximately 3,000 men under Sir James Ramsay, with at least eight pieces of artillery, according to royalist accounts. Ramsay's humiliating experience at Edgehill and subsequent court-martial at St Albans may have made him all the more determined to retrieve his honour by leading a strong resistance to the royalists at Kingston.[38]

On 10 November the Commons was told that the royalist army was 4,000 or 5,000 strong, and that it intended to capture Kingston.[39] This perhaps referred to the horse under Rupert's command and Fielding's infantry regiments. An attack on the troops guarding the town and bridge was, therefore, expected. One parliamentarian newsbook went so far as to describe, in some detail, a stiff fight on the afternoon of 11 November to defend the town. Such a clash is not reported in other sources; the newsbooks' writers were prone to greatly exaggerating the merest skirmish, inflating it into a battle, boosting morale by describing how bravely and successfully the parliamentarian troops had fought. At this stage of the war any success against troops commanded by Rupert would have been very welcome, to try to shatter their growing reputation for invincibility. According to the description of the action at Kingston Bridge, the prince's own troop was engaged in the fighting and was almost cut off by an encircling movement. By the time the royalists had extricated themselves they had lost 600 men, while parliamentarian casualties were roughly 100. This is certainly an exaggerated account, with improbably large casualty figures; according to a royalist source Rupert's cavalry and dragoons did approach the town to assess the strength of the defences and were faced by a small number of parliamentarian cavalry before withdrawing.[40]

Although the royalists were advancing once more and parliament was making preparations to check their approach, neither side was yet fully committed to continuing the war. As with the royalists, the parliamentarians were wavering between negotiation and a renewal of the military campaign. Those members of both Houses who favoured a negotiated settlement had gained support in the aftermath of the arrival of the news of Edgehill and they secured agreement from parliament and Essex, who was consulted, that a letter should be sent to the king. On 3 November the two Houses agreed on the wording of a petition, asking him for a safe conduct for a delegation that was authorized to begin discussions about negotiations. Charles's reply, from Reading, was despatched on the 4th and in it he agreed to grant a safe conduct to a committee of both Houses, although that was not extended to any of its members who had been declared a traitor.[41]

The six men who were to form the delegation had already been chosen. They were the earls of Northumberland and Pembroke, from the Lords, and William Pierrepont, Thomas, Viscount Wainman, Sir John Evelyn and Sir John Hippisley, from the Commons. The senior figures were Northumberland and Pembroke. Algernon Percy, Earl of Northumberland, was known to be a moderate, in favour of peace talks, as was Philip Herbert, Earl of Pembroke and Earl of Montgomery, who had become alienated from the court as the political crisis developed, yet had kept in touch with Hyde, and as recently as July had assured the king of his loyalty. Pembroke had acted in a similar capacity in March, when he and the Earl of Holland had waited on the king at Royston, with a declaration from parliament.[42] Evelyn was a more controversial choice. Member of Parliament for Ludgershall, in Wiltshire, he was one of four men named in the king's declaration and pardon to that county of 2 November, as 'Traitors and Stirrers of Sedition against Us', and so presumably would be ineligible for a safe conduct.[43] Nevertheless, parliament forwarded his name with the others, only to receive a reply from Falkland, dated at Reading on 6 November, confirming that as a declared traitor he could not be given a safe conduct.

The Commons regarded such treatment of one of its members as quite unacceptable and a breach of its privileges, and interpreted it as a refusal to negotiate.[44] The king's offer of a safe conduct for the other members of the committee was therefore rejected and so, although Evelyn was a traitor of only four days' standing, that was enough to prevent negotiations to discuss practical arrangements, let alone the opening of substantive talks.

A hostile interpretation of the king's actions was that, at short notice, he could declare as a traitor anyone nominated to negotiate, and so delay the process, while his army would be free to continue its advance. And so a committee from the Commons was deputed to go to the City and explain to Common Hall that everything possible had been done to arrange a peace treaty, but without success. As an attack was more likely because of the impasse over the safe conduct, and a 'rumour of peace' would produce complacency, the committee was also 'to quicken them to a Resolution of defending and maintaining their Liberties and Religion with their Lives and Fortunes'.[45] Accordingly, Lord Brooke and Sir Henry Vane went to Guildhall and explained the current situation and Pym himself later went there to reinforce the message that 'Printed liberties' without real liberties 'is but to mock the kingdom'.[46]

On the day that the Lords received Falkland's reply, 7 November, they were told that Rupert's men were at Windsor. This news may have brought a sobering realization that the choice between negotiation and a royalist attack was a stark one that could not be delayed much longer, or perhaps more mature reflection had produced a change of heart. Both sides protested that they accepted that further bloodshed should be avoided; parliament especially being aware of the deaths at Edgehill, where 'many of great Quality were lost'. Some MPs were uneasy that insistence on the rights of just one member of the six-man delegation was preventing possible discussions on peace and so 'we would be put into blood'. This prompted a long debate and the conclusion that parliament should again try to present the petition, even if Evelyn was excluded. The proposal for talks was renewed, with the same delegation, and Evelyn himself was offered the choice of whether or not to go. The arrangement was said to have been his, as he was prepared to withdraw from the delegation rather than prevent further progress, and there was clearly a strong feeling in the House that he should not insist on his right. And so on 9 November parliament agreed to renew the request to present its petition to the king. The Speaker of the Lords, Lord Grey of Wark, wrote to Falkland accordingly, that the delegation, reduced to five members, would attend the king on the next day, Thursday 10 November. So as not to incur any unnecessary delay if Falkland should be absent, the letter was directed to him, or to 'any one of the Lords the Peers attending His Majesty'.[47]

Still apprehensive of the royalists' intentions, on the same day parliament ordered Essex to assemble his army on the following morning, and a proclamation was prepared that was to be read that afternoon, ordering all of his troops in London to return to their units, on pain of death. Parliament was clear that it should continue to prepare to defend the city, even though the petition was to be carried to the king. It also sought to reassure the members of the dominant party in the City that they were not about to be betrayed, by a deal struck between parliament and the royalists without reference to them. A committee was appointed to attend a meeting of Common Hall that evening, or at nine o'clock on the following morning, with the reassuring message:

that they will never agree unto any Peace, but what shall be fully for the Preservation of Religion, the Liberty of the Subject, and the settling the Peace of the Kingdom, and if this cannot be effectually done, both Houses are resolved to spend their Lives and their Fortune in the Maintenance thereof.

The committee of four Lords and eight MPs included the earls of Salisbury and Holland, Pym, Sir Thomas Myddelton and Samuel Vassall, one of the MPs for the City, who was not shy of pressing for a military solution to the crisis.[48]

Following parliament's order, Essex made dispositions to prevent the royalists' probing movements. As part of his arrangements to defend the approaches to London, the two foot regiments of Denzil Holles and Lord Brooke arrived in Brentford by the morning of 11 November, with that of John Hampden probably sent to occupy Acton. With the force at Kingston, he now had troops stationed along a front stretching across the approaches to the capital from the west.

For their part, the royalists agreed to receive the commissioners, having carried their point regarding Evelyn. On Thursday 10 November the parliamentarian commissioners set off towards Maidenhead, assuming that the king was still there, only to be met by Sir Peter Killigrew, the king's messenger, as they approached the town, who told them that the king was at that moment riding towards Colnbrook and would receive them there.[49] Colnbrook is on the Great West Road 10 miles from Maidenhead and 4 miles east of Windsor. It seems slightly odd that they were not intercepted and re-directed earlier, especially as the king's movement could hardly have been the result of an unexpected decision, for that part of the army with him could not have moved off at very short notice. The military logic for an advance to Colnbrook was that it would be easier to concentrate the army, by bringing in the horse and the detachment of foot from around Egham and Oatlands, and the remainder of the foot still at Windsor.

The period of six days between the king's arrival in Reading with the bulk of the army and his departure from Maidenhead suggests that so far the council had restrained the swordsmen, so that talks could be arranged. This was not done without difficulty, according to Hyde, who blamed Rupert in particular for 'too much neglecting the council of state (which from the first hour the army overmuch inclined to)'.[50] Faced with such slight parliamentarian opposition the army could have marched at least 10 miles a day, despite the muddy autumn roads and fewer than ten hours of daylight. Indeed, it had achieved that rate of progress from Shrewsbury to Banbury, and Essex's army managed a slightly higher daily mileage in its march from Northampton to London. The royalists could then have reached Brentford within four days of leaving Reading, had that been the intention, and then pressed on to Hammersmith and perhaps even closer to London. The horse would have covered the ground much more quickly, although running the risk of being separated from the foot and cut off. But Forth may have been wary of moving so close to London that he risked finding himself between Essex's army, which could have swung round to approach the city from the west, and the city's defending forces, protected by the new fortifications.

Because of the army's slow progress its commanders had not had to face such decisions and the statesmen could now argue that they had been justified, for negotiations seemed to be very close; the two sides were in touch and were prepared to discuss the arrangements for talks. Even so, the swordsmen could still have pressed for a continuation of the advance, irritated by what they regarded as procrastination by the politicians of both sides. John Belasyse's opinion was that the king himself regarded the delegation's mission in this light, 'imagining it only to gain time'.[51]

Whatever Charles may have felt about the sincerity of parliament's proposal, he received the commissioners soon after his arrival at Colnbrook. Quite reasonably, he told them that he could not make a full reply to them there and then on a matter of such importance, but he did take the opportunity to protest that the war was not of his making. If others had been as careful as he had, it would not have begun. He had acted 'for My own Safety, and to maintain that Government with Honour, which My Father left me'. Having unburdened himself of these sentiments, he told them that he would not delay their return to London while the petition was being considered and would send a full reply to it with his own messengers. Hyde wrote that the reply was delivered to them 'within two or three hours' and that they returned to London the same night, but that is clearly incorrect.[52] The commissioners did not begin the journey back to London that evening, but spent the night at Uxbridge, 5 miles from Colnbrook. After they arrived at Uxbridge they wrote to both Houses, informing the members what had passed so far. They returned to Colnbrook the next day, Friday 11 November, perhaps following the advice of some of the king's entourage.[53]

On the 11th the king and the council considered their reply. Their deliberations and the delivery of the response to the commissioners took some time, Sir Philip Warwick thought that they spent about half of the day at Colnbrook.[54] The king's letter was positive and not evasive; Northumberland and Pembroke described it as 'a full answer'. He was prepared to receive proposals for a settlement and his reaction to parliament's suggestion that he should reside somewhere near London pending talks was to state that Windsor Castle would be suitable, if the parliamentarian forces were withdrawn. But he added that if that offer was not acceptable, he could await parliament's propositions 'at any Place'; that is, if parliament did not agree to remove its troops from the castle, the king would not regard that as an obstacle to proceeding with negotiations. The commissioners then returned to Whitehall with Killigrew, carrying the letter, 'to save Time'.[55]

As the commissioners were returning to London they encountered Essex's men at Brentford. Northumberland later told the Lords that before the commissioners came from the king 'Three Regiments of the Lord General's were at Brainford' and when they reached the town 'they found many Soldiers, both Horse and Foot', there by Essex's orders.[56] Even if Rupert's patrols had not penetrated that far, travellers going west could not have failed to note this recent development, and they would have passed on that information to the royalists.

1. Plan of London, Westminster and Southwark in the mid-seventeenth century, drawn by Wenceslaus Hollar. The City was the densely built-up area to the north of the bridge. Most of the suburbs, along the river and to the north and east, lay outside the City's jurisdiction. To the west was Westminster, with Whitehall Palace. South of the river Southwark was expanding and was larger than many provincial towns.

2. In 1638 Marie de Medici visited her daughter, Henrietta Maria, and son-in-law, Charles I. Her procession is shown passing along Cheapside, the City's principal street, escorted by soldiers of the trained bands, the citizen's militia. Commanded by the corporation, the London trained bands were to support the parliamentarian cause in the Civil War

Above: 3. The Piazza in Covent Garden *c.*1640, drawn by Wenceslaus Hollar. Covent Garden was developed by the Earl of Bedford in the 1630s as a fashionable area for the aristocracy and gentry, who were increasingly spending much of the year in London.

Below: 4. Charles I came to the throne on the death of his father, James I, in 1625. Unable to work with parliament, he did not call one from 1629 until 1640, when the need to raise taxes to finance his campaign against the Scots compelled him to do so. His opponents mistrusted his motives, afraid that he was set upon changing existing constitutional practices. By the summer of 1642 the seemingly irreconcilable differences between court and parliament saw both sides preparing for war.

Opposite: 5. After the two wars against the Scots, royalist officers hung around Whitehall, hoping to receive their pay arrears and perhaps a command should the king raise an army. During the winter of 1641–2 they clashed with apprentices and others demonstrating in Westminster in favour of parliament.

The Tower

Stepney

6. Although obsolete in military terms, the Tower of London was still a powerful fortress, containing the magazine and the mint, a secure place for the merchants to store their wealth and serving as a prison. When parliament took political control of London in the winter of 1641–2, it became a priority to secure the Tower. This was achieved shortly afterwards. It is shown in Claes Visscher's view of London of 1616.

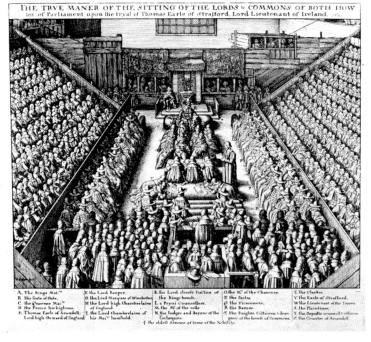

THE TRVE MANER OF THE SITTING OF THE LORDS & COMMONS OF BOTH HOW
ses of Parliament, upon the tryal of Thomas Earle of Strafford, Lord Lieutenant of Ireland. 1641

7. The king's foremost advisor in the crisis which preceded the outbreak of war was the Earl of Strafford. Fearful of his ability and influence, in 1641 his opponents put him on trial. The trial was held in Westminster Hall, before members of both Lords and Commons.

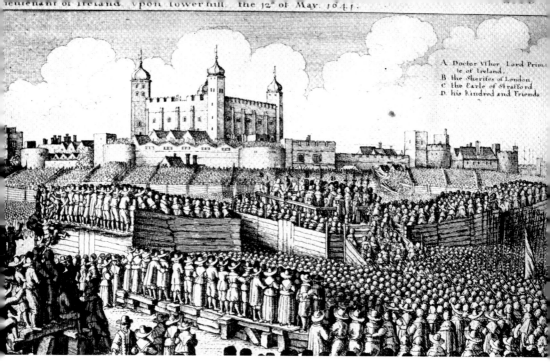

A Doctor Vsher Lord Prima
  te of Ireland.
B the Sheriffes of London.
C the Earle of Strafford
D his Kindred and Friends

Above: 8. Uncertain of being able to secure a conviction, parliament condemned the Earl of Strafford to death by an Act of Attainder. Charles I gave it the royal assent, after much heart-searching. Strafford was immensely unpopular and his execution on Tower Hill in May 1641 was carried out before an enormous crowd.

Right: 9. A Londoner in Cornhill, dressed against the winter cold: 'The cold, not cruelty makes her weare / In winter, furs and wild beasts hair'. Cornhill was one of the City's principal streets, a centre of trade and finance, where the Royal Exchange was built in 1568. The City's wealthy mercantile community was divided politically, but feared the impact of civil war on business and trade.

The cold, not cruelty makes her weare Winter For a smoother skinn at night,
In Winter, furs and Wild beasts haire   Embraceth her with more delight.

Previous page spread: 10. The king levied an army during the summer of 1642 and on 22 August the royal standard was raised on the castle hill at Nottingham in windy conditions, but inauspiciously blew down that night. The raising of the standard was taken to mark the beginning of hostilities against parliament. The scene was depicted by George Cattermole, c.1865.

Top: 11. Prince Rupert was Charles I's nephew, son of his sister Elizabeth and her husband Frederick V, Elector Palatine and briefly King of Bohemia. Rupert was vilified by the London press as a rapacious soldier who would bring the dreadful and destructive practices of the Thirty Years War into England. He commanded the royalist cavalry during the campaign which culminated in the battle at Turnham Green.

12. Robert Devereux, 3rd Earl of Essex, by William Faithorne, 1643. He was appointed by parliament as its Lord General and commanded its army in the campaign during the autumn of 1642. Criticized for being a cautious commander, he nevertheless kept his army together after the battle of Edgehill and returned to London, achieving his objective of securing the capital's safety by successfully halting the royalist advance at the battle of Turnham Green.

13. Robert Rich, 2nd Earl of Warwick, was appointed Lord High Admiral in March 1642 and at the outbreak of the Civil War secured the navy's adherence to parliament. He commanded the army raised to defend London during the autumn of 1642 and was one of the parliamentarian commanders at the battle of Turnham Green on 13 November, before relinquishing his command to the Earl of Essex.

The right Hon.ble Robert Earle of Warwicke.

14. Philip Skippon was an experienced officer who had fought in the wars in the Low Countries. In 1639 he was appointed Captain-Leader of the Society of the Artillery Garden and in early 1642 as Sergeant Major General of the trained bands. He was responsible for organizing London's defences and commanded the trained bands at the battle of Turnham Green. Skippon was subsequently appointed as Essex's senior infantry commander.

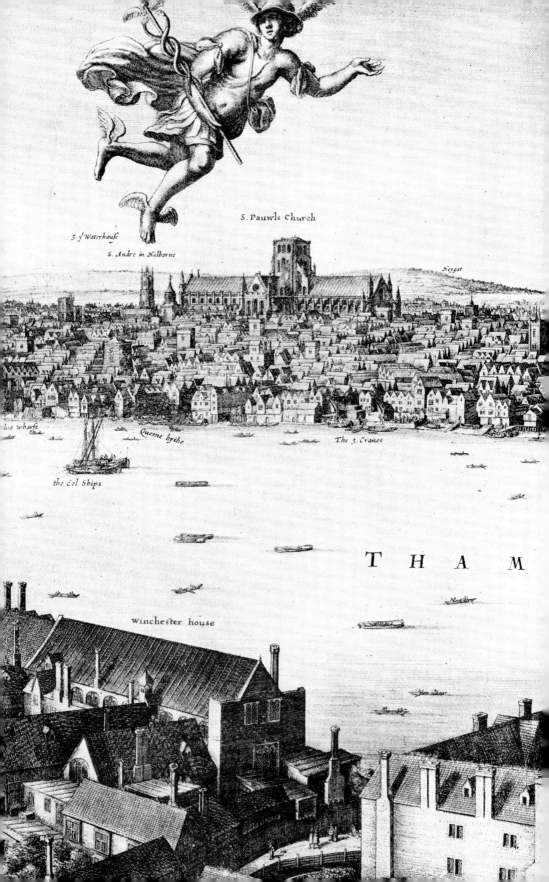

S. Pauwls Church

S. ye Waterhouse

S. Andre in Holborne

Heygat

lis wharfe

Queene hythe

The 3. Cranes

the Eel Ships

T H A M

winchester house

Opposite: 15. A section of Wenceslaus Hollar's 'Long View' of London from Bankside, drawn in 1647. St Paul's Cathedral dominates the skyline, with densely packed houses crowded between it and the Thames. In the foreground is the palace of the Bishops of Winchester, which was commandeered by parliament in 1642, as a prison for those suspected of supporting the king, as they attempted to secure London from subversive activities.

Above: 16. New Palace Yard, with Westminster Hall to the left, behind which was the chamber of the House of Commons, and Whitehall Palace beyond, drawn by Wenceslaus Hollar in 1647. The yard is crowded with the coaches of the aristocracy and gentry in that part of the capital which was the focus of English politics and the centre of government.

Right: 17. George, Lord Digby, after Van Dyck. Digby served as a colonel of horse at Edgehill and may have joined the royal army with reinforcements on 9 November as it advanced on London. He succeeded Lord Falkland as Secretary of State and reverted to a political role, becoming an anathema to the military commanders.

19. Charles I on campaign, dictating instructions to Sir Edward Walker, Secretary at War, artist unknown. Walker, appointed in September 1642, accompanied the king on most of his campaigns.

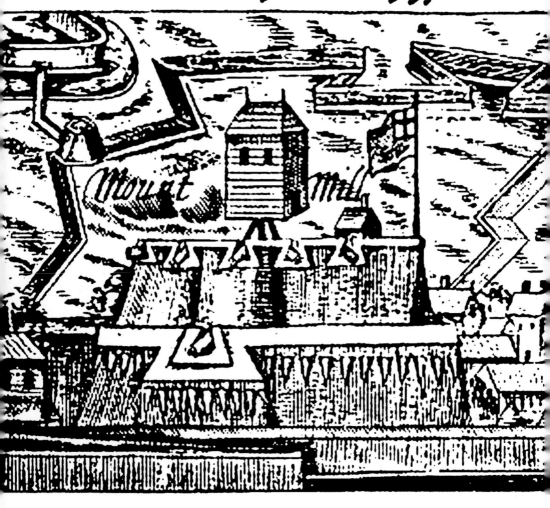

In the next place they intended to seize the For and Out workes to preuent all supplies.

Lord Falkland

Above: 20. The first fortifications around London were erected in October and November 1642. Mount Mill was built on the north side of the City, as a circular fort with an outer line of defence consisting of angled bastions. According to an observer who walked the line of the fortifications during the spring of 1643, it was one of the first forts to be built in the previous autumn. The windmill which gave it its name stood within the fort.

Left: 21. Lucius Cary, 2nd Viscount Falkland, was appointed one of the two Secretaries of State by Charles I in January 1642 and accompanied the king during the campaign in the autumn of that year. He was responsible for drafting the declarations issued by the king before and after the battles at Brentford and Turnham Green. He was killed fighting with the king's cavalry at Newbury in September 1643.

Above: 22. This contemporary depiction of the Battle of Nördlingen, fought by the French/Swedish and Imperial armies in 1645, shows the almost chaotic scenes around the wagon train during a battle.

Right: 23. Robert Bertie, 1st Earl of Lindsey, had a long military career and was appointed Lord General of the royal army. After a disagreement with Prince Rupert concerning the battle formation that the army should adopt, he chose to fight with at the head of his regiment at the battle of Edgehill and was killed

Vandyke pinx.t   *W. I. Taylor sculp.*

The Earl of Lindsey.

Gardes ~~ssoife~~
les Gardes Françoise
les Garde~~s~~ Françoise

24. The battle of Lens between the French and Spanish armies in 1648, with the field artillery placed between of the blocks of infantry, which consisted of musketeers and pikemen. The parliamentarian field artillery at Edgehill was deployed in a similar fashion.

25. The Savoy Palace was built in 1245 by Peter, Earl of Savoy and Richmond. In 1505 it was rebuilt and endowed by Henry VII as a hospital for poor people. When parliament urgently required a hospital for soldiers wounded at the Battle of Edgehill in October 1642, its investigations showed that the Savoy had 150 beds but only two residents, and so it was selected as Parliament's military hospital. It was probably used to treat some of the casualties from the battle of Brentford.

26. Richard Browne was a
Londoner who was appointed
captain of a troop of horse to
be raised in the city in 1642.
He rose though the ranks of
the parliamentarian armies and
was appointed Major General in
1644. Royalist writers who were
sarcastic of the background of
those Londoners who achieved
prominence in parliament's
service sneeringly described him
as a 'woodmonger'. Yet Browne
was knighted by Charles II at
the Restoration, in May 1660,
and was lord mayor in 1660–1.

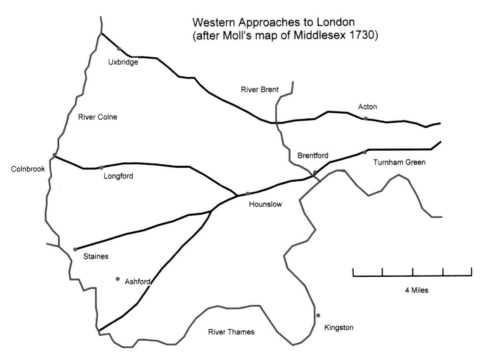

27. Plan of the western approaches to London. On reaching Colnbrook, the royalist high
command decided against an advance on London along the most northern route via Uxbridge
and Acton. Instead, they gathered the royal army at Hounslow Heath and moved along the
Great West Road through Brentford.

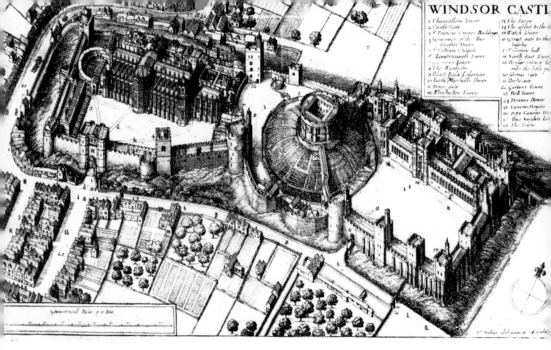

WINDSOR CASTI

1 Chancellors Tower
2 Castle Gate
3 S. Francis Crones Buildings
4 Governor of the Hou
  Knights Tower
5 S. Georges Chapel
6 Lieutenants Tower
7 Gunners Tower
8 The Wardrobe
9 Black Rods Lodgings
10 Earle Marshalls Tower
11 Twoes Gate
12 Winchester Tower

13 The Keepe
14 The ascent to the
15 Watch Tower
16 Great Gate to the
   Inferior
17 S. Georges hall
18 North East Tower
19 Bridge from y Kin
   side the little pe
20 Terras Gate
21 Darke Gate
22 Garters Tower
23 Bell Tower
24 Deanes House
25 Canons House
26 Petty Canons Ho
27 Pore knights Lo
28 The Towne

28. Windsor Castle was secured by parliamentarian forces at the beginning of the Civil War and its garrison refused to surrender when summoned by Prince Rupert. The royalists were compelled to leave it in parliamentarian hands in their rear as they marched on towards London. Charles I proposed it as a possible place where negotiations between the two sides could be held. The perspective view is by Wenceslaus Hollar.

Opposite: 29. Brentford is depicted on Moses Glover's plan of Isleworth Hundred of 1635. The viewpoint is from the town, looking west. Syon House can be seen on the riverside on the left of the view. Sir Richard Wynn's house is marked on the road beyond Brayneford End and before the cross-roads. Fighting there was the first engagement of the battle of Brentford.

Cunduit
Arab
44—2—

past
6—0—0

pa
4—2—9

pa
2—5—9

pa
2—3—

or
0—0—
peneral

D ...... Beatones
Farme
pa
4—0—0

Arab
6—0—0

pa
3—3—

3—0—0
pa & or

113—0—0

3—3—0
pa

Sr Rich Win K. & Baronet
Sr Francis Darcee K.t

pa
3—1—19

4—0—0

pa
3—0—0

Ar
9—0—0

Herings Hall

BRAYNEFORD END
pa
3—1—14

1—2—12
pa

past
3—0—0

pa
3—2—9

2—1—0

1—0—2

3—0—0

M Nore

orchards
3—2—20

1—2—0

Ar
3—2—0

Ar
2—1—0

yHam
Y Bowleing Alley

Ar
4—1—30

orchards
2—1—0

P
5—2—0

M Henderson
Y Minister

Y Brewe house

past
7—2—11

past
7—2—

S George

Brewers
Meade
pa
5—0—0

Y Doves

Thornetus Meade
pa
7—2—0

Boares Head

past
7—2—19

Y Oxe wharfe

The Market

Y Wolfe Wharfe

NEW BRAYNFORDE

Whele Wharfe

Which togather with Y Oulde is Extended
one Mille, in one Streete onely;

M Haleigh

arde

30. Sir Richard Wynn's House, described as Little Syon House. Wynn was a courtier who held offices in the households of Charles I and Henrietta Maria. He was elected an MP for Liverpool in the Long Parliament, but did not join the king's army or support his cause. His property in Middlesex came to him through his wife Anne, daughter and co-heir of Sir Francis Darcy of Isleworth.

Opposite right: 32. The fifteenth-century tower of St Lawrence's church, Brentford. This is shown, topped by a spire, on Moses Glover's plan, close to the River Brent. It gave the parliamentarian defenders a vantage point, but that was of no help on the morning of the royalist attack because of the thick fog that hung over the area.

Above: 31. Syon House was the seat of the Earl of Northumberland, a supporter of parliament and one of the commissioners sent to negotiate with the king in November 1642. The house was captured by the royalists during their attack on Brentford and sustained some damage in the fighting and during attacks on parliamentarian barges on the river.

Next page: 33. John Hassall's painting of 1928 shows royalist cavalry charging across Brentford Bridge to attack an improvised parliamentarian barricade at the end of the street which ran through the town. In fact, the engagement there was between the infantry of both sides and the royalist cavalry were not engaged in that phase of the battle.

Mr. JOHN LILBORNE.

34. John Lilburne fought at Brentford, where he was captured and taken to Oxford as a prisoner. He was condemned to death and reprieved only after strenuous efforts by his wife Elizabeth and parliament's threat that its forces would execute royalist prisoners in retaliation. Contemporary usages of war were clear, but it took cases such as Lilburne's for them to be adapted to the fighting in the Civil War.

35. This account records payments to 20 officers and more than 300 soldiers of Denzil Holles's and Lord Brooke's regiments 'that were taken prisoners and stript att Brentford'.

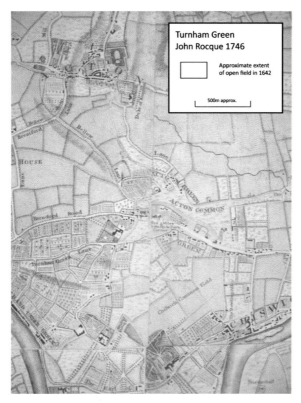

36. The open space covered by Turnham Green, Acton Green and Chiswick common field, superimposed on John Rocque's plan of 1746. Acton is at the north of the map and Chiswick is close to the River Thames. Enclosures had been created since the battle, 104 years earlier.

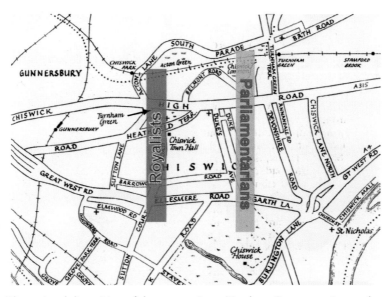

37. The notional disposition of the two armies at Turnham Green superimposed on a twentieth-century plan, redrawn by Malcolm Dickson.

38. In this interpretation of the battle of Turnham Green by John Hassall, painted in 1928, royalist cavalry have broken into the ranks of the parliamentarian pikemen and musketeers. In fact, the two armies did not engage in any fighting at close quarters in the way which Hassall portrays and forays by the royalist horsemen were not successful in luring the parliamentarian foot into combat.

Dauentny

Brimidgham

39. The allegations of barbarous practices that were directed at Prince Rupert during the campaign of 1642 continued throughout the Civil War. Here he is shown, with his dog 'Boy', prancing on horseback and firing his pistol, with Birmingham in flames in the background. Roughly eighty houses in the town were burned and some of its citizens killed when his forces captured it, less than five months after the sack of Brentford.

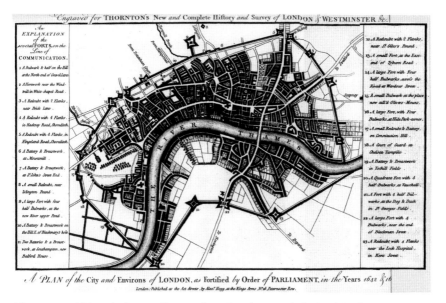

Above: 40. Although the royalist march on London was halted at Turnham Green in November 1642 and the military threat receded, work on London's fortifications was continued in 1643, with more forts constructed and a continuous line of earthworks thrown up by the enthusiastic citizens. George Vertue's plan was first published in 1739 and is not entirely accurate in its depiction of the line of the defences.

Below: 41. The campaign that culminated at Turnham Green demonstrated that the royalist armies would be unable to capture London, and so an armed uprising to seize the city was planned. This was focused around the MP and poet Edmund Waller, assisted by Nathaniel Tompkins and Richard Challoner. The plot was uncovered. Waller got away, but Tompkins and Challoner were tried and executed, in Fetter Lane. The scene on the scaffold was depicted by the Victorian painter J. Quartley.

Left: 42. The memorial to the 1642 battle of Brentford was first erected in 1909 through the efforts of a local historian, Montague Sharpe, though not in its current location. It commemorates two other battles at Brentford, supposedly an opposed crossing of the Thames by Julius Caesar in 54BC and King Edmund Ironside's defeat of Cnut in 1016. Until the establishment of a battlefield trail in 2007 by the Battlefields Trust, this was the only acknowledgement of the battle in the town.

Below: 43. Muskets being fired by a reenactor group.

Hyde later wrote that it was 'believed by many' that if the king and his army had returned to Reading, parliament would have withdrawn its troops from Windsor Castle, as a signal of its good faith, so that negotiations could proceed. In a significant passage, he reported that this was the view of 'those lords who had been with the petition, and some others, who thought themselves as much overshadowed by the greatness of the Earl of Essex and the chief officers of the army as they could be by the glory of any favourite or power of any counsellors'. He was referring to Northumberland and Pembroke and, as he was not present when the parliamentarian delegation was at Colnbrook, his source almost certainly was Falkland, who handled the negotiations and would have met and entertained the delegation. From their conversations, Falkland learned that some senior parliamentarians were prepared to give the king the benefit of the doubt as far as the occupation of Windsor Castle was concerned, and that they were as apprehensive of the growing power of their senior officers as the royalist statesmen were of their own commanders' influence. Even so, in retrospect Hyde himself did not think that the members of the peace party could have persuaded Essex and his senior commanders to give up such a strong fortification, so strategically placed, only in the hope of talks of peace, without any guarantees.[57]

Sir Philip Warwick did not have such a positive memory of the morning that the council spent considering the reply to parliament. He thought that the king could have responded to the commissioners more quickly, yet equally courteously. His version of the meeting was critical of the lack of a swift and decisive response:

> Here our lukewarm temper, or what the French call *entre-deux*, wounded us again for the King and his counsellors about him affecting *inquissimam pacem* &C the worst conditions of peace before the most prosperous warr.[58]

In fact, that Friday was a day of military preparations in the royalist army, the outcome of a meeting between the king and Rupert, who had ridden over from Egham with significant intelligence:

> The P: went from Egham to Colebrook, and told the K: that at Branford were two Regts of Hambens and Hollis and the Prince desir'd of the K some foot force to engage those two Regts and that the K would draw off the army upon Hounslow Heath.[59]

Sir Richard Bulstrode's testimony was that the king's response was to call a council of war, which decided 'that the King's army should advance to Brentford', afraid that if parliament was occupying the town the royalist army 'would be wholly surrounded, and deprived either of moving or subsisting'.[60] The king evidently accepted this advice.

As a result, Sir Jacob Astley, the Sergeant Major General, issued a warrant to Sir John Heydon, the Lieutenant of the Ordnance, which by the king's 'Express Command' required that the artillery train should be ready to march by dawn on the next day, Saturday.[61] It ordered that a by-train of four cannon firing ball of 4lbs or 6lbs (minions or sakers) should be made ready, with gunpowder and shot. This was to advance to Longford, a mile and a half east of Colnbrook. The remainder of the train was to be readied to follow 'as we pass upon the march'. The by-train that Heydon prepared consisted of two minions and two demi-culverins (firing shot of 9lbs), with twenty shot for each type of piece. In addition, Heydon was to supply gunpowder for 4,000 musketeers, with match, shovels and spades.

This was no less than an order to prepare the army to resume its march eastwards, for in addition to the musketeers there would have been a roughly equal number of pikemen. Forth was at Maidenhead early on the Thursday morning, when Heydon received his warrant to re-supply Wentworth's tertia at Old Windsor with powder, match and shot at around 7 a.m. on that day.[62] He then presumably moved with the king to Colnbrook, and probably was followed, later on Thursday or on Friday, by the remaining royalist infantry from Windsor and Maidenhead, which now joined the king at Colnbrook. The detachment at Oatlands was also recalled, marching to Ashford on the Friday, where they spent the night. This accounts for almost all of the royalist foot. The bulk of the horse and dragoons presumably was still at Egham, ready to cross the Thames and join the infantry.[63]

Rupert may have arrived at Colnbrook with the news of the parliamentarian force at Brentford on the Thursday evening, after the commissioners' departure, or early on the Friday morning. The order from Astley was endorsed by Heydon at about ten o'clock on that Friday, presumably the time when he received the order, rather than completed it. It is most improbable that Heydon referred to 10 p.m.; it would have been very late in the day to expect the train and foot to be readied by dawn and would have incurred the obvious risk of handling gunpowder by candlelight. Astley and Heydon were both experienced and competent officers and unlikely to have attempted to equip such a large force in the evening of a late-autumn day. The timing is significant, for it establishes that the decision to advance was taken before the commissioners were handed the king's reply, indeed before the council had completed drafting it.

The order was issued by the king's own command. That is, while the talks about negotiations were being conducted, he was preparing to resume his army's march, and with more purpose than had been the case hitherto. If a probing movement from Oatlands had ever been considered, that was now abandoned and the army was being brought together, for the first time since it had arrived at Oxford. This would not have been done unless a major operation was intended, given the problems of provisioning such a large force concentrated together. That operation was a response to Rupert's intelligence of Essex's regiments at Brentford, which were used as the pretext for assembling the army, which could then resume the advance towards London.

This marked a clear change in strategy, from the cautious approach followed while the possibility of negotiations was being explored, to the out-and-out military option. Hyde's narrative of the campaign describes how Rupert and the horse had led the army throughout, moving forward and obliging the king to bring up the foot and artillery in support. He reiterated this in his description of the events of 11 and 12 November. Pointing out that the king could have withdrawn his army to await a response from parliament, or at least have remained at Colnbrook, he attributed its advance to Rupert's influence. While repeating the claim that the positioning of Essex's troops at Acton, Brentford and Kingston threatened the royalist army, he wrote that Rupert, 'advanced with the horse and dragoons to Hounslow, and then sent to the king to desire him that the army might march after'. Rupert had indeed provided the intelligence about Essex's troops at Brentford and suggested the response, which gives some credence to Hyde's account.[64] But he is misleading in suggesting that Rupert took action on his own initiative, with which the king acquiesced. Charles was the king and commander in chief, he was there at the time, and no course of action could be implemented without his knowledge and approval. He was ultimately responsible for the decision to advance, whatever Rupert, the other officers, or the council advised, and despite the complexities of decision making in the royalist high command.[65] Hyde's claim is consistent with his hostility to Rupert and the swordsmen generally, and can be interpreted in that context. Perhaps more to the point, it deflects direct responsibility for the decisions made over those two days away from the king. By implying that he had responded to actions taken by Rupert, Hyde was attempting to absolve his royal master.

While Hyde may have thought such exoneration to be prudent in retrospect, at the time the king and many of his adherents would not have thought that necessary, for surely the king was dealing with men who by opposing him were traitors. His decision could simply have been made because he regarded the advance on London, not negotiations, as the objective of the campaign. This he now wished to pursue, regardless of the possibility of talks or the stage which the discussions with the delegation from parliament had reached. The beginning of war had produced a clear distinction for him between his supporters, on the one hand, and, on the other, his opponents, whether soldiers or statesmen, who by their actions made themselves his enemies and so traitors. His treatment of the delegation may be construed in those terms, although immediate factors, such as points raised during the discussions, or Rupert's information regarding the presence of the parliamentarians at Brentford, could have tipped the scales and prompted the king to order an advance when he did, rather than a delay while negotiations were being considered.

In a letter to parliament written at Colnbrook on 12 November, the king announced that his intention was:

> to march with our Forces to Brainford; We have thought hereby fit to signify to both Our Houses of Parliament, that We are no less desirous of the Peace of the Kingdom than We expressed in Our aforesaid Answer, the Propositions for which We shall willingly receive where-ever We are; and desire (if it may be) to receive them at Brainford this Night, or early To-Morrow Morning; that all Speed may be made in so good a Work, and all Inconveniences otherwise likely to intervene may be avoided.[66]

The 'any Place' where the king was prepared to receive parliament's response, in his letter written just a day earlier, had now become Brentford, which he acknowledged he knew to be occupied by Essex's forces. They would have to be dislodged, by a negotiated withdrawal or military action.

The king's justification for this military response was that it was defensive; provoked by the forward movement of Essex's troops. In his letter he claimed that the information reached the royalist commanders only after the commissioners had left and neither they nor parliament had notified him of it. The commissioners may not have been aware of Essex's dispositions until they reached Brentford on their return journey, and could not have notified him, and so that part of the king's claim was correct. The royalists could, in any case, have sent riders after them to ask for an explanation, or to have recalled them for another meeting. Furthermore, the timing is not borne out by the evidence, especially Astley's warrant to Heydon, which shows that the preparations were under way while the commissioners were still at Colnbrook and so they could not have been a reaction to news that allegedly arrived after they had departed. This timing is confirmed by Thomas May, who wrote:

> As soon as the Commissioners were gone with this Answer, the King's Artillery (for so all Relations agree) advanced-forward with the Horse, throw Colebrook, after them toward London.[67]

Lucy Hutchinson's memory of this time was also that the royalist advance took place 'Assoone as ever the Commissioners were gone'.[68] May's and Hutchinson's retrospective accounts may have been coloured by how events unfolded, but a note of the Commons' proceedings shows that the members thought that as the commissioners returned through Brentford, the king's armies 'were coming that way'.[69]

The king's letter from Colnbrook could not have reached parliament before the commissioners presented his earlier response. This was anxiously awaited by both Houses. The Lords did not sit on 10 November, but met the next day and transacted a considerable amount of business. Yet the issues which they dealt with were not those that were uppermost in their minds and can have done little to ease the tension. The implicit dangers to themselves and the parliamentarian cause of a hostile army approaching London, and an awareness of the fate of continental cities that had been captured and sacked, must have caused much nervous apprehension. Great efforts had been made to defend London against an attack and to secure it internally, but the outcome of a royalist advance could not be entirely certain. They must also have been eager to learn of the response to their petition to the king. Were they to expect peace or war?

The first business of the day, after prayers, was the reading of the letter from Northumberland and Pembroke, but of course that was just to notify them of their preliminary meeting with Charles. Hopeful of a further communication from them, the Lords decided to meet again at four o'clock and asked the Commons to do the same, which they agreed to. This was because they thought it probable that Northumberland 'may return with some Business as may require Expedition'. But the commissioners had not arrived by the time that the two Houses finally rose for the day, confirming that they did not leave Colnbrook until after noon.[70]

In the period of just over two weeks since the capture of Banbury the royalists had continued their campaign virtually unimpeded, occupying Oxford and replenishing their army, which continued to attract recruits, so that it was at least as large as it had been before Edgehill. They then continued their march towards London, but not quickly or directly. After their horse reached Maidenhead, they moved not eastwards towards the capital, but along the line of the Thames to Egham and Oatlands, suggesting that a strategy that involved a direct approach had not yet been settled. Essex had returned from Warwickshire more purposefully and his army was in London before the royalists got near to it; and military preparations in the capital had gone on apace, with parliament keeping their allies in the City informed of developments. Accompanying the movements of the armies were talks about possible negotiations. The first attempt collapsed because of the king's refusal to allow Evelyn to be a delegate, but when parliament's approach was renewed it produced a meeting between Charles and the parliamentary commissioners, with the prospect of future talks. Yet, just as meaningful negotiations seemed to be close, the royalists at last assembled their army, although this was unknown to the parliamentarians.

6

Surprise at Brentford

In the early morning of Saturday 12 November the two sides had quite differing expectations of the day ahead. Members of the two Houses of Parliament were anticipating the report of their commissioners and the king's response to the proposals for peace negotiations. The royalists, on the other hand, were preparing for military action, while politicians close to the king must have realised that any possibility of negotiations would be suspended until the army's operations were halted.

When Hyde came to write his account of the Civil War, it served his purpose to stress the common ground between the politicians of both sides, trying to sustain a policy in the face of the military's increasing and, as he saw it, disruptive influence. The strained relationship between the statesmen and the swordsmen was one of the underlying themes running through his history. It had an especial significance at this critical point, when a renewal of the fighting could jeopardize the chance of a peace settlement, which seemed to be good, and probably lead to an escalation of the war. At the meetings at Colnbrook, Falkland and the other senior royalists had learned of the dissatisfaction of Northumberland and Pembroke with the growing power of their own military, which gave the two groups of politicians some common ground.

The two earls reported to the Lords at the beginning of the House's business on that Saturday morning, and the king's letter was read, and its contents conveyed to the Commons. The reaction was a wave of relief. Walter Yonge noted that the MPs rejoiced at the king's reply, which seemed to bring safety for the immediate future and, in the longer term, the prospect of ending the war through negotiation rather than fighting.[1]

Both Houses recognized that the military situation had now changed. Essex's response at this stage did not need to be definite on the possible evacuation of Windsor. But he did ask, quite pertinently, what instructions parliament had for the army during the period of negotiations; specifically, would there be a truce, during which military actions would cease? This was the obvious next step, as neither side would wish to negotiate without such security, and it may well have been one of the issues informally discussed by the parliamentarian delegation and the king's councillors at Colnbrook. The Lords accordingly wrote to the king, asking 'how the Armies shall govern themselves, and whether His Majesty resolves not of a Cessation of all Acts of Hostility, upon this Overture of a Treaty of Peace'.[2] The letter was entrusted to Killigrew, who duly set off to find the king, assuming that he was still at Colnbrook.

In fact, Charles and his army were already on the move. Before sunrise the royalist soldiers quartered around Colnbrook, Longford and other places to the west of London readied themselves to march on the capital. The detachment that had spent the night at Ashford marched 'very early' to Hounslow Heath and rendezvoused there with the remainder of the foot; the roads from Colnbrook and Egham to Brentford converged at Hounslow.[3] The horse and dragoons also joined the army. Even at this stage fresh recruits were arriving. John Gwyn was one of a group of five men who left Richmond intending to join the army 'which we met accidentally that morning upon Hounslow Heath'. They were quickly integrated into Sir Thomas Salusbury's regiment.[4]

When it was on Hounslow Heath the royal army was halted and deployed into battle formation, as a defensive manoeuvre 'expecting a bataille'.[5] The royalist commanders had interpreted Rupert's intelligence of parliamentarian forces at Brentford as implying that they were numerous enough to mount an attack and indeed had an aggressive intent. As just two regiments would not have been a serious threat, they must have feared that Brooke and Holles had been reinforced. Forming the army into a battle formation allowed it to check an early morning advance by the enemy towards Colnbrook, rather than have to hastily improvise a defensive formation while on the march. The royalists were being very cautious and acting defensively, their uncertainty increased by the foggy weather, which reduced visibility. Although the concentration of the army had been planned at least as early the previous morning, with an offensive intent, they did not now press on regardless and lost time by forming the army into battalia and then reverting to a marching formation.

The delay gave the opportunity for those regiments which were short of powder, match and shot to complete the process of re-supply with the munitions ordered to be readied the day before.[6] It also allowed the commanders to consider their plans. They did not decide to hold their ground in case an attack materialised, or to send an officer under a flag of truce towards Brentford, to discover if the parliamentarian officers were expecting a cessation of arms (which would also have allowed them to estimate the size of the detachment there). Instead, they resumed the advance across Hounslow Heath, through the village of Hounslow, towards Brentford, 2 miles away, which had been the objective since the previous day.

This was a crucial decision; the army could have been held on the heath in defensive positions until better intelligence was received or contact made with parliament, but the advance already decided on was continued. At some stage the king's self-justificatory letter to parliament explaining this action was despatched. As Killigrew was still at Whitehall, this was entrusted to John White, the Earl of Dorset's secretary (and so familiarly known as 'Dorset' White, to distinguish him from the John White who was an MP for Southwark in the Long Parliament and was known as 'Century White').

By selecting Hounslow Heath as the rendezvous for the army, the royalist commanders had effectively denied themselves the option of taking a route further north, avoiding the parliamentarian detachment in Brentford. The northerly route would have entailed a difficult cross-country march and exposed the royalist right flank to an attack from Brentford until the Uxbridge-Acton road was reached. Once there the army would have been vulnerable to attack on both sides, but could have attempted to outflank the troops in Brentford by crossing the River Brent further upstream and advancing on to the higher ground through Acton. This was held by one or more parliamentary regiments, probably including John Hampden's regiment of foot. At the time Acton was a village of roughly 500 people, a third of the size of Brentford. But both were surrounded by enclosures and it is unclear whether the royalists would have judged Acton a lesser obstacle. If, as suggested above, the royalist commanders had inadequate intelligence of the parliamentarian strength and dispositions, the route through Brentford which they chose had the advantage that the army's right flank was protected by the Thames. This, and the additional time it would have taken the royalists to march via Acton, may have been the decisive considerations.

Brentford consisted of one main street, lined on both sides with houses and shops, which ran for roughly one mile. The town had three distinct parts; Old Brentford to the east, New Brentford to the west of that, running as far as the triple-arched stone bridge over the River Brent, and Brentford End on the western side of the river, a ribbon of houses which stretched for more than 200 yards along the road towards Hounslow Heath. On the north side of the road in New and Old Brentford enclosed burgage plots, forming long narrow gardens, lay behind the properties, while on the south side the houses backed on to the confluence of the Brent and Thames, or the Thames itself. Old Brentford had some substantial houses; a number of them were three storeys high. St Lawrence's church stood, as now, on the south side of the road, its fifteenth-century rag-stone tower, topped by a spire, dominated the skyline of New Brentford and provided a vantage point from which the low-lying land to the west of the town could be scanned.[7]

There, beyond Brentford End, were fields on either side of the London Road, shown on Moses Glover's 1635 map of the Hundred of Isleworth. These were a mixture of arable and pasture; the enclosures bounded by hedges and ditches. To the south-west of Brentford End was Syon House, converted from a Bridgettine monastery after the Reformation and, ironically, owned by the Earl of Northumberland. To the north-east of the town was the open common field, but along the Great West Road towards Turnham Green were further enclosures.

With a population of more than 1,500, Brentford was a busy and congested market town. The weekly market was held along the street, which was also the Great West Road. In Elizabeth's reign the townsmen had moved the market to the rear of the Crown Inn because of the congestion, and Glover's plan shows it vaguely to the side of the street, but by the mid-seventeenth century it had again spilled out on to the main road. A traveller described how, 'The great highway passes through this market place', and he reported that at the market 'a great deal of merchandise' was traded by 'lots of people from the neighbouring villages'.[8] Brentford's position on a main road, and its distance from London, greatly influenced its economy, with inns providing travellers with food and lodging, and their horses with fodder and stabling. It also had a role as a river port, with wharves on the Brent, close to its confluence with the Thames. The town had developed a somewhat sleazy reputation, as a place frequented by Londoners carrying on illicit liaisons, because of its inns and its proximity to the city. This was made much of by Thomas Middleton and Thomas Dekker, whose characters in *The Roaring Girl* resorted to an inn called The Three Pigeons, and they described the town as 'sinful Brentford'. Middleton also referred to horse races there, which were always said to attract disreputable characters.[9] This lively and colourful town lay in the path of the royalist advance on London.

By around eleven o'clock no parliamentarian forces had materialized on Hounslow Heath and the army was ready to continue its march. In the still and misty morning air – Giovannie Giustinian described the weather as a thick fog – Prince Rupert prepared to lead-off the royalist troops, but Forth came up and took overall control of the army, leaving Rupert in command of the horse.[10] Such a late change of commander for an operation is surprising. It suggests either uncertainty in the royalist command structure, which is somewhat implausible, or that a smaller force was allocated to advance to Brentford ahead of the army, initially under Rupert's command. Forth had been appointed Lord General of the royalist army after the death of the Earl of Lindsey at Edgehill and was Rupert's superior. He would, therefore, have been expected to command this operation all along, with the incident perhaps simply referring to Rupert's impatience with the speed of the advance from Colnbrook.

While almost all the royal army, which probably totalled around 12,000 men, advanced to Hounslow, not all were engaged at Brentford. A parliamentary account refers to the royalist strength there being eight regiments of foot, twenty troops of horse and six pieces of artillery.[11] But a royalist account describes six foot regiments being involved in the fighting,[12] while contemporary accounts and petitions presented after the Restoration suggest that elements from at least eight royalist foot regiments were directly engaged. They included those raised in Lancashire by Sir Gilbert Gerrard and Lord Molyneux; Sir Edward Fitton's and Earl Rivers's Cheshire units; and from north Wales one commanded by Sir Thomas Salusbury. Henry Lunsford was commanding the regiment of his brother, Sir Thomas Lunsford, who had been taken prisoner at Edgehill. Thomas Blagge and John Belasyse commanded the other foot regiments that fought at Brentford.

Estimates based on pay warrants from 16 and 24 November suggest that up to 4,000 royalist foot were engaged at Brentford.[13]

All of the Prince of Wales's regiment of horse and at least three troops of horse from the regiments of Lord Grandison and Sir Thomas Aston were also engaged. Based on the Edgehill order of battle this would suggest 600–650 troopers.[14] However, as two of the four troops came from Aston's regiment and represented two-thirds of that regiment, it seems safe to suggest that the remaining troop was also deployed, bringing the likely total to about 700 men. If all three regiments were fully engaged, the cavalry would have totalled around 850 men. In total, the infantry and cavalry deployed at Brentford represented just over one-third of the army.

Denzil Holles's and Lord Brooke's parliamentarian regiments of foot had arrived in Brentford by the morning of 11 November. They were short of arms, match, bullet and powder, and ransacked the shops in the town for supplies.[15] Holles's regiment of red coats was placed in New Brentford and Brentford End. It had started the campaign with 1,130 men, but had been heavily engaged at Edgehill, and deaths, injuries and subsequent desertions are likely to have reduced the numbers to perhaps around 800 men.[16] The regiment had suffered from discontent in the ranks over its Lieutenant Colonel, Henry Billingsley, possibly because his profanity offended the men's godly sensibilities. He had been cashiered on 20 August and replaced by Sergeant Major James Quarles.[17] Brooke's much smaller regiment of 480 men was deployed in Old Brentford.[18] According to John Lilburne, then serving as a captain in Brooke's regiment, the foot were supported by 10–12 troops of cavalry, and they also had two or three pieces of artillery.[19]

Because of the time taken for the royalists to form up, it seems unlikely that their attack began much before midday.[20] The Prince of Wales's regiment of horse cantered down the London Road, having evaded any parliamentarian scouts, and then halted, only to be fired upon by parliamentarian troops, probably belonging to Holles's regiment and totalling no more than a company or two. Sir Richard Bulstrode, serving in the Earl of Northampton's troop in the Prince's regiment, noted that they were forced to retreat after being surprised by parliamentarian artillery placed behind a 'great hedge' and had to await the arrival of the royalist foot before pressing the attack.[21]

The extent of the royalist cavalry's engagement with the parliamentarian troops was limited. The larger arable fields that they passed after leaving the heath were lined with enclosures along the roadside, and they gradually gave way to smaller fields. The enclosures negated the utility of the cavalry, providing the parliamentary infantry with good cover and disrupting the movement of the royalist horse, causing them to become disordered. Henceforward the engagement at Brentford became an infantry battle, primarily, though not exclusively, involving musketeers. The royalists had a strong advantage in the numbers of foot engaged, outnumbering the parliamentarian infantry by more than three to one.

John Gwyn later wrote that the initial clash was in the vicinity of Sir Richard Wynn's house and it would have been the troops placed there who fired on the Prince's regiment.[22] That house, with its outbuildings and garden walls, was a suitable strong-point to serve as an outpost for the parliamentarian advance guard. The field pattern, too, favoured the defenders. Around the house were relatively small enclosures averaging four acres, and from the house to Brentford End they were smaller still, between one and three acres.[23]

Following the withdrawal of Bulstrode's men, Salusbury's regiment was ordered to dislodge the defenders. A parliamentarian spy in Oxford in early November, just a few days previously, described that regiment as consisting of '1,200 poore welch vermins, the off-scouring of the nation'. Although not detailed in contemporary accounts, it was later reported to have performed badly at Edgehill, and just before his regiment went into battle at Wynn's house, Sir Thomas is said to have told his men: 'gentlemen, you lost your honour at Edgehill, I hope you will regain it here'. His encouragement was effective and they succeeded in driving Holles's soldiers from the house.[24]

The fog might have caused some uncertainty in Brentford about the extent of the action and the scale of the force that was engaged in the attack, but the discharge of cannon and musketry must surely have been heard in the town. Yet no parliamentary reinforcements appear to have been sent to support the detachment at Wynn's house. This may have reflected a decision not to dissipate the limited forces available by supporting the outpost there and to concentrate on defending the town. But Lilburne provides another possible explanation for this inactivity. He claimed that, on hearing of the attack, Brooke's regiment began retreating towards London and only his intervention caused them to return to Brentford to fight.[25] As both regiments were without senior officers – neither Holles nor Brooke were with their regiments and Quarles was the most senior commander – the type of command and control problems described by Lilburne, once the self-serving aspects of his account are set aside, are certainly plausible. Such a failure of command, along with the general confusion caused by the surprise attack, could explain why the initial defence was not reinforced from Brentford. In addition, parliament, in the light of the understanding it judged it had with the king to enter into peace negotiations, had ordered that its soldiers 'should exercise no acts of hostility against any of [the king's] people', and this order alone might explain the uncertain response.[26]

Gwyn also wrote that the royalists were engaged with the parliamentarian troops 'by... Thames side' and 'beat them to retreat into Brainforde'. This advance from the south, through Isleworth along Syon Lane and perhaps alongside the Thames, despite the heavy condition of the water meadows at that time of year, would have put the defenders of Wynn's house in danger of being cut off from Brentford, and have exposed any reinforcements to a running fight in Brentford End and the small enclosed fields along the road, as they attempted to reach the house from the town. An orchard covering 15 acres lay between Syon House and the Brent, which could have provided parties of royalist skirmishers with cover to approach the road through Brentford End. Given parliamentarian uncertainty about royalist intentions, a withdrawal of the outposts to Brentford Bridge was a less hazardous option than reinforcing them.

The royalists advancing down Syon Lane would have passed close to Syon House. It is unclear whether parliamentarian troops were billeted there, although, like Wynn's house, it provided a good strong-point as an advance post to protect the approaches to Brentford Bridge. For that reason, and for their own security, the parliamentarian troops would have been well advised to occupy it, but their officers may have ordered them not to do so, for fear of alienating Northumberland.[27] But the household accounts for 1643 record repairs, costing £26 10s, where the house had been shot through with ordnance, the battlements damaged and the 'three ovals in the middle gallery... which were shot through by the King's forces'.[28] While this is a clear reference to the events of November 1642, it is uncertain whether the damage to the gallery refers to royalist forces firing into the house as part of an attempt to dislodge parliamentarian troops at some point on 12 November, or in an exchange of fire on the following day (see page 83).

The parliamentarian officers' response to the initial action was also complicated by the behaviour of their cavalry, most of which fled on hearing of the royalist attack. Only a troop commanded by Captain Robert Vivers remained. As with Salusbury's regiment, this may have reflected the need to recover its reputation, for it had been one of the first parliamentarian cavalry units to flee from the royalist attack at Edgehill.[29] The conduct of the horse doubtless alarmed the foot and lowered the civilian population's morale.

Even without the sight of the horse fleeing from their town and the vacillating response of some of the foot soldiers, the royalist advance presented the Brentfordians with the dilemma of civilians whose community was being attacked. Essentially, this was whether to leave and risk losing their possessions, and perhaps having their houses fired, or to stay, in the hope that they could protect their belongings and property, even though they must have known that they would be powerless in the face of armed soldiers. Parliamentarian propaganda over the previous few weeks would have inclined them to leave, especially those whose political or religious sympathies were unpalatable to the royalists. Understandably, the response appears to have been mixed. Some did flee and William Dunn, a butcher, slipped away, avoided capture by the royalists and arrest by the parliamentarians and brought the shocking news to parliament. The £5 paid him as a reward was an acknowledgement of his loyalty and the risk that he had run. But the parliamentarian sources suggest that others remained in the town, risking their lives by doing so.[30] They faced a harrowing few hours, as the royalist forces pressed on with their attack.

Once the parliamentary pickets at Sir Richard Wynn's house had been cleared the royalists advanced to attack Brentford. Hyde said that the parliamentarians had 'barricadoed the narrow avenues of the town, and cast up some little breastworks at the most convenient places'.[31] Logically, one of these would have been the approaches to the bridge over the Brent, but there is no reference to earthworks there, as cover for infantry and emplacements for artillery, or to Holles's men having followed the common practice of breaking down at least one of the arches of the bridge and replacing it with a makeshift drawbridge. The river provided the best place for the parliamentarians to check the advance into New Brentford, yet the bridge was blocked only by a small barricade. The time which Holles's men had to prepare for a possible attack – a little over twenty-four hours – and probably a shortage of entrenching tools may explain why they had not erected more effective works, and the barricade may have been hastily improvised.

The royalist attack, with overwhelming numbers – one royalist account talks of 1,000 musketeers – dislodged the parliamentarian troops from this defensive position in under an hour. Hyde acknowledged the contribution of Salusbury's regiment: 'Here a Welsh regiment of the king's, which had been faulty at Edgehill, recovered its honour, and forced the barricadoes well defended by the enemy'.[32] With the barricade captured, the defenders were forced to abandon the line of the Brent and retreat to another barricade, between New and Old Brentford, joining Brooke's purple-coated regiment. The approaches to the new position were covered by a brick house and by two small pieces of artillery, but Lilburne was clear that it did not have earthworks or trenches to provide cover for the defenders.[33]

Holles's men could have delayed the royalist advance along the street as far as this barricade by occupying the houses and firing from them, which would have forced the royalists to clear them from each house – a hazardous task – or to have set the buildings on fire. There is no evidence that the parliamentarians did that; perhaps their officers were afraid of splitting their men into the small groups that the tactic would have required, and so risk being defeated piecemeal. Moreover, it would have been counter to their training, which was to form in ranks and fire in volleys. The officers presumably preferred to keep the regiment intact, under their direct command, and fall back to join Brooke's men, forming a stronger unit that might be able to hold the second barricade.

The most likely location for that barricade is at the crest of the rising ground at the western edge of Old Brentford. Brooke's men had more time to construct it than Holles's troops had when erecting the barricade at the bridge, and the royalists had some difficulty in overcoming this second obstacle. One of their number, probably Matthew Smallwood, in Fitton's regiment, wrote a few days after the battle that his regiment:

was the sixth that was brought to assault, after five others had all discharge'd, whose happy honour it was (assisted by God, and a new piece of cannon newly come up) to drive them from that worke too.[34]

Gwyn also implies that the fighting was hard and at close quarters throughout the battle, describing the royalists' tactics as 'after once firing suddenly to advance up to push of pikes and the butt end of muskets'.[35] The parliamentarian soldiers were both outnumbered and handicapped by a shortage of powder, but a letter written from London shortly after the battle described how 'notwithstanding they wanted powder, they fell to it with their swords'.[36] The fight for this barricade was fierce on both sides; in Lilburne's words it was 'a bloody fight', and in Hyde's more gentlemanly phrase 'a very warm service'.[37]

Once this second barricade was cleared, following around two hours of fighting, the troops defending it finally broke; some retreated along the road through Old Brentford towards London, but others were forced down the relatively steep slopes to the Thames, unable to re-form in a body to prevent being pushed down from the higher ground. Some of them ended in the river, a significant number of them drowning, though probably fewer than the 200 reported in a royalist account. One newsbook claimed that the royalists shot at the parliamentarian troops as they swam for their lives.[38] Captain Richard Lacey from Holles's regiment probably was among those who were drowned.[39] The parliamentary troops forced into the Thames must have been prevented from retreating along the London road by royalists who had either worked around the right flank of the parliamentary defensive position through the enclosures, gardens and houses – making the barricade position untenable – or by a sudden royalist breakthrough, exploited with speed. This would have cut off the parliamentarians defending the left flank and forced them to surrender or swim. Lilburne confirmed this when he asserted that the defenders of the barricade 'never stirred off the ground till both [royalist] horse and foot had, as it were, encompassed us round'. This also suggests that the royalist cavalry had enjoyed some success in working its way through the enclosures to the north of the town and was able to manoeuvre to assist the infantry in an attempt to block the parliamentarian retreat.

A detachment was brought up to pursue the retreating parliamentary troops through Old Brentford. One account mentions four regiments of foot, including Belasyse's, and some horse, which pressed on to an open field 'almost as far as Hammersmith'. Another report described it as 'a good spatious field for those parts', which almost certainly refers to the open space covered by Turnham Green and Chiswick common field, the only open field between Brentford and Hammersmith.[40]

Here the advancing royalists encountered fresh parliamentarian troops, including the green-coated men of John Hampden's regiment of foot, who probably had come from Acton. One account described them as having been 'billeted not far-off', and the parliamentarians did have troops there.[41] His regiment was said by a nineteenth-century historian to have come from Uxbridge, but that is most improbable, not least because of the distance involved.[42] Hampden, who was with his regiment, had responded promptly to reports of the royalist attack on Brentford, and he readied his soldiers and marched them to Turnham Green.[43] He may have left a detachment to cover the road through Acton towards London. There were royalist dragoons at Uxbridge, perhaps detailed to protect the army's flank as it marched from Colnbrook and to probe for a weakness in Essex's dispositions, and other parties of royalists may have been carrying out similar operations.[44] According to a parliamentarian report the force at Turnham Green included several elements 'under their several leaders', including trained-band soldiers, while a royalist put its strength at four regiments, which probably was a case of over-estimating the size of an enemy force.[45]

Clearly, this was a force assembling hastily in response to the emergency. It would have been vulnerable in the open field and so Hampden placed his men in defensive positions 'in lanes and closes' along the edge of the open space. The royalists divided their force, with one detachment of horse and foot advancing on the parliamentarian positions and the remainder held in reserve. A royalist wrote a few days later that the fighting had lasted three hours and that they eventually drove the parliamentarians from their positions and took 'manie prisoners and colours and cannon'.[46] According to a parliamentarian account there was indeed a 'most fierce and furious fight about Brentford and Turnham Green'.[47]

Another pamphlet represented it as a full-scale action, during which Rupert with several troops of horse 'charged them with a broad front, into our front of Foot', but they were repelled, the pikemen killing some of the horses and tumbling the riders from their saddles, before the foot on both sides crashed together. As the battle raged, royalist soldiers 'dropped down in heaps' and were saved from further destruction only by the falling darkness. Their dead numbered more than 800 and parliament's army had more than 120 killed. While there were elements in the account which agree with other sources, this was a greatly exaggerated report.[48] Another account stated that Hampden's troops charged the royalist forces five times to cover the retreat of what remained of Holles's and Brooke's regiments, although that would have meant abandoning their defensive positions and so being exposed to attack by the royalist horse.[49] Whatever the truth of these accounts and the extent of the action, the royalists failed to defeat Hampden's men and, with the light fading and the royalist troops exhausted from around four hours of combat, the opposing forces disengaged.

The Committee of Safety commended Hampden for his resolution and judgement, which had helped minimise parliamentary casualties, and Essex's biographer Robert Codrington, in 1646, commented that Rupert 'was so well entertained at Brainford and Turnham Greene' by parliament's forces.[50]

Thomas May, in 1650, also acknowledged the importance of this action, in which Brooke's regiment, withdrawing from Brentford, and Hampden's, covered the retreat during 'a great and bloody fight' that both sides subsequently claimed as a victory.[51]

Hampden's troops stayed in the field after the fighting, to block the road into London while Essex prepared his forces, and to prevent the royalists pushing on to Hammersmith to capture parliament's artillery train there. The train had only 'a slender guard', according to Lilburne, perhaps referring to the seventy-five soldiers armed with firelock muskets who were responsible for its defence.[52] The royalists who had reached Turnham Green also stayed there, with their horse and foot.

Meanwhile, Brentford was sacked. According to Giustinian this was done on Rupert's orders as a punishment for its disloyalty to the king, though how easily he could have exercised control of his soldiers at a time when the laws of war legitimized the plunder of a stormed town is unclear.[53] After drinking heavily the royalist soldiers were said to have taken 'money, linnen, wollen, bedding, wearing apparell, horses, cows, swine, hens. And all manner of victuals. Also pewter, brasse, Iron pots and kettles'.[54] News of the sack quickly spread to London, where Nehemiah Wallington, writing shortly after the battle, noted in his journal:

> for the King's army, poor Brentford is made a miserable spectacle for they have taken from them... all that they have, insomuch that when the Parliament's army came into the town on the Lord's Day at night, the innkeepers and others begged the soldiers a piece of bread.[55]

But another contemporary view which suggested that the pillage at Brentford was comparable to the worst excesses at Magdeburg during the Thirty Years War, in which a town of 40,000 inhabitants was burnt to the ground, was clearly an exaggeration. Only one house was recorded as having been set on fire and, despite the fighting and subsequent looting, there seems to have been few, if any, civilian dead.[56]

The writers of the parliamentary newsbooks made much propaganda from the sack of Brentford, which indeed played into their hands by confirming their earlier warnings of royalist behaviour. But their own soldiers' search for provisions in the town prior to the attack must have been responsible for at least some of the townsmen's losses. To the north-east of Brentford, Ealingbury House was also badly sacked by royalist troops, so much so that by 1647 it was reported as being uninhabitable.[57]

The parliamentary forces suffered considerably in the action at Brentford. According to royalist accounts between six and eleven colours were captured, suggesting at least that many broken companies, and a number of officers were killed or mortally wounded, including Lieutenant Colonel Quarles, who was buried four days after the battle. Hyde later wrote that 'the chief officers and many soldiers' of the parliamentarian regiments were killed.[58] The burial registers of St Lawrence's church for November and December 1642 record the interments of two parliamentary captains and three lieutenants.[59] Among the dead was Captain William Bennett, who, according to his widow Thomasine, was 'the chief instrument' in checking the royalist advance, and was killed at the end of the battle, presumably at the barricade between New and Old Brentford, or in the river. Her narration of his service was accepted, for she was granted a pension of 22 shillings per week.[60] Accounts of casualty and prisoner numbers resulting from the battle vary, but it appears that around 50 parliamentary soldiers were killed in the battle, with perhaps more drowning during the rout.[61] A contemporary account suggests that 140 parliamentary soldiers were killed, which appears credible, and others would have died from their wounds in the days and weeks after the battle.[62]

Many more were captured. A parliamentarian newsbook reported that 400 parliamentary prisoners were taken, but that 140, largely from Holles's regiment, despite being threatened with death and branding, were released shortly after the action; the remainder apparently enlisting with the royalists.[63] The accounts of the committee for maimed and wounded soldiers for November 1642 are a more reliable source and show that 21 officers from both regiments, 57 soldiers from Brooke's and 249 soldiers from Holles's regiments received payments of £1 each for the officers and five shillings each for the soldiers who had been captured and 'strypt' at Brentford.[64] Having been stripped of their coats and outer clothing, and made to swear not to serve against the king in future, these 327 men were released, and so comparatively few men joined the royalists.

Not all were allowed to go free. It was during the rout at Brentford that John Lilburne was captured, and he was held by the royalists, as was Captain Robert Vivers, who had commanded the one troop of horse which remained once the royalist attack commenced. Both Lilburne and Vivers were taken to Oxford and charged with high treason, which carried a sentence of death, although they were prisoners of war. When parliament was informed of this it sent a message to Oxford that, if they were convicted and executed, royalist prisoners would be treated in the same way. Lilburne and Vivers were saved by this timely intervention and later were exchanged for royalist prisoners, but the willingness to try them as traitors indicates the way in which the king and senior royalists regarded parliament's soldiers at this stage of the conflict.[65]

Assuming that the term 'officers' refers to company commanders, lieutenants and ensigns, and allowing for those killed in action or known not to have been present at Brentford, the figures imply that at least 45 per cent of the combined officer totals for the two foot regiments were taken prisoner. This is a greater proportion of prisoners than experienced by the rank and file (an estimated 25 per cent) and reflects how well the parliamentary officers stuck to their task despite overwhelming royalist numbers and the loss of Quarles, the senior officer present. The dogged resistance of the parliamentarian foot produced a high level of losses, with around 470 of the 1,200–1,300 engaged being killed or captured, some 35–40 per cent; the unrecorded number of wounded would have raised the proportion to well over 40 per cent of those engaged. Perhaps the fact which best illustrates the impact of the battle is that Holles's regiment never again appeared on the parliamentarian order of battle; the surviving soldiers appear to have at least in part been drafted into Skippon's regiment, which was formed later in November and early December as part of Warwick's army.[66]

The accounts for the artillery train show that two pieces were lost, both of them drakes.[67] These were light field pieces, wider at the muzzle than the chamber and probably designed to fire case-shot, and so appropriate for use with the two regiments at Brentford.[68] They probably were the two pieces deployed at the barricade between New and Old Brentford. Henry Hexham, in his *The Principles of the Art Military*, published in 1643, described drakes as suitable 'to be drawne to some suddaine peece of service, as in the day of Battle… or for the defence of a Campe, when an ennemy is at hand'.[69]

Royalist losses appear to have been light, despite some parliamentary claims to the contrary.[70] One account details the deaths of sixteen men, including one captain and two lieutenants. The king, in a subsequent letter to parliament, admitted that ten royalists had been killed.[71] An unsubstantiated account suggests that the royalist dead were removed to Hounslow Heath, although why that should have been so is unclear.[72]

The defeat of Holles's and Brooke's regiments was not the end of the action in the Brentford area. Royalist accounts refer to parliamentary troops or equipment being moved down the Thames by boat from Kingston during the night following the battle. Rupert appears to have been sufficiently concerned about the threat of parliamentary soldiers from Kingston landing at Syon that once Brentford was taken he ordered Thomas Blagge's regiment of foot to take possession of the house.[73] As with the responsibility for the sack of Brentford, whether this order was on Rupert's own initiative or after having discussed it with Forth is unclear. It is possible that this implies that Rupert was responsible for directing the attack on Brentford, with Forth in overall command of the army but not directly engaged with the operation. But Forth was made Earl of Brentford by the king in March 1644 and Lloyd described him as 'leading his forces gallantly [at Brentford]', suggesting he had more than a passing involvement in the battle.[74]

Essex withdrew his troops from Kingston to reinforce the defence of London. Most of them marched to London on the south side of the Thames. But artillery, munitions and, possibly, a small number of troops travelled by boat down the river. The most contemporary, royalist, account indicates that fourteen barges with 600 troops and thirteen pieces of artillery passed by Brentford in the early hours of 13 November.[75] These were spotted by royalist musketeers at Syon House and reportedly engaged over a period of two to three hours, presumably by artillery. The royalists claimed that in this action they sank four or five vessels and captured the remainder, with eight pieces of artillery. A separate, parliamentary, account reported that eight barges were laden with cannon, powder, match, bullets and ammunition at Kingston and rowed down the Thames on the night of 12–13 November.[76] They came under musket fire from Syon House and three or four crew members were injured. But between Old Brentford and the site of the modern-day Kew Bridge the royalists had deployed cannon covering the river and, judging that they had no chance of escape, the parliamentarian sailors detonated the powder and scuttled at least some of the barges.[77] One of the barges was carrying six brass cannon and twenty-five barrels of gunpowder. Parliament later rewarded its captain, George Phillips, for his decision to detonate the powder, which sank the boat, and for subsequently recovering the cannon.[78]

Gwyn also refers to a barge with soldiers and ammunition being blown up by Sir Charles Lloyd 'or some other engineer', but he may have conflated this single sinking with a separate incident which appears to have occurred on 13 November.[79] According to a parliamentarian pamphlet, on that afternoon two pinnaces, deployed by parliament to prevent the royalists using boats to land forces at Whitehall or in the City, attacked Syon House with cannon, damaging it substantially.[80] The royalist counter-fire, from cannon on the 'top' of the house and 'lower', was largely ineffective; the former apparently because it overshot the ships and the latter because it was inconvenient to use, possibly because of the heavy, rain-sodden, nature of the ground. However, one of the vessels was sunk by royalist fire, according to the pamphlet, due to the skill of the king's engineers. This appears to fit with other accounts of both sides that refer to one or two vessels being sunk. Some of the repairs reported in the household accounts for Syon House in 1643 probably were necessary as a result of this exchange of fire.[81]

The royalists would have been uncertain of the number of cannon which the parliamentarians lost when the barges and pinnace were sunk. This may explain the high and conflicting figures provided by Giustinian and Hyde. According to Giustinian's report, the parliamentarians lost eight pieces of artillery at Brentford, and Hyde put the number of cannon captured at fifteen.[82]

Little damage appears to have been done to the house during the royalist occupation, perhaps because the high command wished to avoid alienating Northumberland, whose influence provided some hope for a peaceful settlement. This, however, would suggest a degree of control over the royalist soldiery that had been singularly missing throughout much of the preceding campaign, and conflicts with Blagge's subsequent reputation when he was governor of Wallingford.

The fighting at Brentford had resulted in the destruction of two parliamentarian regiments and the loss of two guns, but the royalist march on London had been severely disrupted. The delay caused by the prolonged parliamentarian resistance in the town gave Essex time to prepare his defence of the capital. Unaware of this or the reaction in London, and in any case insensitive to it, Charles was convinced that victory was in his grasp and did not withdraw his forces, having given Essex's army a bloody nose. He would have achieved something positive in propaganda terms if he had shown no further aggressive intent, to counter the unfavourable impression created by the attack on the parliamentarian force and sack of the town. He could indeed have waited there to receive the parliamentarian commissioners, as he had written that he would do. The sack of the town could have been blamed on the senior officers, for exceeding their orders, while the king would be seen to have acted graciously by not pursuing his advantage. Instead, he took the fateful step of bringing up the remainder of the army to reinforce the detachment of his forces which had reached Turnham Green by nightfall.

The battle at Brentford had checked the king's advance on the capital and had lost him the element of surprise. Nevertheless, the objective of capturing the town had been achieved and all now rested on the outcome of the next day, 13 November. If the king could either push on without meeting serious opposition, or defeat those parliamentarian forces which he encountered, he would be in a strong position to dictate the terms of a settlement, with the prospect that the war would be over by Christmas.

7

Turning the Tide at Turnham Green

The attack on Brentford abruptly ended any thoughts of further negotiations and required a swift military response from parliament. Whatever the royalists' intentions were, their actions posed an immediate threat to the parliamentarian forces, their artillery train at Hammersmith and perhaps even London itself. Essex's only feasible response was to concentrate his troops to prevent any further royalist movement eastwards.

Before the news of the attack reached Whitehall, his regiments mustered in Chelsea Field heard the volleys of musket fire, audible 6 miles from Brentford in the still autumn air, and the artillery fire was 'easily heard' in London. Both Houses of Parliament were still sitting. This produced a dramatic moment, with Essex hastily leaving the chamber of the House of Lords to take horse and organize the assembling of his troops, directing them westwards towards the sound of the guns.[1] Only a part of his army was drawn up there, for the foot regiments of Brooke, Holles and Hampden already were at Brentford and Acton, with some units of horse, and those guarding the artillery train were at Hammersmith. The detachment of 3,000 men under Sir James Ramsay at Kingston was described as horse and foot 'of Essex's army', although perhaps in the sense that they were troops who came under his command, rather than all units of the regular army. Another source reported that they were members of the trained bands, although it is unclear whether these included some from the Southwark or Westminster bands. And so the troops mustered at Chelsea Field were by no means the whole of the army available to Essex.[2]

The news 'that the kinges army sett upon our men att Brainforde' was not unwelcome to those members of both Houses of Parliament who were apprehensive of where negotiations with the king may lead, for although it brought the danger of a military threat to parliament and London, it ended the proposed treaty without further argument.[3] The members were now subject to another wave of emotion. Having had their earlier apprehension and foreboding replaced that morning by relief and hope, when the news of the king's willingness to negotiate was presented to them, they must now have felt a renewed sense of alarm, and probably, too, of indignant anger. The justificatory letter sent by the king and carried by 'Dorset' White had not arrived.

Parliament's instruction to Essex not to carry out any acts of hostility while their letter despatched to the king suggesting a cessation was being considered, now had to be rescinded, in case he would feel constrained by it, which would put his army at a military disadvantage. A determined and unwavering response was urgently needed and so it sent to reassure him that he was no longer bound by their letter's contents, as the royalists had 'begun to commit Acts of Hostility'.[4] Parliament needed to know how its Lord General was likely to react and sent William Strode to a meeting with him. Strode was one of the five MPs impeached by the king in January. He had been with Essex at Edgehill and was entrusted to carry his account of the battle to parliament, and so was thought to be someone to whom the earl would speak frankly. He returned to tell the Commons that Essex, 'does not intend to be amused by Treaties; but seeing they have begun the Acts of Hostility, to pursue, and see what they will do'.[5]

Londoners were less sanguine when the news from Brentford spread through the city. The surprise attack on the parliamentarian regiments and the sack of the town, when peace negotiations were being discussed, came as a shock. John Evelyn's entry in his diary expresses the reaction: 'No[vember]: 12: was the Battaile of Braineford surprisingly fought, & to the greate consternation of the Citty'.[6] In Hyde's expressive phrase: 'The alarum came to London, with the same dire yell as if the army were entered into their gates.' But it had the effect of hardening opinion against a settlement and rallied the citizens in favour of a stand against the king. The hostile propaganda directed against his army over the previous weeks had been effective, encouraging the belief that if the royalist soldiers broke into the city they would sack it and their officers would be unable, or unwilling, to restrain them.[7] John Milton penned his sonnet *When the Assault was Intended to the City* to reflect, and gently mock, the prevailing mood, with its appeal to the royalist officers to protect him in his house in Aldersgate Street, should they overrun the city:

> Captain, or colonel, or knight in arms,
> Whose chance on these defenceless doors may seize,
> If deed of honour did thee ever please,
> Guard them, and him within protect from harms.

But this fear, with the wave of dismay which ran through the city, had to be turned into an effective response to the emergency, not allowed to generate despair.

The senior commanders may not have been as stunned by the attack as were the citizens. On the previous day, John Lilburne, before he went to Brentford, had met Essex and Lord Brooke at Essex House in the Strand, when Brooke told him that he expected an imminent clash with the king's army and that he was hopeful of a parliamentarian victory that would bring the war to an end.[8] Whether this was based on intelligence or a perception of the probable conduct of the royalist commanders is uncertain, but suggests that Essex's officers were not taken completely by surprise.

They may have welcomed the attack, for it allowed them to impose discipline on the army, which was becoming something of a problem, and to resolve the uncertainty of the response of the trained bands if such an emergency occurred. This was in some doubt. When Essex discussed with his senior officers the possibility of ordering Ramsay's force at Kingston to advance across Hounslow Heath in the wake of the royalist army and block its rear, some objected that they had no certain idea of how many troops would assemble to face the king's army, or the number that would be required to stop it. They felt that the strategy should be to concentrate all the available forces. And so Essex withdrew the detachment from Kingston to join the army at Turnham Green, even though it would take time to march on the south side of the Thames, across London Bridge and then out of the city.[9]

Their concerns proved to have been unfounded. In the face of a royalist advance on the city, Essex was able to assemble a considerable force. Following the arrival of the news from Brentford and the realization of its significance, the Commons sent a message to the lord mayor, Isaac Pennington, and Militia Committee, asking them 'to send all the Forces of Horse and Foot they can spare, with all Speed, to my Lord General'. They also requested that supplies be sent to the army, consisting of 'Provisions of Bread, Cheese, and Beer, and Men, and Munitions'.[10] Any uncertainty about how the City would react was dispelled by the efforts of Pennington and the committee, who secured the agreement of the Common Council for the service of the trained bands with Essex. Giustinian stressed that this was the first time that they had been asked to serve away from London itself, and their commanders had agreed.[11] He was perhaps unaware that some of them had already been despatched to Windsor.

Whatever problems may have arisen because of the conduct of the troops, or lingering doubts about the propriety of opposing the king – a more immediate issue when he was just a few miles away with an army than in abstract, which had been the case two months earlier – the citizens responded willingly. Imprisonment of the king's foremost supporters had been effective in depriving the London royalists of leadership, and many of those sympathetic to the king would have regarded the city's capture by his ill-disciplined army as a greater evil than acting with their communities to provide men and supplies in its defence.

Those young royalists whose behaviour, in St Paul's and elsewhere, had caused problems for the authorities in the preceding weeks did not now take the opportunity to create a diversion. Yet the call to arms could equally have served to bring them and other royalist demonstrators on to the streets. Small groups noisily running around the city, making sporadic attacks on the guards at the barricades, skirmishing with the pro-parliamentarian apprentices, breaking windows, throwing stones, starting fires, could have caused enough disturbances to occupy all the trained-band troops. Unruly crowds had worked in favour of the parliamentarian cause over the previous two years or more; none now appeared to help the royalists at this crucial moment, with the king's army so close to London. A lack of organization was one reason, as was absence of co-ordination with the army; the news of the attack on Brentford came as a surprise to the adherents of both sides. In any case, the royalist commanders would hardly have considered using popular uprisings as part of their strategy. Careful parliamentarian control of the neighbourhoods and streets was another explanation, although that may have been less complete in the suburbs than in the City. Clearly, by mid-November the king's supporters in London had been cowed and were not numerous or determined enough to make an effective fifth column.

As the trained bands and other soldiers levied in London were not distracted by any violent and threatening disturbances close to home, they could march away with the city securely held behind them. And so:

> all that Saturday Night the City of London poured out Men towards Brainford, who every hour were marching to Turnham-Green, where the Rendezvous was [and where, by the morning,] a wonderful number of armed men were met.[12]

In his parish of St Leonard's, Eastcheap, just north of London Bridge, Nehemiah Wallington witnessed the response, as word of the royalist attack spread:

> This heavie tidings put us all in feare & seeking to the lord for help. Then suddenly Drumes strock up for our souldigrs to goe forth & my man William Grant at that time went forth with the rest. And we heard that the King would come with all his forces against the City the next morning being the Lords day & that night was a troublossom Night the Carts carying magazen all night & morning.[13]

To a puritan such as Wallington, the fact that the royalists were prepared to advance against London on the sabbath was an affront and helped to stiffen his resolve. Certainly, the parliamentarian forces were mobilized without delay and, as well as the forces that 'flockt with the Generall out of London', John Gwyn, with the king's army, reported that 'a great recruit of men' came from Windsor and Kingston to join Essex's army.[14]

Turnham Green was part of an open space between the village of Chiswick, on the Thames, and the enclosures in the adjoining parish of Acton to the north, the only area between Brentford and Hammersmith large enough to provide a battlefield. Neither commander would have wished to commit his forces to irregular skirmishing among the hedged fields, which was likely to develop into confused fighting that was difficult to control. The troops and the trained bands had been prepared for formal combat, with the members of each foot regiment standing together, the musketeers and pikemen providing mutual support, not piecemeal 'hedge fighting'. Given the lack of experience of the trained bands and volunteers, Turnham Green would have been Essex's preferred ground and the royalists either could not prevent him from concentrating his force there, or were willing for him to do so, enabling them to bring up their army and deploy opposite the parliamentarians, prepared for a formal battle. Essex spent the night at Hammersmith and assembled his force by eight o'clock on the morning of Sunday 13 November at Turnham Green.[15]

Most contemporary sources estimated the army's strength at 24,000 men, although some put the figure at only 20,000. An accurate number is difficult to achieve. Some foot regiments were seriously under strength, with fewer than 500 soldiers. Others, such as those of Hampden and Viscount Rochford, were much closer to their nominal complement. The muster lists show the average strength of eight foot regiments, excluding officers and non-commissioned ranks, to have been around 510 men before the clash at Brentford. Hampden's regiment probably escaped relatively unscathed from the fighting on the previous day, but Holles's regiment had been smashed up in the fighting at Brentford and Brooke's regiment, too, had been badly mauled. Holles's regiment ceased to exist shortly afterwards and Brooke's regiment was disbanded on 10 December.[16] If all of Essex's foot regiments were present at Turnham Green, then the foot would have numbered around 9,000, allowing for the losses to Holles's and Brooke's regiments. Shortly after the battle the horse were numbered at 2,700, and the dragoons should have provided roughly 900 more, while the artillery's nominal strength was 570.[17] The regular army's strength was, therefore, more than 13,000 men. It was reinforced by two regiments of the City's trained bands, numbering at least 2,600 men, the 1,200 strong regiment that had been raised by the City under Colonel Randall Mainwaring, the majority of Warwick's army, roughly 3,000 strong, sailors from the fleet organized into at least two regiments, an unknown number of other volunteers and probably 2,400 men from the trained bands of Westminster and Southwark.[18] The royalists' impression was that Essex's army was reinforced by 'at the least ten thousand of the train'd bands out of the city'.[19]

Essex's full force was well over 20,000 men, not including the four City trained band regiments kept back for such duties as manning the defences and the Tower, guarding parliament and Guildhall, and patrolling the city. Ramsay's force, probably consisting of the Surrey, Middlesex and perhaps Berkshire trained bands, some horse and part of a regiment in Warwick's army, now marching towards Southwark was not yet part of the army.[20] It may be prudent to assume that none of the various elements were at full strength at Turnham Green, but the army grew in size during the day, as volunteers continued to arrive. Some failed to reach the battlefield in time, including a party of about 100 seamen, who rode 'singing and rejoycing out of Towne hoping to have a fling at the Cavalliers, but they were gone before they came'.[21]

Among the volunteers were some very senior figures. The presence of a hostile army so close to the capital put the members of both Houses, and parliament's prominent supporters, on their mettle. They could not be seen to be unwilling to appear in arms in the face of such an imminent danger and so Essex was joined by many gentlemen volunteers and 'Many of the most substantial citizens', some of whom formed their own troops.[22] Among them were members of the Lords with recent military experience. Warwick's brother Henry Rich, Earl of Holland helped in the disposition of the army. He had served in the Low Countries as a young man, had been given command of a force that was raised to reinforce

Buckingham's army at the Île de Ré in 1627 – although it was assembled too late to see action – and, more recently, was General of the Horse in the First Bishops' War in 1639.[23] Essex was also advised by the Earl of Northumberland, the negotiator now turned soldier, and he, too, had military experience. He had been appointed by the king as general of the forces raised for the Second Bishops' War. Although prevented by illness from taking part in the campaign, he had been active in organizing the army, for example issuing a set of 'Lawes and Ordinances of Warre Established for the Better Conduct of the Service in the Northern Parts'. Even so, this dramatic change of roles in just three days, from senior politician leading the delegation that had met the king to discuss peace, to appearing in arms at the head of an army confronting his majesty's forces, may have been intended by the earl as a statement of his response to the royalist breach of faith in launching an attack while peace talks were being discussed.

The presence of the members of both Houses may have caused some difficulties within the parliamentarian command, especially as the events of recent years had left a legacy of ill-feeling, such as that which existed between Essex and Holland. This partly arose from the latter's appointment in 1639 ahead of Essex, which was generally accepted to have been due to the queen's influence, and partly from his intemperate reaction to Essex's quite proper response to an approach from the Scottish leaders, when he had gone so far as to describe him as a traitor.[24] The royalists were not alone in having problems among their commanders.

The parliamentarian army was an impressive sight. Walter Yonge proudly noted that it was 'as brave an army as ever was in Christendome' and even Hyde grudgingly described it as 'a full army of horse and foot, fit to have decided the title of a crown'.[25] The addition to the army of the City forces, sailors and other volunteers produced an unusually high proportion of foot, although the horse regiments, recovered from their mauling at Edgehill, matched the royalist horse in terms of numbers.[26]

Both Essex and Skippon were conspicuous in going from regiment to regiment, encouraging the troops. Essex rode from one regiment to another and when he had finished his harangue the soldiers threw their caps in the air and shouted 'Hey for old Robin'. Skippon also went to each of the companies under his command, exhorting his men, shrewdly appealing to their religious convictions and their need to defend their families, playing on the fears of a royalist army running amok in London, telling them: 'Come my boyes my brave boyes, let us pray heartily & fight heartily.'[27]

Essex had no alternative but to block the road to London at the most westerly point where he could deploy the army. The royalist commanders, on the other hand, did have a choice and even on the Sunday morning could have withdrawn their advanced forces from Turnham Green and remained in and around Brentford, without confronting the parliamentarian army. But they were unaware of parliament's offer of a cease fire. Sir Peter Killigrew, carrying parliament's letter to the king, did not succeed in delivering it. He set off on the Saturday, but when he reached Brentford the fighting had already begun and he was unwilling to try to make his way through the warring soldiers. He then attempted to go around the obstruction by going to Uxbridge, but there found a party of royalist dragoons 'and upon that he returned back'. His rank as king's messenger had not been a convincing enough reason for the royalist soldiers to let him through, and on the following Monday he returned the letter to the Lords.[28]

Whether the letter would have prompted the king to keep his forces at Brentford is uncertain, now that the army was so far committed, but it would at least have allowed the politicians the opportunity to make one more attempt to halt the advance and agree a truce, so that talks could be considered. Without that inducement, the royalist commanders pressed on with the campaign and ordered the army up through Brentford to be assembled facing the parliamentarians at Turnham Green. Killigrew's lack of success in reaching the king was an unfortunate missed opportunity.

The royalist army may have been as large as at Edgehill. It had sustained losses at Brentford and Rupert ordered a party of 500 to guard Brentford Bridge, to safeguard the army's rear from an attack by the parliamentarian forces from Windsor and Kingston.[29] Nevertheless, the force available at Turnham Green would have totalled approximately 12,000 men, with the horse constituting more than a fifth of the army's strength.

The hope, and perhaps even expectation, in the king's entourage was that, because of royalist support in London, and fear of a confrontation, the trained bands and volunteers would not march out of the city to join Essex. If the hearsay that Giustinian reported – that some of the trained band captains had resigned and those still serving had 'loudly refused to go outside London to oppose the King' – had also reached the king's army, then this was not as unrealistic as it seemed in retrospect.[30] John Belasyse's secretary Joshua Moore wrote that the king:

> expected those of London would not stand out... [but] At break of day our hopes from the City were disappointed, for they drew out all their trained bands against us in such infinite numbers as, if we had fought them, we must have been overpowered.[31]

No accounts mention the foggy weather that had helped the royalist approach to Brentford on the previous morning, and looking across the open space the royalists realised that they were heavily outnumbered, perhaps by as much as two to one.

This was not such a clear-cut advantage as it appeared. A part of Essex's numerical advantage came from Warwick's newly raised force and the miscellaneous volunteers, who were neither well trained nor dependable, nor had they come under fire before. On the other hand the trained bands provided a prepared and self-confident force serving under its own dependable officers, although they, too, lacked experience of battle. Essex and Holland attempted to overcome the inexperience of the trained bands and volunteers by alternating their regiments with those of the army.

The disposition of the foot was not described, but in both armies may have followed that adopted at Edgehill. As the intention of the royalist commanders was to continue the advance as far as possible, and so be more likely to attack the parliamentarians than fight a defensive action, they may have used the Swedish system at Turnham Green, as they had done at Edgehill, despite the poor performance of their infantry during that battle. On the opposite side of the battlefield, Essex probably drew his infantry up following the Dutch system, as at Edgehill. The horse regiments were placed in the conventional way on the flanks.

The armies stood on open ground that consisted of Turnham Green, Acton Green, Stamford Brook Green and, on their south side, Chiswick common field. In the 1640s, 100 acres of the green lay within the parish of Chiswick and perhaps a further 30 acres in Acton.[32] The modern open spaces of Turnham Green, Chiswick Back Common, Acton Common and Acton Green are the remnants of Turnham Green, although it was more extensive in the seventeenth century than the overall area now covered by them would suggest. The Stamford Brook and the Bollo Brook flowed roughly south-east across the open space. On the north side were hedged fields on the rising ground towards the common fields of Acton, with the village beyond that, and there were also enclosures on the west side of the green towards the riverside village of Strand on the Green. To the east the green continued as far as Stamford Brook.[33] On its south side, Chiswick common field extended almost to the village of Chiswick and the walled gardens of the Jacobean Chiswick House. On the west side of the field was the small hamlet of Little Sutton.[34]

Access to the battlefield was relatively uncomplicated for both armies. East of Old Brentford the London road diverged. The southern branch, Turnham Green Lane, ran eastwards to the south-west corner of Turnham Green and then roughly along the south side of the green and on to Hammersmith. The northern one also ran across the green, and then to Stamford Brook along the line of the modern Bath Road. The two roads were connected by a third one that ran across the centre of the green. This, now the High Road, was lined with small cottages and a windmill. On the north side stood an inn, recorded in 1632, called 'The King of Bohemia', named after Prince Rupert's father, the Elector Palatine.[35] These three roads on to the west side of the green would have allowed the royalist troops to be drawn up relatively quickly and Sutton Lane, running southwards from its south-west corner, provided access to the west side of the common field, until it turned westwards to loop around an area of enclosures. The parliamentarians had been able to approach along the roads from Hammersmith and Stamford Brook.

The royalist historian Sir Philip Warwick referred to the battlefield as 'a large fair heath' and in 1662 the Dutch artist William Schellinks described Chiswick as lying 'in a great plain', which was the open space formed by Turnham Green, Acton Green and the common field.[36] Despite these impressions of a wide open tract of ground, the battlefield was a constricted one for the 36,000 or more men drawn up there and the parliamentarian army must have been quite tightly packed, helping to give a sense of security to those who had not stood in a battle formation before.

In numerical terms this was close to being the largest ever military confrontation in the British Isles. Essex's success in concentrating all of the available men can be measured by the fact that his army was the largest that either side deployed on a battlefield during the first Civil War, with the sole exception of Marston Moor in 1644, where three parliamentarian armies were combined to form a rather larger force than that at Turnham Green. Only at Marston Moor, Worcester in 1651, and possibly at Towton in 1461 (for which the figures are much more uncertain), were so many troops assembled on a British battlefield.

On the east side of the battlefield the parliamentarian front probably ran from the enclosures fringing the north side of the green to the garden walls of Chiswick House. Musketeers and dragoons placed in the gardens would have secured their left flank. Beyond the house was an expanse of meadows that was unsuitable for troop movements, especially so late in the year, and a party of troops attempting to cross them would have been countered relatively easily before it could reach Chiswick village. The enclosed fields around the green and common field were described as 'thick enclosures, with strong hedges and ditches, so lined with men as they could well stand one by another'.[37] Clearly, Essex was able to use his numerical advantage to good effect by positioning adequate numbers of men to protect the army's flanks.

Essex placed his artillery, protected by earthworks, to cover the roads running across the battlefield.[38] The artillery available to him consisted of five heavy guns – four demi-culverins and one twelve-pounder – and twenty-four lighter pieces: nine sakers and fifteen drakes.[39] Given the short distance from the artillery park at Hammersmith to Turnham Green, and the time and the resources available to Essex, it is possible that all of the field pieces were brought up with the army. As well as the chief engineer, a further four engineers were attached to the train 'for ordering trenches Fortifications and approaches', who would have set out the emplacements, and sixteen 'guides or conductors for the Workes of approaches for Fortifications & trenches' for overseeing the work.[40]

The royalist front probably ran from Acton Green across the modern Turnham Green and east of the line of Sutton Court Road. The gardens of Sutton Court on the south side of the Bollo Brook – at the junction of the modern Fauconberg Road and Sutton Court Road – gave cover for troops protecting their right flank. Enclosures in this area may have caused this section of the royalist front to have been pushed forward somewhat. The parliamentarian front extended for roughly 1,200 yards (approximately 1,100m), but the royalists' line was rather shorter. The frontage available at Turnham Green was much less than it had been at Edgehill and Essex now had twice as many men to deploy.[41] This notional disposition of the fronts places them roughly 550 yards (503m) apart; a contemporary account describes them as being separated by about half a mile.⁴²

On the north side of the battlefield the royalist left was outflanked by the horse opposite to them, who, according to John Gwyn, 'stood upon more ground than the King had horse to face them'.⁴³ This may have been because Rupert preferred to keep all of the horse on the south side of the brook here, rather than divide his force on either side of it, even though this risked being outflanked.

The royalist left flank was their weakest point and Forth attempted to reduce its vulnerability by deploying infantry 'towards the hill at Acton', to line the hedges of the enclosures, hoping to prevent the parliamentarians from carrying out an outflanking movement. When a parliamentarian force of foot and horse, including Hampden's regiment, was sent to drive them out, the royalist musketeers had some initial success, killing some men and horses in a lane between the green and Acton before they were forced to withdraw. Essex was then able to deploy a larger force of four foot regiments (including Hampden's) and two of horse, instructing them to march around through Acton and get behind the royalist rear, so that 'upon a signal' a simultaneous attack would be launched on the king's army, from both front and rear. According to one account the foot regiments included that of Denzil Holles, although this may be an error, given the losses it had sustained at Brentford, and fresher regiments would have been employed.⁴⁴

The six regiments, containing roughly 3,000 men, marched around the north side of the two armies into Acton. This is higher ground than the battlefield, which stands on the flood plain. To the south of Acton was Mill Hill and, on its south side, Turnham Field, with enclosures separating the field from Acton Green. Mill Hill and Turnham Field occupied a spur of relatively high ground, which commanded the royalist left. Hampden would have been familiar with the topography from the events of the previous day, and aware of the potential for disrupting the royalist left wing. Yet he did not have any artillery with his detachment, and so he sent Essex a request for cannon. Essex despatched two pieces, but then changed his mind and not only recalled them before they had reached Hampden, but countermanded his previous order by withdrawing the six regiments to rejoin the army on the battlefield.

Essex's Sergeant Major General, Sir John Meyrick, brought the order to Hampden and was asked by his friend Bulstrode Whitelocke why this decision had been taken, by which they lost 'so great an advantage against the enemy'. Meyrick betrayed a certain amount of frustration by replying, rather indiscreetly, that he was afraid that 'some were false who had given this advice to the general', but Hampden facetiously told him to be quiet, for he was risking being shot as a mutineer.⁴⁵ Indeed, these or some other disgruntled remarks by Meyrick led on 17 November to the House of Commons considering a rumour that he had slandered some of its members, although on investigation it concluded that it retained its 'good Opinion of him, and his Service'.⁴⁶ Whitelocke's account conveys the controversial nature of the decision and the dissatisfaction of the detachment's commanders, who could appreciate what a good position they held. The royalists, too, realized the danger which the detachment presented, with the possibility that it could press on past Acton and then turn southwards to the Thames to mount an attack on the rear of their army, or to Brentford, cutting them off from their supplies and line of withdrawal.[47]

Attacks on the royalist front and rear would have been difficult to co-ordinate and Essex's commanders may have thought them to be too hazardous to risk. Had Ramsay's detachment still been at Kingston, it could have been ordered to clear Brentford of any royalist troops left in the town and then join with the six regiments, but the reinforcement of the main army had been thought to be the more prudent course. Furthermore, the clearance of Brentford may not have been quick or easy, as the royalists had learned the previous day; a force in the royalist rear would have had to negotiate hedged fields before they could launch an assault, fragmenting it and making deployment and control difficult; while attacks from opposite directions ran the risk of casualties from friendly fire. Yet, even though the risks of simultaneous attacks may have been too great, the six regiments could have been kept in place on the rising ground above the royalist left, able to bombard the enemy and threaten to launch an attack in conjunction with the parliamentarian horse on that side of the battlefield, to drive in the royalists' left flank. Their very presence was a threat that could not be ignored; Whitelocke noted that when they reached the high ground the royalists 'began to gaze & be amused at it'. They would have needed to consider strengthening their left wing, at the expense of other sections of their line. But Essex reverted to his strategy of blocking a royalist advance, with as many troops as possible on the battlefield itself.[48]

The withdrawal of the six regiments relieved the royalist commanders of a major threat, but they were unwilling to launch an attack, against an army that was numerically so superior to their own. This decision must also have owed much to the knowledge that many of their men would have been unfit to fight a second battle in two days, after the exhausting efforts they had made in the fighting at Brentford. Those who had not been engaged in the battle, but had helped to consume the town's food and drink, would also have experienced some reaction, which by the Sunday morning could have meant a heavy drowsiness, at the least. Matthew Smallwood wrote that overnight 'most lay in the cold fields'. The horse had been less involved in the fighting at Brentford, but because of the constricted nature of the battlefield at Turnham Green they lacked an open space in which they could charge the parliamentarian horse and drive them from the battlefield, and so the king 'having no convenient room for his horse (which is the greatest pillar of his army) to fight' could not employ them successfully.[49]

Despite the military disadvantages, the royalists were prepared to keep the troops in position, partly in the hope that a delegation from the parliamentarians would invite the king to accompany them to Whitehall, to resume negotiations there. Some of the senior figures with Essex reportedly had a similar expectation; that under a flag of truce members of the king's entourage would be prepared to negotiate his return and a resumption of talks. Their hopes were based upon the notion that he was badly advised and that this provided the best opportunity, being 'so neare to his Parliament... to have rescued himselfe from those that have thus misled him'.[50] This probably was why Essex withdrew Hampden's outflanking force, so that the parliamentarians were not undertaking any offensive action that the royalists might construe as a reason for not sending a message across the battlefield.

The hopes of those who preferred to explore the possibility of a negotiated settlement, rather than attack the royalists, would have been raised by the arrival of 'Dorset' White at the parliamentarian lines, accompanied by a trumpeter. White was taken to Essex and he showed him the king's letter, written the previous day, but not delivered then because of some unspecified 'Stops by the Way'.[51] As was customary, the letter was directed to the Speaker of the House of Lords, but as the House was not sitting Essex took it upon himself not only to accept the letter, but also to read it. He and the peers with him probably did so anticipating that its contents related to the current situation and possibly offered a political alternative to the military impasse. This would have been a reasonable expectation, with the two armies confronting each other, but they were to be disappointed, for the letter was, of course, out of date. The king's army had taken possession of Brentford, as he had anticipated, but he had not waited there to receive parliament's message and had moved on with the army towards London.

The king's actions showed him at his most capricious, neither waiting to arrange with parliament an alternative to Windsor, nor halting at Brentford, his own designated choice. Northumberland and Pembroke had travelled and conversed with Sir Peter Killigrew on the Thursday and Friday and now might have been able to discuss matters with him and gain some sense of how things stood, had he been the bearer of the letter, rather than White. His failure to reach the royalists on the Saturday was therefore doubly unfortunate, for not only had he been unable to deliver parliament's letter concerning a ceasefire, but he was now unable to act in his accustomed role as trusted messenger from the king. White would have been known to the commissioners as the Earl of Dorset's secretary, who, incidentally, was returned as an MP for Rye in both the Short and Long Parliaments.[52]

White may have been regarded as a committed royalist and perhaps was uncooperative, for Essex held him for some time before sending him on to parliament as a prisoner rather than a courier. Even though he could be regarded as a renegade member of the Commons, this went against the common usages of war, which provided for formal communication by someone acting under a flag of truce. Sir Philip Warwick objected that White was ill treated and blindfolded, and taken into London 'like a common drummer or trumpeter'. Hyde also complained that he was treated 'very roughly' and threatened with execution as a spy. Essex's disappointment at the dashed hopes of possible talks and the royal council's decision to forward a letter that was no longer relevant, except as a post-facto justification for the previous day's shocking events, may have contributed to his treatment of White.[53] An account of the battle suggests that the royalists at Syon firing on the parliamentarian barges from Kingston coincided with White's delivery of the letter. Essex heard the gunfire and interpreted it as another example of the royalists' lack of sincerity, continuing fighting while holding a parley.[54]

Essex's response would have seemed less improper subsequently, for as the war progressed little attention was given to the practice of granting immunity and freedom of passage to those carrying messages between commanders. A royalist officer in Cheshire wrote to his parliamentarian counterpart in April 1645:

> As for the custom of war in not taking trumpets prisoner, I am sure this war has not yet used it on either side, nor shall I be ambitious to begin the custom, having had my own trumpet taken.[55]

Essex's high-profile treatment of White so early in the war may have contributed to this attitude.

The failure of White to return with a reply from Essex did not encourage the royalists to send another letter, and so, with neither party willing to make an approach to suggest negotiations, the armies continued to face each other for 'many hours'.[56] But the period of stalemate was not without action. Essex read the king's letter at about ten o'clock, and both before and after then, 'the King's Forces gave an Alarm to Battle'.[57] According to one account, published in London a few days later, while Essex was reading the letter, a royalist cannonball flew close by. This describes in colourful terms how:

> the hope and harmony of peace was lost in the lowd voice of a Canon, which at that instant had discharged a bullet amongst his Excellencies Troupes, and whizzing by his Excellencies eare, gave him counsell, where ever he heard of that, to looke unto himself.[58]

The anecdote is supported by the observation from another parliamentarian source that the royalist cannon shot 'flew up in the air over our quarters', because the west side of the green was higher than the east, where the parliamentarian army was drawn up.[59] This is indeed the case, although the rise is a gentle one of only roughly 10–15ft. It suggests that the royalists' battery was sited on the higher and drier ground of the green. The common field to the south would have been ploughed after the harvest, making it difficult to manoeuvre artillery on the softer surface, with the risk of the heavier pieces getting bogged down. The royalist gun crews had had the same experience at Edgehill, again firing from higher ground, where their shot had either fallen short and failed to ricochet into the enemy ranks, or had passed over their heads. That may indicate the difficulty of judging the fall of shot and perhaps, too, the inexperience of the gunners. Balfour's men had killed some of the royalist artillery crews at Edgehill.[60]

Essex may not have needed the near miss to help him come to a decision and he did have other members of the Lords with him. There was nothing in the king's message to which they could respond, leaving military action the only option. Even so, the parliamentarians did not return the royalists' fire until late in the afternoon, when two cannon fired fourteen times at the royalist positions, although their effect was disputed. Parliamentarian sources claimed that the fire inflicted casualties, according to one account it 'cut off diverse ranks of their horse', but Hyde stated that it killed only four or five horses and not one man, and another account reported that 'some few shots of cannon are made, six of the King's horse killed, it is said'.[61]

As well as trying to unsettle the enemy soldiers with artillery fire, the royalist horse probed the parliamentarian positions. They made feints as if to attack on a number of occasions; according to the parliamentarian account prepared by members of the Committee of Public Safety, 'they made many offers as if they would have charged'.[62] Early in the day some of them rode along the hedges, firing their carbines at the infantry placed there, who replied with musket fire. There was also a small-scale skirmish between the cavalry. More determined attempts to try to break the deadlock were made by squadrons of royalist horse riding in front of the parliamentarian foot, to test their nerve and try to draw out soldiers from the inexperienced units by luring them forward. Had they done so they would have broken the line and lost the mutual support which ranks of pikemen and musketeers provided. If a group had edged forward far enough in their nervous response to being threatened, the royalist horsemen would have attempted to get behind them and so break into the regiment. A parliamentarian pamphlet described royalist horsemen:

> hovering up and down the Green, without the reach of our muskets, our red coats, being divers of them London prentices, could scarcely be restrained from falling on those cavaliers.

The royalist cavalry also tried the ploy of 'flurting out to try if they could kill or surprise any of our perdues or sentinels'. Flurting in this context means a sudden darting movement by a party of horse, again to unnerve the parliamentarian foot.[63] Neither Essex's soldiers nor the untried troops of the trained bands fell into the trap of being drawn out of their positions to confront the enemy horse and the royalists' tactics proved ineffective.

Almost as unsettling as the manoeuvres of the royalists was the reaction of 'some hundreds' of spectators who had gathered behind the parliamentarian lines. Unwilling to miss such a momentous event so close at hand, or perhaps so anxious as to its outcome that they preferred to witness the action and judge for themselves, rather than having to rely on hearsay, these formed a nervous addition to the parliamentarian army. When a party of either army advanced, or the soldiers gave a shout, some of them would take fright and 'ride apace towards London, to the discouragement of the army, & some of the soldiers would slink from their colours towards the City'.[64] But most of the troops were unaffected by the reactions of those fearful civilian onlookers and helped to maintain their own morale during the hours of anxious confrontation by singing psalms.[65]

While the presence of spectators from London was a drawback, a major advantage for Essex of operating so near to his base was that the army could be kept supplied almost indefinitely with provisions, and it received 'carefull supplies of ammunition'.[66] Following the appeal of the House of Commons, the lord mayor requested the preachers at the morning services to urge their congregations to play their part in defending the city, by sending to the troops food and drink that they were preparing for their Sunday dinners. And they responded with enthusiasm, for roughly a hundred cart-loads of supplies, including barrels of beer, bottles of wine and 'good things', were taken from London to the army. With this plentiful supply of food and drink, according to Whitelocke the soldiers 'were refreshed & made merry'. The operation was well organized, with carts waiting in every parish to carry the provisions to Turnham Green under the supervision of 'honest and religious gentlemen'.[67] The distribution of the supplies when they reached the army was less efficiently done, however, and a few days later a complaint was made in the Commons that beer and biscuit had been left around without anyone taking responsibility for allocating it.[68] Evidently, there was more than enough. The carriages probably were provided by the citizens, for the army was short of transport and on 22 November the wagon-master general was said to have only fourteen serviceable wagons available.[69]

The royalists, in contrast, were low on supplies and ammunition and had no prospect of being re-supplied while they were on the battlefield.[70] Unwilling to attack the superior army facing them and unable to sustain their position for too long, and facing the possible risk of being trapped by troops advancing from Windsor through Brentford, during the late afternoon they withdrew. A royalist account later justified the decision on the grounds that as the king's army could not 'be absolute victors, it was thought fit to retreat with honour and safety'.[71] This was a potentially hazardous operation in the face of a superior army and its skilful execution was a tribute to the ability of the royalist officers.[72] A half of the horse went first, followed by the carriages and artillery train, then the foot, with 1,000 musketeers covering their retreat, and then the dragoons, who took over the musketeers' positions as they withdrew, and finally the remainder of the horse.[73]

For a time Meyrick's officers seem to have been unaware of what was happening and, when the parliamentarian command did realize that the royalists were retreating, they were unwilling to commit their troops to an attack among the enclosed fields in the growing darkness. The simple explanation was that, 'It being now growne dark, it was not thought good to follow them.'[74] Essex's 100-strong lifeguard of horse 'in the highways' were best placed to lead a pursuit and later attracted sarcastic allegations that they were afraid of being ambushed and trapped. But Whitelocke and John Rushworth attributed the decision not to attack the rearguard not to the troops' pusillanimity but the influence with Essex of the professional soldiers, who assured him that it was enough that the king had retreated and London had been secured, so far as parliament's honour was concerned.[75] Essex did use his artillery during the royalist withdrawal, when most of the army had left the battlefield, and 'with no harmful success at all'.[76] He would have been loath to move it forward in the darkness in case of a sharp counter-attack or ambush.

The royalist dragoons and horse continued to cover the retreat through Brentford. The bridge was potentially a point where the pursuing troops could be delayed, but when Rupert reached it he found not a force of around 500 men, as he had ordered, but 'Sir Jacob Ashly almost alone'.[77] This incident suggests a lack of effective communication during the retreat, or perhaps a reluctance to be among the rearguard. But the royalists may have fought a delaying action, which is implied in a contemporary pamphlet, and the twenty-two royalist prisoners taken that evening perhaps were members of an organized covering force captured during a fight, rather than stragglers.[78]

Kingston bridge and town, left undefended, that evening were occupied by a detachment of royalist horse, probably those who had led the way from the battlefield at Turnham Green, who, not having met any resistance in Brentford or beyond, were able to push on and reach Kingston. They were followed by much of the army, according to a parliamentarian account, which reported that, 'they march in a great confusion without opposition to Kingston where most of the horse was quartered'.[79] The greater part of the army did not enter the town, 'standing all night on battalia on Hounslow Heath' in case Essex launched an attack.[80] But he did not pursue the king's forces and 'the Citizens marched home to London the same day'. They were partly replaced by the contingent from Kingston, which arrived at Turnham Green 'late on Sunday, and much tired'. The king returned to Hanworth Park, Lord Cottington's seat near Hounslow, where he had spent the previous night.[81] And so that Sunday ended with a success for the royalists; their approach to London had been halted, but they had achieved their earlier objective of securing the bridge over the Thames at Kingston, opening the possibility of an attack on Southwark, or an advance into Kent.[82]

The parliamentarian commanders had the greater reason to be satisfied, for the army had succeeded in blocking the royalist advance. Because of the prompt response of the trained bands and volunteers, Essex's army had been too large for the royalists to attack, especially on a battlefield which allowed little room for manoeuvre and did not favour the royalist horse. And this had been done at relatively small cost, with an estimate of no more than twenty killed on the parliamentarian side. Another impression was that 'more were slaine on the Kings side', although royalist losses are unlikely to have been significantly higher.[83] But the number of lives lost was not a true reflection of the significance of the battle, or its consequences.

8

The Aftermath

With the withdrawal of the royalists from both Turnham Green and Brentford the balance had swung in favour of Essex, who now had the opportunity to take the initiative and press closely after the king's army. Yet his very success at Turnham Green removed the immediate threat to London and so the trained bands had returned home, considerably reducing the size of his forces. These now consisted of the army with which had returned to London from Edgehill, the Earl of Warwick's regiments and detachments of volunteers, raised specifically to defend the city and, in any case, of uncertain military capability. In such circumstances, a vigorous pursuit of the royalist army was not a secure option, and Essex may have judged it imprudent to carry out any manoeuvres that might put his army at risk of defeat or fragmentation so close to London, having achieved his major objective of securing it from attack.

As Essex was not in pursuit of the royalist army, and Kingston was now in its hands, it was free to cross into Surrey. The king spent the Monday waiting for a response to his letter carried to parliament by 'Dorset' White. When he received no reply, rather than move eastwards to threaten the capital from the south, he left most of his army around Kingston and went to Oatlands, close to Walton-on-Thames, where Prince Rupert established his base.[1]

From the riverside towns, the royalist horse spent the next few days raiding into south-west Surrey and by the following Friday, 18 November, they had taken 200 prisoners.[2] They also plundered the civilian population, who later complained that they had lost sheep, cattle, corn, hay and oats; provisions, including butter, cheese, wine and beer; coal and timber; household goods, pewter, clothing, and even bedding and books. Kingston itself was said to have been 'miserably plundered'. Charles Bentley had goods 'taken' from him there, and he obtained an order of the Commons for a search to be instituted for them.[3] The inhabitants of Byfleet estimated that, 'When the Kinges Souldiers were in these partes, and went to Brainford and comeinge back againe, our parish was damnified, in goods, and victualls at the leaste the sume of £200.' At Egham twenty-two householders valued their combined loss much higher, at £1,901 3s, while Robert Marsh at Leatherhead declared that 'the Kings forces plundred my house & tooke away my goods to the value of £12-0-0 on the 16th day of November 1642'. Stephen Cheeseman at Walton-on-Thames put his losses at £96 and the vicar of the parish, Leonard Cooke, complained that he had lost goods worth £200 and some of his papers had been burned.[4] More strategically, the troops destroyed the gunpowder mills at Chilworth, which the parliamentarians had put out of action earlier.[5]

Parliament gave greater attention to Brentford and the inhabitants there who had been plundered. On the Wednesday following the battle, John Rushworth, clerk-assistant to the Commons, was directed by the House to submit a report on the depredations of the royalists in the town. This was read the next day, and seems to have been received with a degree of scepticism, for two MPs were deputed to go to Brentford and interview the inhabitants to verify the contents of Rushworth's paper. They reported on 19 November and were asked to make further enquiries, reinforced by three other members. Their findings were that the town had been plundered indiscriminately; the losses were valued at almost £4,000. On 26 November a collection was ordered in London and Middlesex, with the ministers urged to 'excite the People to a compassionate Consideration' of the victims. They included John Transham, a bargeman, whose barge had been blown up and who was given separate consideration by the Commons.[6]

The writers of the London newsbooks did not share the members' doubts and had no compunction in printing vivid accounts of the effects of the royalists' behaviour. Their descriptions of some incidents over the previous few weeks had doubtless been exaggerated and may have contributed to the MPs' sceptical reaction, although many of their readers may not have had such reservations. But just the kind of atrocity that they had been predicting had now occurred, so close to home. The account in one newsbook reported that at Brentford the royalists:

> had taken from divers of the inhabitants, their goods, from some the value of
> 400 pounds, some 300 pounds, some more some less, and from the poorer
> sort, all that ever they had, leaving them not a bed to lie on, nor apparel, but
> what they had on their backs, nor a pair of sheets, nor a piece of bread, and
> what beer they drank not, they spilt it in the cellars, divers families of repute,
> with their wives and children, were reduced to such extreme poverty thereby,
> that they begged ever since; and taking divers of the townsmen (who never
> opposed them) after they had plundered them putting them in irons and tying
> others with ropes, and so led them away like dogs to Oatlands.[7]

Another told its readers that when Essex's troops recaptured the town they found the inhabitants:

> most woefully pillaged for they had not left anything that they could carry
> away, or devour and what they could not they spoiled, breaking bed heads,
> cutting their feather beds, scattering their feathers about the streets they
> broke, chests and tables, making all the spoil they could.[8]

But the writers of the newsbooks neglected to tell their readers that parliamentarian soldiers who occupied Brentford had also ransacked the shops when the royalist attack began, because they were short of supplies.[9] Moreover, while condemning the behaviour of the royalist troops, *The True proceedings of both armies* also described how parliamentarian soldiers had captured three women, camp followers of the king's army, and had drowned two of them in the Thames, and the third, who would not sink, even when pushed down by a pike, had been put in the stocks before being killed. The feeble justification for this atrocity was that the women had been paid to cut the throats of the parliamentarian wounded after the battle. This may have been the incident related to the Commons, that a pregnant woman was flung into the river and had dirt thrown at her before she was killed by parliamentarian soldiers. Some said that 'it was an Irish woman'.[10] Thus, brutal treatment of civilians by the royalists was condemned, but the killing of women, assumed to be whores, and possibly Irish, was recounted without any sense of inconsistency. This was an early example of the treatment of royalist women camp followers that was to recur throughout the war, culminating in the savage attack on those with the baggage train in the aftermath of Naseby, when roughly a hundred were killed and many others slashed across the face and disfigured by the troopers of the New Model Army.[11]

The needs of Brentford's inhabitants were immediate, but collection and distribution of the relief funds took time, although money was distributed among them as compensation for their losses. Soon other places were clamouring for assistance. Marlborough was captured and sacked by Wilmot's troops on 5 December, just over three weeks after the attack on Brentford, when fifty-three houses were burned and the inhabitants' goods and stocks of food were plundered. This was given sympathetic attention in the London newsbooks and by the author of a pamphlet expressively entitled *Marlborowe's Miseries, or, England turned Ireland*.[12] Two months later, on 2 February, the royalists captured Cirencester and plundered the inhabitants, deliberately setting some houses on fire in the process. This, too, was given wide coverage, with the horrified readers of one pamphlet being told: 'The value of the pillage of the towne is uncertaine, but very great, to the utter ruine of many hundred families.'[13] Those who wished to help the victims of such royalist atrocities found themselves presented with an increasing number of such requests.

The general expectation in London during the week following the battles at Brentford and Turnham Green was that the royalist army would march eastwards across Surrey. An intercepted letter mentioning that Prince Rupert was expected in Kent seemed to confirm this.[14] Parliament therefore strengthened the force guarding the bridge over the Medway at Rochester. Closer to London, a bridge of boats spanned by 'great boords' was constructed between Putney and Fulham, to make the movement of Essex's troops across the Thames easier, 'the better to inable his men to assault the cavaliers in their march from Kingsone into the county of Kent'. This was protected at both ends by artillery and detachments of musketeers. It cost £343 8s 8d. It is unlikely that the boats used were the set of twenty 'boates for bridges' bought in September for £15 each, to be carried with Essex's army as an emergency bridge if it came to a river where the bridges had been broken down, as they had been sent to Gloucester and were used during the Newbury campaign of 1643. The army's Bridge-Master and his assistant may, however, have assisted in the construction of the bridge at Putney.[15]

On the Monday, parliament ordered that the guard in Southwark and Lambeth should be reinforced 'in regard 'tis thought there will be Alarms from the Enemy's Forces in those Parts this Night'.[16] Londoners remained nervous of an attack and when, two nights later, the guards at the fort in Hyde Park fired on a small group of rowdy drunks, the alarm spread and the citizens were roused from their beds, 'all concluding that the Cavaliers were come to cut their throats'.[17]

Despite the potential advantages of inflicting a defeat similar to that at Brentford, as well as adding to the citizens' fear and foreboding, the royalist commanders were unwilling to undertake such an attack. Nor were they prepared to march into Kent, even though they anticipated finding 'very affectionate and considerable' support there.[18] Control of a section of coastline with one or more ports would have made it easier to receive help from France and the Low Countries, where the queen was actively gathering arms, but would have taken them further from their new base at Oxford and from recruits arriving from the north, the west and Wales. Even their position around Kingston and Oatlands was unsuitable in that respect, although it did allow them to block traffic along the Thames and prevent supplies reaching London. But the area proved to be incapable of maintaining the army, even with the provisions brought in by the marauding horse, and on Friday 18 November the king withdrew to Bagshot and then marched back to Reading and on to Oxford. Some saw this as an admission of the weakness of his army, while others judged it to be a sensible stratagem not to stay so close to the enemy, who would be able to follow all his movements and draw upon the city for support and provisions when needed.[19] As they retreated, the royalists placed five regiments in Marlow, for 'some days', before ordering two of them to garrison Reading, with Sir Arthur Aston appointed governor, and the others to march to Abingdon.[20]

Essex was ordered to move his army, now merged with Warwick's regiments, up the Thames to Windsor.[21] The parliamentarians immediately set about fortifying Windsor, Eton and Wokingham, as outlying defences for London. Essex then sent detachments to Wiltshire, Hampshire and Buckinghamshire, and decided early in December against a further campaign that winter, anticipating a period of skirmishing.[22] Although both sides placed garrisons in the smaller towns, to control territory from which their troops could be maintained, there was no further campaigning in the Thames valley below Reading and this phase of the war ended with the king's departure from that town.

As well as having to withdraw his army from a potentially good position astride London's communications with the south-west, the king had to face the political consequences of the campaign. These were bound to be dominated by accusations of his duplicity, in permitting the attack on Brentford after having agreed with the parliamentary delegation that further negotiations should be held. The timing of events showed a lack of sincerity, to put it mildly, for the operation was under way so soon after the commissioners had left the king that it was evident that it must have been planned earlier.[23] Although they could not have known that the royalist decision to march had been taken on the morning of 11 November, they had enough evidence to conclude that the king had acted in bad faith. As Sir Peter Killigrew was at Whitehall, the royalists must surely have been expecting him to return carrying a message from parliament to the king, yet they had not waited for him before launching their attack. Hyde's view was that those senior parliamentarians who had been most in favour of a treaty felt betrayed 'by his majesty's making so much haste towards them after their offer of a treaty, that he meant to have surprised and taken vengeance of them without distinction'.[24] The king's council was now on the back foot, facing the difficulty of having to defend the almost indefensible and overcome distrust born of treacherous dealing.

The two Houses expressed their bitterness and disappointment in a letter sent to the king on 16 November, using their reply to his letter carried by 'Dorset' White to make some strong points:

> We thought it a strange Induction to Peace, that Your Majesty should send Your Army to beat us out of our Quarters at Brainford, and then appoint that Place to receive our Propositions, which yet it plainly appears Your Majesty intended not to receive till You had first tried whether You could break through the Army for Defence of this Kingdom and Parliament, and take the City, being unprovided, and secure in Expectation of a fair Treaty made to secure the City: If herein Your Majesty had prevailed, after You had destroyed the Army, and mastered the City, it is easy to imagine what a miserable Peace we should have had; and whether these Courses be suitable to Your Expressions Your Majesty is pleased to make in Your Answer to our Petition, of Your Earnestness to avoid any further Effusion of Blood, let God and the World judge!

The king and his councillors were not given the benefit of the doubt. He had not planned to wait at Brentford, as he had informed them in his letter, but had acted with the intention of attacking London, hoping to catch the parliamentarian army off guard, while arrangements were under way for a ceasefire pending negotiations.[25]

Justifying their own actions, the two Houses pointed out that Essex's troops were in Brentford before the commissioners returned from their meeting with the king at Colnbrook and that, when they received their report, they instructed Essex not to undertake any hostile operations. Killigrew had been prevented from delivering their letter as a result of the king's own actions, by 'the Fury of Your Soldiers, thirsting after Blood and Spoil'. They expressed their hope that they could 'free Your Majesty from those destructive Counsellors, who labour to maintain their own Power by Blood and Rapine'.[26]

His response came in a letter to parliament written by Falkland from Oatlands on 18 November. This stated that Essex had threatened his position by moving troops westwards from London and occupying places near his army, after the commissioners were sent to him. As far as he could judge they may have planned to continue their march towards Colnbrook. In other words, parliament had been the aggressor and his troops had responded. This part of the dispute hinged upon the significance of the timing of Essex's regiments moving into Brentford. The king's related claim that he had not received any letter suggesting a suspension of military action was correct, and it was also true that neither side had broken a truce, for none had been agreed. But the royalist advance had begun before a reply could have been received, and even if Killigrew had persisted in trying to deliver the letter entrusted to him, he would have arrived after the attack on Brentford.[27]

The king assured parliament that he had no intention of attacking London or even moving his army there. This was clear both from his assurance and his actions in:

> not pursuing his Victory at Brainford, but giving Orders to his Army to march away to Kingston as soon as he heard that Place was quitted, before any Notice or Appearance of further Forces from London.

His account, therefore, omitted the day-long confrontation with a large parliamentarian army at Turnham Green, as though it had not happened at all. Yet the advance was halted not out of choice, but because Essex's much larger and unflinching army stood in the way, and surely that was a 'further force' from London. This was an extraordinary alteration of the facts and rewriting of recent events, and Hyde's later summary of the letter, included in his history of the Civil War, omits this passage. Had the king indeed captured Brentford and advanced no further, then he would have carried out his intentions as stated in his letter, but the events of 13 November had no justification in any communication which he had sent to parliament, hence the attempt to expunge them from history. This could not be expected to mislead the members of the two Houses, many of whom had been at Turnham Green, and it can have done little to impress them of the king's integrity and sincerity.

The king was also being disingenuous in claiming that he would withdraw his army because the Londoners were afraid of their city being surprised and sacked, thus removing its proximity to the capital as an obstacle to the renewal of talks.[28] His army was so close to the city as to be seen as a threat because of his own decisions after offering talks. And its withdrawal was due to the presence of an army which greatly outnumbered his, presenting the real possibility of a military defeat. These statements were obviously designed to mislead a wider readership than the parliamentarians and Londoners, and were aimed at potential supporters in the provinces and perhaps even foreign governments, by presenting an image of a king who could act decisively and forcefully when threatened, but display magnanimity in victory.

The letter ended with the king's offer that he would receive proposals for further negotiations, or that a single battle should be fought, to decide the outcome of the political crisis.[29] A similar proposal had been made by Rupert in a letter sent to Essex shortly after the skirmish at Powick Bridge in which he proposed 'an encounter in a pitched field', naming the place as Dunsmore Heath, near Rugby, and the date as 10 October. Alternatively, 'if you think it too much labour and expense to draw your forces thither' he suggested that the two of them engage in 'a single duel'.[30] A duel between the commanders was an absurd idea, for many reasons, but the notion of one battle to end the conflict was evidently still a possibility in the minds of some senior royalists, even after Edgehill.

Their suggestions for a trial by battle, a kind of tournament fought by armies, with the future of the kingdom as the prize, came from an earlier and more chivalric age, when such challenges had indeed been made. This was an honourable course to take, ensuring that the two sides had an equal opportunity and neither was put at a disadvantage. But even when a place and date were agreed, the battle did not always take place.[31]

The appeal to the royalists of such an arranged combat was that it would neutralize the advantages which parliament had gained, by the repulse at Turnham Green and the clear evidence that London would not switch its allegiance and support the king. For those who were apprehensive of the effects of an all-out war, and had hoped that the conflict would be ended as quickly as both of the Bishops' Wars had been, it also had the considerable attraction that it would halt the war before it could develop to engulf the whole country, bringing in its wake the much-feared devastation that the warfare in Germany had caused. If Rupert's earlier letter was serious and sincere, he favoured such a solution, and the inclusion of the proposal in the one now sent to parliament may also have owed much to Falkland, who, according to Hyde, was 'one of those who believed that one battle would end all differences, and that there would be so great a victory on one side, that the other would be compelled to submit to any conditions from the victor'.[32] This had not happened at Edgehill or Turnham Green, but could yet be contrived by a single set-piece battle.

Essex had ignored the earlier suggestion and parliament was not going to agree to such a winner-take-all engagement, having ensured that the king could not use his army to return to his capital and dictate a settlement. Its mistrust of the king had been greatly increased, and it had reason to be optimistic, having secured London and the Tower, and control of the navy. But, while Rupert's challenge to Essex had been in a letter, this new proposal was in a document that was made public, and for parliament to spurn the challenge could be seen to be dishonourable. And so the Commons had to respond, which they did with the comment:

They think it strange that the King of England should send a Challenge, and an Invitation to a Battle, seeing heretofore His Majesty hath seemed to decline the Effusion of Blood, and professed to use all Means to prevent the same; therefore the House of Commons resolve to be in a Readiness; and, if His Majesty will withdraw Himself from His Cavaliers, the Army will so behave themselves as to be ready, and will not decline, if they have a Mind, to give a Battle, if the Place and Time shall be appointed.[33]

They could have pointed out that, although the proposed fight on Dunsmore Heath had not taken place, Edgehill had been such a battle, or have asked if Turnham Green had not provided another suitable opportunity, while the two armies were drawn up facing each other. Could not the royalists have called a parley and suggested such an arrangement, for the war to be decided in that one battle? It seems doubtful whether parliament really expected its response to be taken up, any more than the royalists anticipated that their own proposals would prove acceptable.

Yet the notion of a single set-piece battle recurred over the following months. In January 1643 Lord Grandison was approached with a similar idea, but when he referred the matter to the royalist commanders at Oxford they refused him permission to go ahead, despite their own proposal to parliament just a few weeks earlier. But the royalists were not consistent, for shortly afterwards the Earl of Newcastle made a similar proposal to Lord Fairfax, to follow 'the examples of our heroic ancestors'. Fairfax rejected the challenge. In the summer of 1643, when parliament's military fortunes were at their lowest ebb, Essex himself was prepared to suggest risking all on a single battle. When his letter to the Committee of Safety was read in the Commons, those who favoured continuing the war showed their hostility to the suggestion by pulling their hats over their eyes.[34]

The possibility of an arranged battle in the aftermath of Turnham Green was very remote, yet, although the king's actions during the campaign and his subsequent self-justificatory account had alienated some members, parliament did not dismiss the possibility of further negotiations out of hand. Indeed, this was debated for two days in the Commons, when a clear division emerged between the peace party and those, guided by Pym, who were not prepared to compromise. Perhaps surprisingly, the 'doves' were not diminished or completely discredited by recent events and were now joined by Holles, whose enthusiasm for the war had all but evaporated following the dismaying experience of seeing the effects on his regiment of the fighting at Brentford. A few others who had been opposed to negotiations now supported an approach to the king. Nevertheless, some members, such as Sir Henry Marten and Samuel Vassall, were resolutely against further talks and the motion that propositions should be sent to the king was carried in the Commons by just a single vote.[35]

Pym distrusted the growing influence of the soldiers in the king's entourage and perhaps, too, the importance given to parliament's own senior commanders. Essex had been treated with great consideration in the days leading up to the battle at Brentford. Those apprehensive that the professional soldiers would continue to prosecute the war, and could forestall negotiations by aggressive action, would not have been reassured by the events of the autumn. Some must have realised how difficult it would be to demobilize the armies, now that the first campaign had not been decisive. The soldiers could establish their own agenda, hence Pym's proposal that both armies be disbanded so that discussions could resume. This was not acceptable, or indeed realistic, but in other respects his views prevailed. He could count on the City's support, expressed in a petition that there could be no settlement until the king returned to Westminster, without his army. Its stance remained crucial to the cause because of its financial support.[36]

In addition to the political exchanges, a war of words in the newsbooks and pamphlets followed the battles of Brentford and Turnham Green. No longer respectful of the king, the London press did not shrink from condemning him, both for condoning the behaviour of his troops and his own perfidious conduct, in launching the attack on Brentford. The kind of accusations levelled at Rupert were now aimed at the king, who could be accused of being party to the 'barbarous outrages' of his men because he had been with them at Turnham Green, although not, admittedly, at Brentford. This posed little difficulty for the writer of *Speciall Passages*, who claimed that as the king came through Brentford after the battle he had encouraged the troops to press on to London, promising them 'brave and plentiful pillage'. Even worse, he passed through the town 'glorying at the sight of the dead bodies of our men as he went along, commending his souldiers for their valour in slaying of them'. And he left Turnham Green:

> no doubt with a troubled conscience, for that he had consented to such a treacherous, Jesuiticall, unchristianly, and unkinglike accommodation, in being a cause of the shedding of so much blood, under the signed expression of calling God to witness.

He then encouraged his readers with the news that parliament was so incensed with the king's 'horrible and unnatural' conduct that there would be no military truce and that Essex had vowed to revenge 'this bloody act' of the cavaliers. He also made the perceptive assertion that the king's actions in this brief campaign had disillusioned those who, until then, had been willing to accept his sincerity in seeking talks, and, put simply, had lost him the support of many in and around London who had been sympathetic to his cause. Other pamphleteers told their readers of plundering by the royalists at Banbury, and in Berkshire and Buckinghamshire, but it was the thorough sack of Brentford which took most attention.[37]

The royalists attempted to limit the damage by publishing the king's response to the allegations of duplicity and misconduct in a pamphlet, which set out to clarify his 'True Intentions in advancing lately to Brainceford'. This appeared on the London streets by the beginning of December, offered no explanation for Turnham Green, but included the assertion: 'Wee had not the least thought, by so advancing, to surprise and sack London (which the malignant party would infuse into that Our Citty).' This, of course, begged several questions. Why the army was advanced so near to London, if the intention had not been to attack and capture it? Why had it been ordered to continue beyond Windsor, leaving the parliamentarian garrison there as a potential threat in its rear, if there had not been another objective? And what could that have been other than London? And why the haste, in not halting to secure Windsor, if not to try to reach the capital before Essex had time to prepare his army to confront the king's forces? Arguments along such lines had no clear conclusions, but the royalists could hardly deny that their troops had plundered Brentford.[38]

They did attempt to recover some political ground by emphasizing that the initiative lay with parliament, as the king's propositions sent from Colnbrook still held good:

> to meet both Houses in any Place free and convenient for Us and them. But We could never receive the least Satisfaction in any of these Particulars; nor for those scandalous and seditious Pamphlets and Sermons which swarm amongst you.

The royalists referred to the attack on Brentford – described as 'the late and sad Accident' – but must have known that the events there and at Turnham Green could not be passed over so lightly.[39]

The optimism that had existed when the king's reply from Colnbrook was read in parliament had all but evaporated and little vigour was left in the political process. Two days after the battle of Turnham Green, Sir John Coke the younger, MP for Derbyshire, wrote that 'We... suppose the treaty wholly broken off.'[40] A fortnight later the MP Sir Simonds D'Ewes wrote that 'the whole kingdome [is] like to be sett in [com]bustion at once', and the problem of Ireland and 'those bloodie murtherers' there would be neglected.[41] In fact, a new submission to the king was prepared, but not with any urgency, and it was not completed for despatch to him until 20 December. Yet the strong desire for peace among some MPs, including D'Ewes, was enough to overcome the sceptics and the Commons agreed to the propositions. Perhaps they hoped that the king's direct experience of war and a realization of the weakness of his position, if he could not subdue London, would make him amenable to negotiations.

He was asked to accept the Militia Ordinance and all subsequent ordinances and the abolition of bishops, deans and chapters. Many of the points covered indemnity for the actions taken since the Long Parliament had met. If negotiations were to be arranged, parliament, mindful of the events of mid-November, requested 'a Cessation from all Manner of Acts of Hostility for Fourteen Days'.[42] The proposals were not acceptable to the king, who would not agree to the Militia Ordinance and so yield control of the armed forces, and he wanted to ensure the continued use of the Book of Common Prayer in worship. In the New Year delegations from the City and parliament waited on the king at Oxford, but could not find enough common ground for negotiations. Failure to agree a basis for talks can only have been a major disappointment for those who, for just a few hours on the morning of 12 November, had thought that they were possible, perhaps even imminent.

Parliament had seized the moral high ground in the aftermath of the battle of Brentford, yet military matters could not be neglected. The king's idea of a set-piece decisive battle was interpreted by Sir Henry Vane, one of his most vociferous opponents, to indicate that the royalists were confident of the strength of their army. Parliament was indeed anxious that Essex should not be too cautious while communication with the king continued, but was aware of the potential weakness of its army.[43] Warwick relinquished his independent command, to avoid the dangers of divided control, and perhaps to placate Essex, who, according to Giovannie Giustinian, seemed increasingly dissatisfied and even bitter.[44] But supply and recruitment problems remained. Many troops of horse were under strength, one was said to contain only twenty-eight troopers, and the foot regiments, too, were short of men, their actual size being disguised by false musters. Some officers were spending time in London, away from their regiments, and desertion was a problem, for 'many men do run from their Colours'. Complaints had also been made about the equipment supplied, with the allegation that some musket barrels were bored for only a part of their length, and that pike staves were of fir, coloured to resemble ash. Some soldiers were selling their weapons, perhaps because they had not received their pay.[45]

A vigorous prosecution of the war was required, now that it was evident that it would continue into the new year. The City offered to provide additional troops and a report was submitted to the Commons that the gunsmiths could supply 1,500 muskets a week. A more certain method of financing the war effort than voluntary contributions was essential, for the weekly cost of maintaining the army was £20,000 and the navy required £6,000 each week.[46] Pym requested a further loan from the City, of £30,000, which was agreed, and on 29 November he steered through parliament an ordinance which imposed a levy on all citizens of London and Westminster, effectively imposing parliamentary taxation without royal consent.[47] Draconian measures were taken with those who would not meet the requirement of paying half the sum within six days and the remainder within twelve, having their goods distrained for sale, or being put in prison.[48] Many must have found it difficult to meet the demands. Nehemiah Wallington had earlier noted in his journal the problems caused by 'this dead time... of traiding' and was unable to pay the collectors the whole amount required when they called.[49]

These were gloomy times in London, as the days got shorter and the prospect of a prolonged war increased. The authorities at the Middle Temple decided that during the coming winter:

Commons may be kept in the House... without any music, gaming, public noise, or show, whereby company may be drawn into the House; and this in respect of the danger and troublesomeness of the times.[50]

The gloom was financial as well as seasonal, and the sense that London was bearing the cost of the war came not only from increased taxation but also from growing economic problems. Merchants who had been trading through London were switching their business to Holland and the customs officials complained that they were receiving only a half of the expected revenues. Internal trade was disrupted by the depredations of royalist soldiers, who were intercepting shipments of cloth from the producing areas.[51] This could be prevented by maintaining the armies and extending their role beyond countering the king's forces, to guard the movement of goods and protect from plundering counties not directly affected by the war, especially those in East Anglia that were producing the 'new draperies', the most profitable branch of the woollen-cloth industry. And the navy had to be kept up to strength to safeguard shipping from capture by privateers. Inevitably, in protecting resources to ensure that the forces could be paid and provisioned, the size and cost of those forces were increased.

The capital was also supporting the royalist war effort, for money was being taken out of the city and donated to the royalist administration, helping to pay the king's armies.[52] Parliament admitted that:

Powder, Money, Ammunition, and other Provisions in considerable Proportions, are carried out of this City daily to the King's Army; and that many ill-affected Persons do withdraw their whole Estates out of the City; to the end they may avoid such equal Contributions to the Parliament as are or may be appointed by both Houses.

The royalists were, therefore, acting in their own best interests, not being magnanimous to the city which had defied them, when the Council of War agreed at Reading on 5 November that trade with London should continue without restraint. The king confirmed this policy in a proclamation issued on 8 December and it was not reversed until the following July.[53] Ironically, it was parliament, which had just secured the capital, that took steps to limit freedom of movement when it acted to try to prevent money and provisions being taken out of the city, by authorizing the search of 'all Waggons, Carts, Carriages on Horseback, or on Foot, that go forth of this City'. Money, arms, ammunition and provisions that were found would be seized. As well as movements by land, the guards could also stop and examine:

all Persons, Ships, Barques, Boats, and other Vessels, that shall pass or go into, or out from, the City of London, or upon the River of Thames; and, if any shall be found offending in the Premises, to seize and detain the same.[54]

Furthermore, as the royalists had begun to collect tolls from the crews of the colliers carrying coal from the Tyne and Wear, which had their largest market at London, parliament's ships blockaded the ports in the north-east to prevent the coal vessels from leaving. This denied the royalists a potentially lucrative source of revenue, but with the inevitable effect of producing fuel shortages and high prices during the coming winter. In January 1643 coal was said to be selling at 'intolerable prices' in London.[55]

Taxation, controls and economic hardship, combined with latent support for the king, contributed to unrest that erupted in riots in early December, both in the City and Westminster. The crowds that demonstrated on 8 December, to the cry of 'a pox of all roundhedds', complained of goods being forcibly distrained in lieu of taxes, against the policies of Common Council, and in favour of peace, believing that, once it was achieved, 'truth will follow'. Alarmed by this, a delegation of citizens went to the Commons to explain that the protesters were 'malignants', raising a petition solely to give the royalist forces time to recover. Its response was an order to the lord mayor and sheriffs 'to prevent any tumultuous Gatherings together of people', but this was more than they could achieve, for on 12 December a crowd estimated to be at least 1,000 strong presented a petition at Guildhall amid chaotic scenes, with swords drawn, wounds inflicted and the rioters threatening to cut the throats of the lord mayor and aldermen. Soldiers of the trained bands were called out to suppress the disorder. Towards the end of the month Lord Saye's coach was stopped by unruly apprentices, demanding the release of their masters, who were imprisoned in Lambeth Palace. The steps which parliament had taken during the autumn to secure the city were drawing a hostile response, now that the immediate danger from the royalist army had been removed. By the beginning of January the House of Lords, prompted by the arrival of yet another crowd of apprentices, was so wearied of 'the coming of Multitudes to the Parliament' with petitions that it ordered that only a few individuals should be allowed to hand over those petitions.[56]

Such petitioning and disorder was just the kind of reaction that would have helped the royalists in the middle of November, as their army pressed on to Brentford and Turnham Green. It had not occurred then, but that peaceful period of acquiescence proved to be short-lived. This was partly because the doubts of those citizens uneasy with the political developments had been accentuated by the measures taken to impose taxation and enforce collection, and partly because of the disappointment that the war had not been settled by a single campaign. Indeed, neither negotiation nor military action had solved the crisis, which was now set to continue.

9

The Significance of London's Defence

In the aftermath of the two battles the various parties on both sides sought to grapple with and understand the significance of the events of those two days in mid-November. The peace party at Whitehall was encouraged because the two sides had come so close to agreeing to negotiations, although the failure to do so was frustrating. But the exasperation was all the greater among those who wanted to pursue the war vigorously and anticipated that a political solution would come only after a military victory. The royalists, too, were disappointed at the outcome, which fuelled divisions within the leadership, although the campaign provided lessons that influenced their future strategy.

For those parliamentarians who wanted a decisive victory and so a swift end to the war, Turnham Green was seen as a missed opportunity, a chance to defeat the royalist army which had been allowed to slip away. This view was current soon after the battle. On the following Thursday the writer of a letter, in London, expressed it succinctly:

> If the Parliaments forces had set upon them upon Sunday in all likelihood they had ended the quarrell, for the Earle of Essex was before them, the Earl of Warwicke behind them, & Colonell Hollis with some others on one side of them.[1]

He was mistaken in placing Warwick's forces in the royalist rear, and perhaps in identifying Holles's as one of the outflanking regiments, although his assessment of the potential for striking a decisive blow may, nevertheless, have been a widely held opinion. Certainly, a few days later a newsbook felt the need to print a refutation of the notion that Turnham Green had presented the chance to put 'a short period to these Warres'. It pointed out that it would not have been easy for parliamentarian troops to have got round the rear of the king's army, and if they had done so, they would have been ambushed by a royalist detachment concealed in 'a great wood'. The force and the wood may have been imaginary, and are not mentioned in other accounts, but the real point that the writer was making was that to have marched the parliamentarian detachment behind the royalist army 'would have proved a service of much difficulty'. There was the risk that it could have been trapped, or that the royalists would not have waited patiently until the manoeuvre was completed and have retreated earlier and so escaped.[2] As with other military engagements, the temptation for armchair strategists to re-fight the battle proved irresistible.

The number of casualties and the extent of the damage caused by military campaigns were relatively modest by the end of 1642, compared with the loss of life, goods, livelihoods and property that was inflicted across the British Isles during the next ten years. As the scale of the war grew, so did the resentment at the failure to end it at Turnham Green. Essex's recall of Ramsay's men from Kingston was seen as a major cause of the outcome, by allowing the king to withdraw his army unscathed, and that was done 'by their procurement who designed the continuance of the war'.[3] The insinuation was that the professional soldiers, described by Bulstrode Whitelocke as 'the officers of fortune', did not wish the war to end so suddenly, because that would terminate their employment. Whitelocke wrote that they had also opposed the suggestion that Essex should attack the royalist army at Turnham Green, which, according to his account, was supported by most members of the Commons at the time.[4] Essex himself could have been castigated for the outcome, and subsequent campaigns were to demonstrate that he was a cautious commander. The defensive posture which he adopted at Turnham Green was suited to his inclinations, and he had been in the unenviable position of having members of both Houses present with him on the battlefield, scrutinizing his decisions.

The influence of the professional soldiers had been anticipated at the start of the war and the events at Turnham Green could be fitted into the pattern feared by those who wished to end the conflict through an outright military victory. Lord Brooke had summarized this before the start of the campaign, commenting that mercenaries 'rather covet to spin out the wars to a prodigious length, as they have done in other countries, than to see them quickly brought to a conclusion'.[5] Meyrick and Dalbier were the principal targets of such allegations after Turnham Green, yet Meyrick's critical comments at the withdrawal of the outflanking detachment during the battle had been so strong that they had landed him in trouble. Dalbier was more vulnerable, for he had been an unpopular figure during the 1620s, when he served as paymaster to Ernst von Mansfeld. Indeed, he had been denounced in the Commons in 1628 with a wide-ranging condemnation of him as untrustworthy, disloyal, incompetent, and a papist. He continued to serve during the first Civil War under Essex and Sir William Waller, although, like Meyrick, he did not secure a command in the New Model. But he joined the royalist uprising during the Second Civil War and was killed at St Neots.[6]

The Earl of Holland was also suspected of not wishing for an outright victory at Turnham Green. His commitment to the parliamentarian war effort proved to be so lukewarm that he defected to the king in 1643, fighting with the royalist army at the first battle of Newbury, before abandoning the cause and returning to London. Like Dalbier, he joined the royalists in the Second Civil War, was captured at St Neots and executed in 1649.[7]

The battle at Brentford and, perhaps even more, the outcome of the confrontation and skirmishing at Turnham Green revealed and widened, but did not initiate, the divisions within the parliamentary camp, between those suspected of being apprehensive of the effects of defeating the king, and so unwilling to press home an advantage, and those who saw that a military solution to the crisis was necessary. Those rifts grew as the war dragged on.

But the divisions were more apparent with hindsight than in mid-November 1642, when relief at the favourable conclusion of the campaign must have been a common emotion. The notion that the conflict had been deliberately drawn out was given extra weight over the longer term, in the context of the dreadful consequences that ensued from a prolonged and bitterly fought war. Londoners saw the impact themselves, through the parties of bedraggled refugees, wounded soldiers and royalist prisoners who streamed into the city over the following years. The grand houses of those senior royalists who had left to join the king were packed full of destitute people with nowhere else to go. Many Londoners must have had cause to bemoan the long and destructive war.

For the royalists the disappointment was more immediate, especially after the high hopes produced by the advance so close to London and the victory at Brentford. News of the battle there had reached Oxford on the Sunday evening and senior royalists left in the city had ordered celebrations, with 'Bells ringginge and bonfires made in Oxford &c. abundantly by the Lords'. On the following day 'came the like tidings of another victory at Brainford uppon the Sundaye, when fifteene hundred of the parlament side were blowen up &c'. This account was optimistic, confused and exaggerated, but no good news followed and the return of the army without further success surely was an anticlimax after the celebrations. Of course, the 'armies successe over the Lundoners' was welcome in Oxford, and the soldiers had been allowed to plunder Brentford, but Brentford was not London, and hopes had been high.[8]

A letter from a member of the queen's entourage, written from Holland on 12 November and intercepted by the parliamentarians, was critical of the delay in advancing on London, citing the similar example of Hull, which the royalists had failed to capture during the summer, partly due to their prevarication. Encouraged by royalist accounts of Edgehill, the writer was optimistic about the outcome of the campaign, believing that in the aftermath of the battle Essex's force was 'so lame an Army, without Horse or Cannon', and was sure that in London 'the King's Party there are very considerable, and full of that Expectation' of the royalist approach.[9]

James II's 'Life' comments that 'a person of quality, who was then with the Earle of Essex' later said that if the royalist army had pressed on after the capture of Brentford they would have captured London, because Essex's men were so widely dispersed. This fails to take account of the swift concentration of his army at Turnham Green, blocking the way. Hyde noted that he had heard the opinion of 'many knowing men', including some who were in the City trained bands at Turnham Green, that if the royalists had charged, the parliamentarian regiments would have given ground, and that so many in Essex's army were royalist sympathizers that they would have offered little resistance. But, in his view, that would have been an unjustifiably rash thing to do and the decision to retreat had been the right one.[10] As an eyewitness, John Gwyn drew a similar conclusion, that the royalists could not have advanced any closer to London, being so heavily outnumbered and faced with Essex's skilful placing of his troops and artillery.[11]

The campaign had ended in recrimination and had widened the rifts among the senior officers, which made co-operation more difficult in the future. Hyde, an unfriendly observer of the soldiers' actions, commented that the outcome of the campaign was seen as unsatisfactory, and it had 'raised much faction and discontent among the officers, every man imputing the oversights which had been committed to the rashness and presumption of others'.[12] The military action had not succeeded and had poisoned the atmosphere so far as further attempts at negotiation were concerned. Yet the royalists were able to draw some conclusions from the campaign that informed their future actions. It had demonstrated that they would be unable to capture London by military means. A successful coup or an uprising were the only ways in which the king could expect to regain control of the capital. But their hope of a strong royalist presence there that would be essential for such a coup to succeed was much reduced, for the citizens had turned out in large numbers to support Essex and oppose the king's army, without provoking an uprising in the city. His chances of capturing London were further reduced in the following spring, when the fortifications constructed in 1642 were extended and connected by a continuous line of earthworks. This was done by the citizens themselves, with thousands turning out willingly to carry out the work, in a burst of popular enthusiasm. Only by diminishing that willingness, by comprehensively defeating the parliamentarian field armies, or by engendering a weariness with the war, could the royalists hope to drive a wedge between parliament and the Londoners.[13]

This was something which the royalist commanders needed to know, and never again during the first Civil War did they attempt to bring an army so near to London. It argued for a negotiated settlement, a course of action still favoured by the politicians around the king, but opposed by the swordsmen. The outcome of the campaign widened divisions within the leadership about future strategy. The fear that the military commanders would direct policy rather than implement it was a concern to senior royalists, who, according to the royalist historian Philip Warwick, were not inclined to trust Rupert, in particular, 'lest he should be too apt to prolong the warr'.[14] The events of November 1642 must have done much to strengthen their opinion. On both sides, therefore, the campaign fuelled the apprehension of those who were concerned that professional soldiers would continue the war, in their own interests. Indeed, the politicians felt uncomfortable that their freedom of action lay quite so much in the hands of the swordsmen.

The royalists' failure to either capture London or galvanize a response in their favour within the city clearly demonstrated their inability to subdue it. This was now apparent to parliament and to other states and continental merchants who were considering supplying the king with money and arms. Backing a monarch excluded from the capital city by its citizens might not produce a worthwhile return, in diplomatic or financial terms.[15]

This was one reason why parliament clearly had the better of the campaign, despite failing to defeat the royalist army and so be in a strong position to negotiate a favourable settlement. London was secured and the support of its citizens, which had been decisive, was maintained. And the military worth of the trained bands had been demonstrated, in their readiness to march out of the city and join with the army, and their ability to stand in the line with Essex's regiments and unflinchingly endure a cannonade. This evidence of their capability in action added considerably to parliament's military resources and freed Essex's army from being restricted by the need to defend London, especially after the fortifications were completed.[16]

The self-confidence of the trained bands must have been increased by the crucial part which they played in blocking the royalist advance at Turnham Green. Although the performance of the county militias during the Bishops' Wars had been disappointing, to say the least, the London citizen-soldiers would have disassociated themselves from such shabby conduct and were more likely to identify with other civic militias in north-west Europe. Those in the Dutch cities had played important roles in the sieges during the revolt against Spain, which could be compared with the defiant action at Turnham Green, where the metropolis had been protected from a hostile army by its own citizens' forces.

Parliament's cause was also strengthened by the behaviour of the royalist troops, which gave validity to the claims made in its propaganda campaign in the preceding weeks. Allegations of their misconduct and rascality were confirmed by the sack of Brentford and looting of other places in the Thames valley, so close to London that refugees arrived in the city soon afterwards, to tell their tales of their sufferings at first hand. This had far more impact than published accounts of plundering in places remote from the capital and helped to further alienate the population in and around London from the king's cause. And the word spread further afield. John Rous, the minister of Santon Downham, in Suffolk, heard that a German visitor who went to check the extent of the damage had said that he had not seen any town in Germany as 'ruined and defaced' as was Brentford.[17] The inability of the commissariat to pay the troops or ensure a supply of provisions in this early stage of the war partly accounts for the royalist soldiers' conduct. But the wisdom of moving so close to London with an army which could be maintained only by pillaging surely was questionable, especially at a time when negotiations were being discussed.

It could not be claimed that the king and his entourage had blundered unwittingly into a propaganda trap, for the nature of the wars in Germany had been well enough known over the previous twenty years or more. Even if they had overlooked, or disregarded, the pamphlet campaign aimed at their army since the war had begun, they should have been aware of the wider context and the danger of being accused of similar brutality and plundering. Perhaps they were, and yet were confident enough of ultimate success to be contemptuous of a popular reaction against them.

Not only was repugnance at the conduct of the cavalier army increased during the November days of 1642, but so was Charles's regrettable reputation for deceitfulness, making agreement with him difficult. As on other occasions, a period of doubt and prevarication over which course to follow, hence the sluggishness of the advance along the Thames valley, was followed by decisive action. The chance of a peaceful settlement being agreed in the following weeks was so slim that both sides set about preparing for the prolonged war which the outcome of the campaign had made inevitable.

The war in southern England was fought chiefly in the midlands and south-west, not in the vicinity of London. In April 1643 Essex moved up the Thames valley and captured Reading, after defeating a royalist attempt to relieve it. The focus then shifted to the west country, where a succession of royalist victories culminated in their capture of Bristol on 26 July. They then moved not against London, but besieged Gloucester, prompting a concerted effort by parliament to relieve it, and the London trained bands again joined Essex's army, in a march which met with success when the royalists were compelled to raise the siege. Royalist attempts to block Essex's return to London failed at the first battle of Newbury. They were able to re-occupy Reading, but could not prevent the trained bands from returning home after another successful campaign.

The trained bands' experiences under Waller in 1644 were less happy and his own early success at Cheriton in Hampshire was followed by the near disintegration of his army after the battle of Cropredy Bridge, north of Oxford, on 29 June. The royalists had already abandoned Reading for a second time and did not exploit Waller's problems by moving towards London, but instead pursued Essex's army westwards into Cornwall, forcing its surrender. This ended Essex's military career and seemed to have given the royalists an advantage, but the other parliamentarian armies were still in the field and combined to face the king at a drawn battle near Newbury. The parliamentarians had the better of the year's campaigns, having completely defeated the Marquess of Newcastle and Prince Rupert at Marston Moor and gained control of much of the north of England. Yet, as after Turnham Green, the second battle of Newbury led to recriminations among the parliamentarian commanders and suspicions of a lack of resolve to defeat the king. Negotiations followed, at Uxbridge, but they were not successful. Parliament then enacted the Self Denying Ordinance which barred members of both Houses of Parliament from holding military command, and created the New Model Army early in 1645, under Sir Thomas Fairfax's command. This showed a determination to win the war. The New Model achieved that, and its victory at Naseby in June 1645 effectively ended any military threat to London.

Negotiating with the king became no easier as the decade progressed and, after the Second Civil War, in January 1649 he was put on trial. The charges included the allegation that he had 'traitorously and maliciously levied war against the present Parliament, and the people therein represented'. The places where he had appeared in arms during 1642 were cited as Beverley, Nottingham, Edgehill and Brentford. Turnham Green was not mentioned, perhaps because the task of preparing the indictment was so complex and was completed in some haste, or because the small number of fatalities did not advance the case that was being made.[18] Surely its authors had not found the royalist account of those crucial two days so convincing that they really had disregarded the battle?

When Philip Warwick wrote his history of Charles's reign a quarter of a century later, he seems to have been influenced by it, for in his somewhat indistinct description of the campaign he does not refer clearly to the confrontation at Turnham Green, although he admitted that he was writing 'from a frail memory and some ill-digested notes'.[19] Sir William Dugdale's strongly pro-Royalist account of the war, published in 1681, was also strangely vague about the campaign. After a short and clear summary of the royalists' success at Brentford and an admission that they were 'intending to march forward on the next day', he wrote that the king:

> having advertisement that Essex had drawn his Forces from Kingston, and joining with the London-Auxiliaries, lay in his way at Turnham Greene, he chose rather to make a safe retreat, than hazard his Army by a second Battel.

This implies that the king retreated having received information of Essex's dispositions at Turnham Green, rather than after the two armies had confronted each other there.[20]

Royalist chroniclers had good reason to gloss over the events at Turnham Green, but Essex's biographer Robert Codrington was no more emphatic about the success there, which he gave only a glancing mention, devoting more space to explaining the parliamentarian defeat at Brentford. Curiously, he did not take the opportunity to claim this as one of the earl's major military successes. Codrington was writing only four years after those events, but perhaps some memories had begun to fade. When Lodewijck Huygens travelled from Hammersmith to Brentford in 1652, presumably as he was crossing Turnham Green he was told that it was the site of a battle where the king had beaten 800 parliamentarians led by Essex. Those who explained this to him surely had conflated the two battles in their minds and greatly diminished their scale.[21]

By the time that Daniel Defoe wrote his fictional account of the war, published in 1720, he was able to draw upon several published histories and memoirs, especially those by Hyde, Whitelocke and Ludlow. As its title suggests, *Memoirs of a Cavalier* purports to be the recollections of a soldier in the royalist armies, who had earlier served in the Thirty Years War. Defoe was a keen student of the Civil War and its battles, and he skilfully used his sources to write judicious and largely accurate accounts of both actions. He was aware of the issues raised; for example, his cavalier opposes the attack on Brentford while the possibility of negotiations was still open, but then exonerates it 'as there was no Cessation of Arms agreed on'. Defoe also expresses the royalists' sense of missed opportunities; both the decision to turn and offer Essex battle at Edgehill, instead of pressing on to London, and the failure to attack his army at Turnham Green. Defoe was writing to a Whig agenda and the parliamentarian accounts that were available to him had been adapted before publication to suit the politics of the late seventeenth century. Whitelocke's text was heavily edited and that by Ludlow covering the period of the war was rewritten before publication.

Not until the late twentieth century was Whitelocke's diary published in full and Ludlow's original is lost.[22] But Ludlow's account of the late 1650s and early 1660s has survived and contains his summary of the justification for the king's trial, which includes the fact that he issued commissions:

> by which severall of the good people of England were slayne, as at Keinton battle, at Brainford, Causham [Caversham], Glocester, Newbery, Cornewall, Marston Moore, Naisby, and many other places in England and Wales, where many thousands were slayne by his express command.

He did not mention Turnham Green.[23]

The dilution of two of the principal parliamentarian sources may have contributed to some understating of the importance of Brentford and Turnham Green. This may also have been caused by those royalist accounts which were unavoidably vague or sought to excuse their army's missed opportunity of advancing on London more quickly. Even when its significance is acknowledged, Turnham Green's status as a battle has been questioned, even though it was a confrontation between 36,000 soldiers, with skirmishing and loss of life. This may owe something to the relatively few casualties, reflecting the curious notion that the more combatants that were dead at the end of an engagement the greater its importance must have been. Such ambivalence is succinctly expressed in the summary that Turnham Green 'was a critical point in the war, and it was a battle which was not a battle'.[24]

This ambivalence regarding the battles has lingered despite the acknowledgement of their importance by the foremost historians of the Civil War. The great Victorian historian Samuel Rawson Gardiner compared the engagement at Turnham Green to the battle of Valmy in 1792, where the French army under Dumouriez and the Austrians and Prussians under the Duke of Brunswick faced each other and exchanged heavy cannon fire, without the troops coming into action. Brunswick withdrew after the cannonade at Valmy, ending the threat to Paris and the revolutionary regime. Over the following years the French armies went on to a string of victories across Europe, as the parliamentarian forces had eventually won the wars in the British Isles. This was an apt comparison, although with the important difference that while Valmy is 140 miles from Paris, Turnham Green is just 7 miles from London, and so Essex had less leeway for failure than did Dumouriez.[25] Subsequent historians of the Civil War have not challenged Gardiner and have recognized the significance the two actions. The battles were given thorough treatment by Austin Woolrych, and Charles Carlton described Turnham Green as 'one of the decisive confrontations of the civil war'.[26]

The battles also achieved local recognition. The editors of the late-Victorian history of Chiswick reprinted the pamphlet *A true and perfect relation of the chief passages in Middlesex* and added their own judgement, that Turnham Green 'may be considered one of the decisive encounters of this war, since it prevented the advance upon, and possible capture of, London by the Royalists'. Their successor, Warwick Draper, described the battle as 'one of the critical engagements by which Englishmen then settled their politics', but his uncritical acceptance of the evidence provided by *A true and perfect relation* led him to both misdate the action to the 12 November and to believe that the two armies were fully engaged and more than 900 soldiers were killed.[27]

Interest in the battle of Brentford has been more limited. In 1753 the French Ambassador to London, Monsieur le Duc de Mirepoix, who had a house at Turnham Green, was noted by Horace Walpole:

> walking slowly in the beau milieu of Brentford town, without any company, but with a brown lap-dog with long ears, two pointers, two pages, three footmen, and a vis-a-vis following him... survey[ing] the ground of the battle of Brentford, which... he has much studied, and harangues upon.

In 1922, Fred Turner, a local historian and the librarian at Brentford, published his *History and Antiquities of Brentford* which covered the battle of Brentford and reproduced, with some mistakes, Matthew Smallwood's account of the fighting. However, it was not until 1991 that a study dealing specifically with the battle, by Neil Chippendale, was published.[28]

Some uncertainty about the significance of the battles may have arisen because their sites had not received the attention which other battlefields of the period attracted. Unlike other major actions of the Civil War, they were greatly affected by urbanization during the nineteenth and twentieth centuries, which obscured some of their essential features. C.V. Wedgwood wrote in 1945 that 'the battlefields of the Great Civil War remain for the most part neglected sites'. This is no longer the case, but battlefields in urban settings provide much greater difficulties of appreciation and understanding than those in open countryside.[29] Only with the installation of a series of information boards by the Battlefields Trust, in 2007, were the sites of the two battles marked and explained.

Brentford developed into an industrial district, with a gas works which opened in 1820 and grew to be a significant employer. In 1873 the local newspaper described the town as 'the filthiest place in England'. Almost sixty years later it was thought to be 'extremely ugly'; the essential pattern of a main street containing former coaching inns had survived, but surrounded by 'a large industrial population, which is employed at the gas-works, soap works, timber yards, and brewery'.[30] Syon House still stands in its extensive parkland, but Sir Richard Wynn's house has been demolished and its exact whereabouts are uncertain. Parts of Chiswick, too, have remained as open ground, notably the meadows along the river and the grounds of Chiswick House, but they have been much altered. Like Brentford, Chiswick has a riverside brewery and it too attracted industries during the nineteenth century, although the area around Turnham Green developed rather as a residential area of some gentility, with the country houses of Londoners and those who had chosen to retire there. Much of the open land, including the former common field, became market gardens. Only slowly during the nineteenth century was the district built over, largely for housing and shops. The Royal Horticultural Society took a lease of 33 acres of the former field in 1821. A part of its ground was built over in 1881, during a period of more rapid development, stimulated by the opening in 1869 of the London & South Western Railway from Richmond to the City. This had a station close to the north-east corner of Turnham Green and given that name, although there is nothing to suggest that this was a commemoration of the battle.[31] The Society finally left the area in 1903. With the obliteration of the market gardens and considerable encroachment on the green by buildings, and the fragmentation of the residue by railway embankments, it became difficult to visualize the area as the large open space where two armies had confronted each other.[32]

The creeping urbanization which has transformed the landscape where the two battles were fought should not disguise their importance, which deserves greater recognition than Charles I's dismissive account gave them, as he attempted to excuse himself from having made another serious error of judgement. The dogged defence of Brentford by the parliamentarians gave Essex the time he needed to assemble his forces and confront the royalist army at Turnham Green. There, the king and his advisors discovered that the Londoners were prepared to defy him, even when he was backed by an army that had defeated two parliamentarian regiments on the previous day. Not only had the parliamentarian army been reinforced by citizen-soldiers and numerous volunteers, but there had been no uprising in London in his support. Both sides realized that any further royalist march on London was likely to fail; the significance of that realization can hardly be overestimated.

The inability of the royalists to capitalize on their success at Brentford with a victory at Turnham Green, followed by the surrender of London, ensured that the war continued, with all of the political consequences which stemmed from that. Essex achieved a significant victory at Turnham Green, with only about twenty of his soldiers killed, and parliament was ultimately victorious in two civil wars. The king's reputation was harmed by what was seen as the treacherous attack on the regiments at Brentford, while negotiations were pending and the political process still had a chance of success. The choice between peace and war hung in the balance on the morning of 12 November; the royalists' action swung that balance sharply against peace. Had the attack not been launched, or if the king had exploited the confrontation at Turnham Green as a way of returning to Whitehall, and the planned negotiations had taken place over the following weeks, perhaps an acceptable settlement could have been achieved. In any event, the arrangements would surely have been quite different from those which eventually emerged from the long and bloody years of civil war, the execution of the king, and its aftermath. Without the battles of Brentford and Turnham Green, Britain's constitutional development might have followed a very different path.

Notes

Abbreviations

BL – British Library
Bodl. – Bodleian Library
CJ – *Journals of the House of Commons*
Clarendon, *History* – D. Macray (ed), Edward, Earl of Clarendon, *The History of the Rebellion and Civil Wars in England*, Oxford: Clarendon Press 1888
CSPD – *Calendar of State Papers Domestic*
CSPVen – *Calendar of State Papers Venetian*
Davies, 'Battle of Edgehill' – Godfrey Davies, 'The Battle of Edgehill', *English Historical Review*, 36 (1921)
GL – Guildhall Library
Harl. – Harleian
HMC – Historical Manuscripts Commission
LJ – *Journals of the House of Lords*
LMA – London Metropolitan Archives
ODNB – *Oxford Dictionary of National Biography*, OUP 2004
RO – Record Office
Roy, *ROP* – Ian Roy (ed) *The Royalist Ordnance Papers, 1642–1646*, Oxfordshire Record Soc., vols 43, 49, 1964, 1975
SBTLA – Shakespeare Birthplace Trust Library and Archives
TNA – The National Archives
TT – Thomason Tracts
VCH – Victoria County History
Yonge, *Diary of Proceedings* – Christopher Thompson (ed) *Walter Yonge's diary of proceedings in the House of Commons: 1642–1645, Vol. 1, 19th September 1642–7th March 1643*, Wivenhoe: Orchard Press 1986
Young, *Edgehill* – Peter Young, *Edgehill 1642: The Campaign and the Battle*, Moreton-in-Marsh: Windrush 1998

1. THE CROWN & THE CAPITAL

1. Francis Sheppard, *London: A History*, Oxford: OUP 1998, pp.126–47. Stephen Inwood, *A History of London*, London: Macmillan 1998, pp.149–215.
2. C.H. Firth, *Cromwell's Army*, London: Greenhill Books 1992, p.11. Keith Roberts, 'Citizen Soldiers: The Military Power of the City of London', in Stephen Porter (ed), *London and the Civil War*, Basingstoke: Macmillan 1996, pp.97–100.
3. Brian Manning, *The English People and the English Revolution*, 2nd edn, London: Bookmarks 1991, p.63.
4. The relations between the government and the City are examined in, Robert Ashton, *The City and the Court, 1603–1642*, Cambridge: CUP 1979.
5. Valerie Pearl, *London and the Outbreak of the Puritan Revolution*, Oxford: OUP 1961, pp.49–62.
6. Pearl, *London and the Outbreak*, pp.107–32.
7. Quoted in, Robert Ashton, 'Insurgency, Counter-Insurgency and Inaction: Three

Phases in the Role of the City in the Great Rebellion', in Porter (ed), *London and the Civil War*, pp.50–1.

8. Pearl, *London and the Outbreak*, pp.132–41.
9. G.W. Groos (ed), *The Diary of Baron Waldstein. A Traveller in Elizabethan England*, London: Thames & Hudson 1981, pp.65, 71.
10. H.L. Blackmore, *The Armouries of the Tower of London: I Ordnance*, London: HMSO 1976, p.288.
11. Martin J. Havran, *Caroline Courtier. The Life of Lord Cottington*, London: Macmillan 1973, pp.147–8. Clarendon, *History*, I, p.448.
12. Conrad Russell, 'The First Army Plot of 1641', *Trans. Royal Historical Soc.*, 5th series, 38 (1988), 85–106. CJ, II, pp.353–5. Ian Roy, 'The Tower of London and the Outbreak of the Civil War' (1980); we are very grateful to Dr Roy for allowing us to consult this unpublished paper.
13. Lawson Nagel, 'A Great Bouncing at Every Man's Door': The Struggle for London's Militia in 1642', in Porter (ed), *London and the Civil War*, pp.69–71.
14. Nagel, 'The Struggle for London's Militia', pp.71–2. Clarendon, *History*, I, p.162.
15. Pearl, *London and the Outbreak*, pp.148–55.
16. Nagel, 'The Struggle for London's Militia', pp.75–6.
17. TNA, SP16/488, f.96.
18. CJ, II, p.355.
19. Robert Brenner, *Merchants and Revolution: Commercial Change, Political Conflict, and London's Overseas Traders, 1550–1653*, Cambridge: CUP 1993, pp.428–9.
20. CJ, II, p.559.
21. CJ, II, p.653. LJ, V, pp.284–5. Keith Lindley, 'London's Citizenry in the English Revolution', in R.C. Richardson (ed), *Town and Countryside in the English Revolution*, Manchester: Manchester University Press 1992, p.33.
22. David Cressy, *England on Edge*, Oxford: OUP 2006, p.396.
23. Clarendon, *History*, I, p.591.
24. C.V. Wedgwood, *The King's War 1641–1647*, London: Collins 1958, pp.72–4.
25. Cressy, *England on Edge*, p.430. Clarendon, *History*, II, p.1.
26. TNA, SP16/489, f.44.
27. CJ, II, pp.520, 523, 530–1, 508, 637.

2. Raising the Armies

1. Mark Charles Fissel, *The Bishops' Wars. Charles I's campaigns against Scotland 1638–1640*, Cambridge: CUP 1994, pp.224, 251.
2. Fissel, *Bishops' Wars*, p.195.
3. Fissel, *Bishops' Wars*, pp.164–6, 171–3.
4. Clarendon, *History*, I, p.76.
5. George Johnson (ed), *The Fairfax Correspondence*, London: Richard Bentley 1848, p.406. BL, Harl. MS 6851, ff.150, 177, 178. Clarendon, *History*, II, p.93.
6. Sir Henry Slingsby, *Memoirs Written During the Great Civil War*, Edinburgh: Constable 1806, p.36. Peter Newman, *Royalist Officers in England and Wales, 1642–1660*, New York: Garland 1981, p.346.
7. BL, Harleian MS 6851, ff.150, 173, 176, 181, 182, 187.
8. Slingsby, *Memoirs*, p.37. Clarendon, *History*, II, pp.249, 267. The phrase 'weary of their service' was struck out in the manuscript.
9. Clarendon, *History*, II, pp.213, 347. Roy, *ROP*, I, p.15. John Rushworth, *Historical Collections*, The Third Part, I, p.601. CJ, II, p.651.
10. Peter Edwards, *Dealing in Death: The Arms Trade and the British Civil Wars, 1638–52*, Stroud: Sutton 2000, p.197. Roy, *ROP*, I, p.15–16.
11. Clarendon, *History*, II, p.255. Ian Roy, 'Rupert, prince and count palatine of the Rhine and duke of Cumberland (1619–1682)', ODNB.
12. Samuel Rawson Gardiner, *The Constitutional Documents of the Puritan Revolution*

1625–1660, Oxford: Clarendon Press, 3rd edn 1906, p.260.

13. Anthony Fletcher, *The Outbreak of the English Civil War*, London: Edward Arnold 1981, pp.362–3. J.S. Morrill, *The Revolt of the Provinces*, London: Allen & Unwin 1976, pp.40–2, 155–8. Ronald Hutton, *The Royalist War Effort 1642–1646*, London: Longman 1982, pp.5–19.

14. Fletcher, *Outbreak*, pp.356–68.

15. BL, Harl. MS 6852, f.253.

16. C.R.Long and Ian Roy (eds), *Richard Symonds's Diary of the Marches of the Royal Army*, Cambridge: CUP 1997, pp.160–1. Clements Markham, *The Life of the Great Lord Fairfax*, London: Macmillan 1870, p.27.

17. BL, Harl. MS 6851, f.173. Young, *Edgehill*, p.277. Clarendon MSS, Vol.23, no.1738, reproduced in Alan Wicks (ed), *Bellum Civille*, Leigh-on-Sea: Partisan Press 1988, pp.2–3, 9.

18. Gervase Holles, *Memorials of the Holles family 1493–1656*, Camden Soc., 3rd series, vol.55 1937, p.186. Hutton, *Royalist War Effort*, p.22. Newman, *Royalist Officers*, p.284. M.D.G. Wanklyn and P. Young, 'A King in Search of Soldiers: Charles I in 1642. A Rejoinder', *Historical Journal*, 24 (1981), 150.

19. These commissions went to: Earl Rivers and Sir Edward Fitton in Cheshire; Sir Thomas Salusbury, John Owen, John Herbert, Sir Edward Stradling and the Earl of Carbery in Wales; Sir John Beaumont in Staffordshire. Hutton, *Royalist War Effort*, p.23. Young, *Edgehill*, pp.207–25.

20. *Civil War Tracts*, Chetham Soc., old series, vol.2 1844, p.16. Ernest Broxap, *The Great Civil War in Lancashire 1642–51*, Manchester: Manchester University Press 1973, p.13.

21. CSPD *1641–1643*, p.344. Young, *Edgehill*, pp.168, 202–4. BL, Add MSS 36,913, ff.145–55; we owe this reference to the kindness of Prof. Malcolm Wanklyn. Clarendon, *History*, II, p.320. Clarendon MSS, Vol.23 no.1738, in Wickes (ed), *Bellum Civille*, p.3. HMC, *Fifth Report*, p.191, quoted in, Wanklyn and Young, 'A King in Search of Soldiers... A Rejoinder', p.150.

22. CSPD *1641–1643*, p.390. Newman, *Royalist Officers*, p.116.

23. Clarendon, *History*, II, pp.312–13.

24. Clarendon, *History*, II, pp.318, 320.

25. The foot regiments were probably those of Sir Ralph Dutton, Sir William Pennyman, John Belasyse, Sir Lewis Dyve and the Earl of Lindsey.

26. *CSPD, 1641–43*, p.389. Andy Wood, 'Beyond Post Revisionism? The Civil War Allegiances of the Miners of the Derbyshire 'Peak Country'', *Historical Journal*, 40 (1997), pp.32, 35. Young, *Edgehill*, p.217.

27. Iter Carolinum, in John Gutch, *Collectanea Curiosa*, II, Oxford 1781, p.429. Clarendon, *History*, II, pp.338–9. Nicholas to Sir William Boswell, HMC, *Fifteenth Report*, Bouverier MSS, p.86. Also in William Phillips, 'Ottley Papers', *Trans Shropshire Archaeological Soc.*, 2nd series, VII, 1895, p.246. Wanklyn and Young, 'A King in Search of Soldiers... A Rejoinder', p.150.

28. Clarendon, *History*, II, p.350. Stuart Peachey, *The battle of Powick Bridge, 1642*, Bristol: Stuart 1993, p.3.

29. Clarendon, *History*, II, pp.350–2. Peachey, *Powick Bridge*, p.12.

30. Clarendon, *History*, II, p.363.

31. R.N. Dore, *The Civil Wars in Cheshire*, Chester: Cheshire Community Council 1966, p.14. Hutton, *Royalist War Effort*, p.29. Young, *Edgehill*, pp.205, 207, 215, 224. Iter Carolinum, in Gutch, *Collectanea Curiosa*, II, p.429. Clarendon, *History*, II, pp.364, 367, 369.

32. David Hey (ed), Richard Gough, *The History of Myddle*, Harmondsworth: Penguin 1981, p.71. BL, Harl. MS 6851, f.211. Young, *Edgehill*, pp.210, 217. Hutton, *Royalist War Effort*, p.30.

33. TNA, SP28/2B, ff.665–8.

34. Clarendon, *History*, II, p.364.
35. Clarendon, *History*, II, pp.365-7. Hutton, *Royalist War Effort*, p.30. Edward Besly, *Coins and Medals of the English Civil War*, London: Seaby 1990, pp.24, 29-33.
36. Young, *Edgehill*, pp.70, 211, 219. BL, Harl. MS 6851, f.211. Clarendon, *History*, II, p.374. Newman, *Royalist Officers*, pp.55, 130, 403.
37. Stuart Reid, 'Ruthven, Patrick, earl of Forth and earl of Brentford, (d.1651)', ODNB. Young, *Edgehill*, p.62.
38. David Lloyd, *Memoires of the Lives, Actions, Sufferings and Deaths of those noble; reverend and excellent personages that suffered by death, sequestration, decimation or otherwise for the protestant religion, and the great principle thereof, allegiance to their soveraigne, in our late intestine wars, ... and from thence continued to 1666. With the life and martyrdom of King Charles I*, 1668, p.674.
39. Clarendon, *History*, III, p.345.
40. C.H. Firth (ed), Margaret, Duchess of Newcastle, *The Life of William Cavendish Duke of Newcastle*, London: Routledge 1906, p.13.
41. CJ, II, p.668. LJ, V, p.208.
42. Clarendon, *History*, II, p.64. CJ, II, pp.530-1.
43. Gardiner, *Constitutional Documents*, pp.248-9.
44. Clarendon, *History*, II, pp.84-5.
45. Bodl., Carte MS 80, f.78; we owe this reference to the kindness of Prof. Malcolm Wanklyn.
46. LJ, V, pp.123, 142, 185. Essex's Commission is printed in, Young, *Edgehill*, pp.192-3. CJ, II, p.673.
47. Thomas Ballard was referred to as a Sergeant Major General in August 1642 while commanding a brigade-sized force from Essex's army in Buckinghamshire and Warwickshire, but this seems to have been a temporary rank relating to this particular command. CJ, II, p.672. LJ, V, p.321. TNA, SP28/2A, f.289. *CSPD, 1641-3*, p.367.
48. TNA, SP28/2A, ff.65, 158, 184, 199, 211, 239, 240; /2B ff.360, 372. Edward Peacock, *The Army Lists of the Roundheads and Cavaliers*, London: John Camden Hotton 1874, reprinted 1983, pp.20, 23. CJ, II, p.694.
49. Fletcher, *Outbreak*, pp.348, 350.
50. LJ, V, p.122. CJ, II, p.629.
51. TNA, SP28/1A, ff.1-16. SP28/1A, f.132 identifies Capt. George Withers as serving in Col. John Middleton's regiment of horse on 16 August 1642, but it was not until November 1642 that Middleton became a cavalry colonel when he took over command of Lord Feilding's regiment.
52. TNA, SP28/1A ff.89, 140, 167, 201, 230; /2A, ff.151, 242; /2B, ff.321, 421, 453; /3A, f.251. Peacock pp.47-8.
53. Snow, *Essex*, p.316.
54. Godfrey Davies, 'The Parliamentary Army under the Earl of Essex, 1642-45', *English Historical Review*, 49 (1934), p.33.
55. Bodl., Carte MS 80, f.70a. TNA, SP28/129 pt 1, f.2.
56. TNA, SP28/1A, ff.29, 38-41, 64, 65, 67-9, 87, 100, 112, 117, 144, 150, 286; /261, ff.11, 16.
57. Norman Tucker (ed), *The Military Memoirs of John Gwyn*, in Peter Young and Norman Tucker (eds), *Military Memoirs: The Civil War*, London: Longman, Green 1967, p.46. Stuart Peachey, *The Edgehill Campaign and the Letters of Nehemiah Wharton*, Leigh-on-Sea: Partisan Press 1997, p.5.
58. TNA, SP28/1A, f.172.
59. Based upon an analysis of, TNA, SP28/1B, SP28/2A, /2B and /3A.
60. TNA, SP28/1A, ff.172, 177-9, 298-9, 301-2; /2A, ff.88-90, 134, 154-5; /261, f.44.
61. LJ, V, pp.357, 363.
62. Peachey, *Edgehill Campaign*, p.15. TNA, SP28/3B, ff.352-3.
63. TNA, SP28/1A, f.164; /146, ff.400-06.

64. TNA, WO55/1937, unfol. Peachey, *Edgehill Campaign*, p.17.
65. Peachey, *Edgehill Campaign*, pp.7–8. LJ, V, p.321. TNA, SP28/183. Philip Tennant, *Edgehill and Beyond*, Stroud: Sutton 1992, pp.45–6.
66. BL, TT E118/12 *Good News from Banbury in Oxfordshire* [20 Sept. 1642]. *CSP Ven, 1642–3*, p.165. Snow, *Essex*, p.328. Peachey, *Edgehill Campaign*, p.15. Anne Lawrence, *Parliamentary Army Chaplains 1642–1651*, Woodbridge: Royal Historical Soc. 1990, pp.92, 151, 171–2. The preachers were respectively, Obadiah Sedgwick, his brother John, Stephen Marshall and Simeon Ashe.
67. Andrew Clark, *The Life and Times of Anthony Wood, antiquary, of Oxford, 1632–1695, described by Himself*, I, Oxford Historical Soc. 1891, pp.61–7. HMC, *Thirteenth Report, Portland MSS*, I, p.67. BL, TT E122/13 *A Perfect and True Relation of the Daily Passages of the Soldiers which are under Lord Sayes Command*, 9 Sept.–6 Oct. 1642; E240/11 *A Perfect Diurnall of the Passages in Parliament*, 19–26 Sept. 1642. TNA, SP28/261, f.186.

3. The Opening Campaign

1. Young, *Edgehill*, p.57.
2. Vernon Snow, *Essex the Rebel. The life of Robert Devereux, the Third Earl of Essex, 1591–1646*, Lincoln, Ne: University of Nebraska Press 1970, pp.1, 21–2, 91–124, 129, 149.
3. Stuart Peachey, *The Edgehill Campaign and the Letters of Nehemiah Wharton*, Leigh-on-Sea: Partisan Press 1997, pp.17–19. Philip Tennant, *Edgehill and Beyond*, Stroud: Sutton 1992, pp.50–2.
4. BL, TT E200/64 *A Worthy Speech Spoken by His Excellence The Earl of Essex*, cited in Snow, *Essex*, p.330.
5. TNA, SP28/143, dated 1 Oct. 1642.
6. Philip Styles, 'The City of Worcester during the Civil Wars, 1640–60', in his *Studies in Seventeenth Century West Midlands History*, Kineton: Roundwood Press 1978, pp.222–3. Shelagh Bond (ed), *The Chamber Order Book of Worcester, 1602–1650*, Worcestershire Historical Soc, new series, 8, 1974, pp.357–8.
7. Peachey, *Edgehill Campaign*, p.25.
8. BL, TT E123/5 *Special passages and Certain Informations*, 11–18 Oct. 1642, p.83; E240/42 *England's Memorable Accidents*, 10–17 Oct. 1642, p.47; E121/34 *Weekly Intelligence from several parts of the Kingdom*, 11 Oct. 1642, p.3.
9. CJ, II, p.791.
10. Young, *Edgehill*, p.71. Clarendon, *History*, II, p.349.
11. Iter Carolinum, in John Gutch, *Collectanea Curiosa*, II, Oxford: 1781, p.429. M.D.G. Wanklyn and P. Young, 'A King in Search of Soldiers: Charles I in 1642. A Rejoinder', *Historical Journal*, 24 (1981), p.151. Clarendon, *History*, II, p.356. John Harland, *The Lancashire Lieutenancy under the Tudors and Stuarts*, Chetham Soc., old series, 49, 1859, pp.281, 283.
12. Young, *Edgehill*, p.75. Roy, *ROP*, p.153.
13. CJ, II, pp.810–11.
14. LJ, V, p.412.
15. BL, TT E124/14 *Special Passages & Certain Information*, 18–25 Oct. 1642, p.92. Iter Carolinum, in Gutch, *Collectanea Curiosa*, II, p.429.
16. BL, TT E124/14 *Special Passages & Certain Information*, 18–25 Oct. 1642, p.93; E126/38 *A Most True and Exact Relation of Both the Battels fought by his Excellency and his Forces against the bloudy Cavelliers*, 9 Nov. 1642 p.4. Tennant, *Edgehill and Beyond*, p.55.
17. Young, *Edgehill*, p.273.
18. The dispute over the royalist formation is discussed in: Young, *Edgehill*, pp.79–82; Christopher L. Scott, Alan Turton and Eric Gruber von Arnim, *Edgehill: The Battle*

Reinterpreted, Barnsley: Pen & Sword 2004, pp.34–6. A more detailed discussion of the Swedish formation used by the royalists at Edgehill can be found in, Keith Roberts, 'Battle Plans: The Practical Use of Battlefield Plans in the English Civil War', *Cromwelliana* (1997), 4–14. Discussions with Keith Roberts also informed this section.

19. We owe this information to the kindness of Glenn Foard.
20. Young *Edgehill*, pp.78–123.
21. Staffordshire RO, Sutherland MSS, D868/2/67.
22. Young, *Edgehill*, pp.124–6. Jon Day, *Gloucester and Newbury 1643: The Turning Point of the Civil War*, Barnsley: Pen & Sword 2007, p.219.
23. TNA, SP28/2B, ff.665–8. Roy, *ROP*, I, p.155. Staffordshire RO, Sutherland MS D868/2/67.
24. LMA, Journals of Common Council, XL, f.41b. TNA, SP28/3B, f.424; /298, f.606; /2A, f.289; /2B, ff.415, 424–5, 460; /4, f.262; /143, unfol. Capt Vernon's accounts; /3B, f.336; /136. pt 11; /3A, f.207. SBTLA, DR98/1704 unfol. Ann Hughes, 'Feilding, Basil, second earl of Denbigh (c.1608–1675)', ODNB.
25. TNA, SP28/136, pts 11, 19; /184; /253B has John Bridges, at this time nominally a captain in Lord Brooke's regiment of foot, but probably at Warwick during the battle and who was later made governor of Warwick Castle, quoting a figure of 3–400 wounded taken to Warwick. SBTLA, Borough of Stratford-upon-Avon Chamberlain's Accounts, 1622–47, f.175, reproduced in Scott, Turton and Von Arnim, *Edgehill*, pp.160–1.
26. Young, *Edgehill*, pp.270, 279.
27. Clarendon, *History*, II, p.374.
28. Young, *Edgehill*, pp.174–5. Clarendon, *History*, II, p.373.
29. Clarendon, *History*, II, p.374.
30. TNA, SP28/136, pts 11, 19.
31. TNA, SP28/136, pts 11, 19.
32. TNA, SP28/298, ff.605,606; /171, pt 5 unfol.
33. Lord Nugent, *Memorials of John Hampden: His Party and his Times*, London: Chapman & Hall 1880, p.323.
34. LJ, V, p.430. Nugent, *John* Hampden, p.323.
35. BL, TT E242/6, *England's Memorable Accidents* 31 Oct.–7 Nov. 1642, p.70; E669/6 *The Vindication and Clearing of Sir James Ramsay...*, unfol.
36. BL, TT E242/6 *England's Memorable Accidents*, 31 Oct.–7 Nov. 1642. W. Harry Rylands (ed), *Visitation of Buckinghamshire, 1634*, Harleian Soc., 58, 1909, p.71. BL, TT E127/2 *A true relation of the taking twelve cavaliers at Watford by the Earl of Essex. Also declaring how the Towne of Colebrooke was plundered by Prince Robert*, unpag.; E127/3 *A continuation of certain speciall and remarkable passages*, 4–11 November, p.5. For further information on the death of Hampden's son see Roy Bailey's article, 'The Life and Death of John Hampden Junior' on the John Hampden Society website (www.johnhampden.org/archives.htm).
37. BL, TT E242/10 *England's Memorable accidents*, 7–14 Nov. 1642; E242/11 *A perfect diurnall of the Passages in Parliament*, 12 Nov. 1642, p.1. LJ, V, p.435. CJ, II, p.838.

4. PREPARATIONS IN LONDON

1. TNA, SP28/131.
2. CJ, II, p.829.
3. TNA, SP28/261, f.284. Peter Edwards, *Dealing in Death: The Arms Trade and the British Civil Wars, 1638–52*, Stroud: Sutton 2000, pp.71, 103, 199, 110, 133–4, 149–50.
4. Yonge, *Diary of Proceedings*, pp.97–9, 107–8. CJ, II, 787, 798, 815, 821, 828, 843. LJ, V, pp.420, 438.
5. Yonge *Diary of Proceedings*, p.107.
6. TNA, WO55/1754, f.14a; /1937, unfol.

7. *CSPVen*, 1642–1643, pp.192, 198. BL, TT E127/4 *The Last Newes from the Kings Majesties Army now at Maidenhead*, 11 Nov. 1642, p.3. CJ, II, p.837.

8. BL, TT E126/6 *Special Passages and Certain Information*, p.111; E127/26 *The English Intelligencer*, 12–18 Nov. 1642, p.7. TNA, WO55/1937, unfol.

9. CJ, II, p.826. LJ, V, p.447.

10. LJ, V, pp.307-8. LMA, COL/AD/01/041 Court of the Common Council Letter Book QQ, 1640–1647, f.52a.11. TNA, SP28/262, ff.75, 132.

11. TNA, SP28/262, ff.75, 132.

12. TNA, SP28/3A, f.171.

13. CJ, II, pp.821,823. *CSPVen*, 1642–1643, pp.192, 198.

14. Yonge, *Diary of Proceedings*, p.103.

15. TNA, WO55/1937, unfol. CJ, II, pp.835, 846.

16. LMA, COL/AD/01/041 Court of the Common Council Letter Book QQ, 1640–47, f.45a. G.A. Raikes (ed), *The Ancient Vellum Book of the Honourable Artillery Company*, London: Bentley 1890, p.20. TNA, SP28/126; /261 ff.294, 296; /262, f.467. Lawson Chase Nagel, The Militia of London 1641–1649, unpublished PhD Thesis, King's College, University of London, 1982, pp.71, 85.

17. CJ, II, pp.803, 812, 813, 818, 819. LJ, V, pp.414, 416. Yonge, *Diary of Proceedings*, pp.75, 78, 79.

18. *CSPVen*, 1642–1643, p.188.

19. CJ, II, 828, 838, 844–5. Lawson Nagel, "A Great Bouncing at Every Man's Door': The Struggle for London's Militia in 1642', in Stephen Porter (ed), *London and the Civil War*, Basingstoke: Macmillan 1996, p.81.

20. BL, TT E127/9 *A Speech Spoken unto his Excellencie the Earle of Warwicke by Captain Farres, in the behalfe of the whole County of Essex*, 1642, pp.5–6. TNA, SP28/3A, ff.79, 116, 212; /3B, ff.471, 479; /261, f.311; /262, f.14.

21. TNA, SP28/136, pt 56; /262 f.179; /3A; /3B; /4, passim. Ian Beckett, *Buckinghamshire in the Civil War*, Aylesbury: Buckinghamshire County Museum 2004, p.13. John Adair, *Cheriton 1644. The Campaign and the Battle*, Kineton: Roundwood Press 1970, p.111. Little is known about John Holmstead and his regiment, which appears to have been disbanded by the end of 1643, see Peachey, *Edgehill Campaign*, p.53; *Calendar of State Papers Domestic Committee for the Advance of Money 1642–1656*, I, p.419.

22. LMA, COL/AD/01/041 Court of the Common Council Letter Book QQ, 1640–47, f.45a.

23. TNA, SP28/131 pt 5; /144 pt 2, /262, ff.268, 344. Alan Turton, *Chief Strength of the Army*, Leigh on Sea: Partisan Press undated, p.23. Lawson Nagel, The Militia of London, 1641–1649, Ph.D. thesis, King's College, University of London 1982, pp.110–11. Buller may be the Anthony Buller who became Captain-Lieutenant of Skippon's troop. The number of horses acquired by Buller in the horse account outlined in SP28/131 pt 5 is small relative to the other officers and it may be the troop was never completed and was instead amalgamated into Skippon's.

24. TNA, SP28/262, ff.58, 268, 344; /4, ff.209, 261, 350, 359, 362, 361–3; /5 ff.203, 206.

25. William Beamont (ed), *A Discourse on the Warr in Lancashire*, Chetham Soc., old series, 62, 1864, pp.22–3, 108.

26. Bodl. MS Tanner 64, f.87, letter of 12 Nov. 1642.

27. Nagel, 'The Struggle for London's Militia', pp.81–2. Ferdinand Tönnies (ed), Thomas Hobbes, *Behemoth or The Long Parliament*, London: Simkin, Marshall 1889, p.122.

28. CJ, II, p.842.

29. *CSPVen*, 1642–1643, pp.181–2, 188.

30. HMC, *Fifth Report, House of Lords MSS*, p.56. David J. Crankshaw, 'Community, City and Nation, 1540–1714', in Derek Keene, Arthur Burns and Andrew Saint (eds), *St Paul's: The Cathedral Church of London 604–2004*, New Haven & London: Yale University Press 2004, p.61.

31. LJ, V, p.403. CJ, II, p.819.

32. Nagel, 'The Struggle for London's Militia', p.80.

33. HMC, *Fifth report, House of Lords MSS*, p.51. LJ, V, pp.385, 386.

34. For an analysis of the divisions during this period see, Keith Lindley, 'London's Citizenry in the English Revolution', in R.C. Richardson (ed), *Town and Countryside in the English Revolution*, Manchester: Manchester University Press 1992, pp.19–45.

35. LJ, V, pp.416, 420, 437, 439, 443. CJ, II, pp.769, 801, 812, 818–20, 830–1, 834–5, 839, 843, 840–1. Yonge, *Diary of Proceedings*, pp.103, 110. *CSPVen, 1642–1643*, p.198.

36. CJ, II, pp.771, 783, 803, 807, 826.

37. *CSPVen, 1642–1643*, p.198.

38. Marvin Arthur Breslow, *A Mirror of England. English Puritan Views of Foreign Nations, 1618–1640*, Cambridge, Mass: Harvard University Press 1970, pp.10–44.

39. *CSPVen, 1642–1643*, p.177.

40. Bodl, MS Tanner 64, f.83. George Malcolm Thomson, *Warrior Prince. The Life of Prince Rupert of the Rhine*, London: Secker & Warburg 1976, pp.34–6.

41. CJ, II, p.848. BL, TT E127/42 *The wicked resolution of the Cavaliers*, pp.2–5.

42. BL, TT E127/16 *Prince Robert his Plot Discovered*, p.2; E127/18 *Prince Roberts Disguises*.

43. BL, Add MS 40,883, f.48r.

44. BL, TT E127/6 *An Extract of Severall Letters*, 1642, p.4. Yonge, *Diary of Proceedings*, p.98. CJ, II, p.838.

45. BL, TT E127/4 *The Last Newes from the Kings Majesties Army now at Maidenhead*, 12 Nov. 1642, p.3; E127/3 *A Coninuation of Certaine Speciall and Remarkable Passages...*, 4–11 Nov. 1642, pp.5–6; E127/6 *An Extract of Severall Letters which came by the last Post*, Nov. 1642, pp.4–5.

46. A.L. Beier, 'Engine of manufacture: the trades of London', in A.L. Beier and R. Finlay (eds), *London 1500–1700: The making of the metropolis*, London: Longmans 1986, pp.147–9. P.J. Corfield and N.B. Harte (eds), F.J. Fisher, *London and the English Economy, 1500–1700*, London: Hambledon Press 1990, pp.121–2.

47. BL, TT E127/38 *Gods Rising, His Enemies Scattering*, 1644, p.49. LJ, V, p.423.

48. Clarendon, *History*, II, pp.376–8.

5. The Royalist Advance on London

1. Ian Roy and Dietrich Reinhart, 'Oxford and the Civil Wars' in Nicholas Tyacke (ed), *The History of the University of Oxford, Volume IV Seventeenth-Century Oxford*, Oxford: Clarendon Press 1997, pp.695–6.

2. Roy and Reinhart, 'Oxford and the Civil Wars', pp.697–8. Ian Roy, 'The City of Oxford 1640–1660' in R.C. Richardson (ed), *Town and Countryside in the English Revolution*, Manchester: Manchester University Press 1992, p.140.

3. M.G. Hobson and H.E. Salter (eds), *Oxford Council Acts 1626–1665*, Oxford Historical Soc. 1933, pp.111, 369. Roy and Reinhart, 'Oxford and the Civil Wars', p.699.

4. A.C. Wood (ed), *Memorials of the Holles Family, 1493–1656, by Gervase Holles*, Camden Soc., 3rd series, LV, 1937, p.187. Christopher L. Scott, Alan Turton and Eric Gruber von Arnim, *Edgehill: The Battle Reinterpreted*, Barnsley: Pen & Sword 2004, p.153.

5. Staffordshire RO, D686/2/68. Bodl., Ashmole MS 830, ff.292–3.

6. Lord Nugent, *Memorials of John Hampden: His Party and his Times*, London: Chapman & Hall 1880, p.323.

7. Nugent, *John Hampden*, p.323.

8. Richard Ollard, *Clarendon and his Friends*, Oxford: OUP 1988, pp.80–1.

9. Clarendon, *History*, II, p.388.

10. Clarendon, *History*, II, p.390.

11. Clarendon, *History*, II, p.390.

12. Ian Roy, 'George Digby, Royalist intrigue and the collapse of the cause', in Ian Gentles, John Morrill and Blair Worden (eds), *Soldiers, writers and statesmen of the English Revolution*, Cambridge: CUP 1998, pp.68–76. Richard Ollard (ed), *Clarendon's Four Portraits*, London: Hamish Hamilton 1989, pp.55–65.

13. Andrew Clark, *The Life and Times of Anthony Wood, antiquary, of Oxford, 1632–1695, described by Himself*, I, Oxford Historical Soc. 1891, p.71.

14. His commission is reproduced in David Smurthwaite, *The Complete Guide to the Battlefields of Britain*, London: Michael Joseph 1984, p.133.

15. Ollard, *Clarendon*, pp.63–70. For Clarendon's portrait of Colepeper, see G. Huehns (ed), *Clarendon: Selections from The History of the Rebellion and The Life by Himself*, Oxford: OUP 1978, pp.332–7.

16. Clarendon, *History*, III, p.443.

17. Clarendon, *History*, II, pp.389–90.

18. Clark, *Life and Times of Anthony Wood*, I, p.70. Yonge, *Diary of Proceedings*, p.96. BL, TT E127/3 *A Continuation of Certaine Speciall and remarkable Passages...* 4–11 Nov. 1642, p.7.

19. 'The Journal of Prince Rupert's Marches', *English Historical Review*, XIII (1898), p.731.

20. Yonge, *Diary of Proceedings*, p.100. Bodl., MS Tanner 64, f.83.

21. Young, *Edgehill*, p.131.

22. Yonge, *Diary of Proceedings*, pp.97, 98. BL, TT E126/23 *Truths from Severall Parts of the Kingdom*, 7 Nov. 1642. TNA, WO55/1937, unfol.

23. SBTLA, DR98/1704, 25 Nov. 1642.

24. BL, TT E127/12 *Speciall Passages*, 8–15 Nov. 1642, p.117.

25. *Cal. of the Committee for the Advance of Money*, p.155. BL, TT E127/10 *Exceeding joyful news out of Surrey...*, 1642.

26. Philip Warwick, *Memoires of the Reign of King Charles* I, 1701, p.231. TNA, SP28/126.

27. Clarendon, *History*, II, p.389.

28. Warwick, *Memoires*, p.231.

29. Young, *Edgehill*, p.131.

30. Ian Roy, 'The Royalist Council of War, 1642–6', *Bulletin of the Institute of Historical Research*, XXXV (1962), pp.153–4.

31. Yonge, *Diary of Proceedings*, pp.107, 110, 111. CJ, II, p.846.

32. Clark, *Life and Times of Anthony Wood*, I, p.70.

33. Bodl., Carte MS 76, f.3.

34. Roy, *ROP*, I, p.162.

35. Bodl., Ashmole MS 830, f.293.

36. Roy, *ROP*, I, p.12.

37. BL, TT E127/10 *Exceeding joyful news out of Surrey*. 'Journal of Prince Rupert's Marches', *English Historical Review*, XIII (1898), p.731. Roy, *ROP*, I, p.162; II, p.462 n.24.

38. TNA, SP28/136 Pt 56, part of Holborn's regiment was to be 'relieve[d]' with victuals on 14 November 1642.

39. Yonge, *Diary of Proceedings*, p.107.

40. BL, TT E127/10 *Exceeding joyful news out of Surrey shewing the proceedings of Prince Rupert and his mischievous cavaliers since he came into these parts*, pp.5–7. Bodl., MS Carte 76, f.3.

41. LJ, V, pp.432, 433.

42. David L. Smith, 'Philip Herbert, first earl of Montgomery and fourth earl of Pembroke (1584–1650)', ODNB. Anthony Fletcher, *The Outbreak of the English Civil War* (London: Arnold 1985 edn), p.277. S.R. Gardiner, *History of the Great Civil War*, Moreton-in-Marsh: Windrush 1987, I, p.53.

43. LJ, V, 435, 436.

44. CJ, II, p.838. Yonge, *Diary of Proceedings*, p.100.

45. CJ, II, p.838.

46. Gardiner, *History of the Great Civil War*, I, p.56.

47. Yonge, *Diary of Proceedings*, p.105. LJ, V, p.440. CJ, II, p.841.

48. LJ, V, pp.439–40. CJ, II, p.842. Yonge, *Diary of Proceedings*, pp.105–6, 114.

49. LJ, V, p.440.

50. Clarendon, *History*, II, p.393.

51. HMC, *Ormonde MSS*, II, new series, 1903, p.381.

52. Clarendon, *History*, II, p.392.

53. LJ, V, p.440. The 'Journal of Prince Rupert's Marches' is in error in dating the King's journey from Maidenhead to Colnbrook to 9 November, *English Historical Review*, XIII (1898), p.731.

54. Warwick, *Memoires*, p.255.

55. LJ, V, p.443.

56. Yonge, *Diary of Proceedings*, p.115. LJ, V, p.443. CJ, II, p.849.

57. Clarendon, *History*, II, pp.393–4.

58. Warwick, *Memoires*, p.232.

59. Young, *Edgehill*, p.274.

60. Sir Richard Bulstrode's account, cited in Young, *Edgehill*, p.261.

61. Roy, *ROP*, I, p.163; II, p.462 n.27.

62. Roy, *ROP*, I, p.162.

63. 'The Journal of Prince Rupert's Marches', *English Historical Review*, XIII (1898), p.731. Bodl., Ashmole MS 830, ff.292–3.

64. Clarendon, *History*, II, pp.389, 394.

65. John Adair agrees that it is 'nearly impossible' to believe Hyde on this point: *A Life of John Hampden. The Patriot (1594–1643)*, London: Thorogood 2003, p.196.

66. LJ, V, p.443.

67. Thomas May, *A Breviary of the History of the Parliament of England*, in Francis Maseres, *Select Tracts relating to the Civil Wars in England, in the Reign of Charles the First*, I, London: 1813, p.57.

68. James Sutherland (ed), Lucy Hutchinson, *Memoirs of the Life of Colonel Hutchinson*, Oxford: OUP 1973, p.60.

69. Yonge, *Diary of Proceedings*, p.115.

70. LJ, V, p.440.

6. Surprise at Brentford

1. Yonge, *Diary of Proceedings*, p.111.

2. LJ, V, p.443.

3. Bodl., Ashmole MS 830, ff.292–3.

4. Norman Tucker (ed), *The Military Memoirs of John Gwyn*, in Peter Young and Norman Tucker (eds), *Military Memoirs: The Civil War*, London: Longman, Green 1967, p.46.

5. Bodl. Ashmole MS 830, ff.292–3.

6. Roy, *ROP*, I, p.163.

7. Description based upon Moses Glover's annotated survey of Isleworth Hundred, 1635. See VCH, *Middlesex*, III, opp. p.90.

8. Joan Thirsk (ed), *The Agrarian History of England and Wales*, Volume IV 1500–1640, Cambridge: CUP 1967, p.480. Maurice Exwood and H.L. Lohmann (eds), *The Journal of William Schellinks' Travels in England 1661–1663*, Camden Soc., 5th series, I, 1993, p.81.

9. James Knowles (ed), *The Roaring Girl and other City Comedies*, Oxford: OUP 2001, pp.xxxv, 286. Alan Brissenden (ed), Thomas Middleton, *A Chaste Maid in Cheapside*, London: A&C Black 1968, p.99. For the image of Brentford projected in Elizabethan and Jacobean drama see, Charles Nicholl, *The Lodger: Shakespeare on Silver Street*, London: Allen Lane 2007, pp.233–8.

10. Young, *Edgehill*, p.274, quoting 'Rupert's Diary'. *CSP Ven, 1642–1643*, p.201.

11. BL, TT E127/12 *Speciall Passages and Certain Information from Severall Places*, 8–15 Nov. 1642, p.119.

12. Bodl., Ashmole MS 830, ff.292–3.

13. HMC, *Calendar of the Marquess of Ormonde*, Vol. II, new series, 1903, pp.381–2. *A Brief Relation of the Life and Memoirs of John Belasyse Written and Collected by His Secretary Joshua Moore. Military Memoirs of John Gwyn*. Extracts from the following: Young, *Edgehill*; Rupert's Diary; Somerset RO, Cheshire RO, Lancashire RO, quarter sessions papers; Sir Richard Bulstrode, *Memoirs and Reflections*, 1721; Edward Walsingham, *Brittannicae Virtutis Imago*, 1644. Young, *Edgehill*, pp.178, 179, quoting BL, Add. MS 34,713, f.1.

14. Young, *Edgehill*, pp.84–7. Bodl., Carte MS 76, f.3.

15. BL, TT E314/21 *Innocency and Truth Justified*, 1645, p.40; E242/11 *A Perfect Diurnal of the Passages in Parliament*, 1642, p.8.

16. TNA, SP28/2A f.280; /2B, f.466.

17. Godfrey Davies, 'The Parliamentary Army under the Earl of Essex, 1642–5', *English Historical Review*, XLIX (1934), p.52. Stuart Peachey *The Edgehill Campaign and Letters of Nehemiah Wharton*, Leigh-on-Sea: Partisan Press 1997, p.7.

18. TNA, SP28/3A f.177.

19. BL, TT E314/21 *Innocency and Truth Justified*, p.41.

20. BL, TT E127/19 *The Valiant Resolution of the Seamen Under the Command of the Earle of Warwick*, 1642, unfol.; E127/12 *Speciall Passages and Certain Information from Severall Places*, 8–15 Nov. 1642, p.119; E127/24 *A Declaration and Manifestation of the Proceedings of both Armies*, p.2. The latter claims the attack on Brentford commenced in the afternoon, while the other reports imply midday.

21. Bulstrode, *Memoirs and Reflections*, quoted in Young, *Edgehill*, p.261.

22. Gwyn, *Memoirs*, p.46.

23. Glover's survey of Isleworth Hundred, 1635.

24. Lord Nugent, *Memorials of John Hampden: His Party and his Times*, London: Chapman & Hall 1880, p.323. William Cobbett, *Complete Collection of State Trials*, IV 1809, trial of Charles I, testimony of John Thomas of Llangollen, quoted in Revd John Webb, *Memorials of the Civil War in Herefordshire*, London: Longmans 1879, I, p.199. Lloyd, *Memoires of the Lives...*, p.661.

25. BL, TT 314/2 *Innocency and Truth Justified*, p.41.

26. John Rushworth, *Historical Collections* Part 3 1642–1644, II, 1659, p.62.

27. Archaeological finds near the south-east corner of the house are inconclusive as regards the extent of any action around the buildings. An exploration of the Brigettine Monastery of Syon in 2003 unearthed a probable musket ball and carbine ball and subsequent investigation in 2007 found three further musket-sized balls around the house. Information kindly supplied by Richard Pailthorpe, Estate Manager Syon House in May 2004 and Harvey Sheldon, Birkbeck College Archaeology, June 2007.

28. Alnwick Castle MSS, U.1.6/20.

29. Cobbett, *State Trials*, p.1299; Edward Peacock, *The Army Lists of the Roundheads and Cavaliers*, London: John Camden Hotton 1874, p.56. BL, TT E126/38, *A most True and Exact Relation of Both Battels fought by his Excellency and his Forces against the bloudy Cavalliers*, p.2.

30. Nehemiah Wallington, *Historical Notices*, 1869 edn, II, p.120. *A True and Perfect Relation of the Barbarous and Cruell Passages of the Kings Army at Old Brainceford 1642* quoted in Neil Chippendale, *The Battle of Brentford*, 1991. TNA, SP28/141B, pt 3.

31. Clarendon, *History*, II, p.395.

32. Clarendon, *History*, II, p.395.

33. Bodl., Ashmole MS 830, ff.292–3. BL, TT E314/21, *Innocency and Truth Justified*, p.41.

34. Bodl., Ashmole MS 830, ff.292–3.

35. Gwyn, *Memoirs*, p.46.

36. Bodl., MS.Don.c.184, f.29r.

37. Clarendon, *History*, II, p.395. BL, TT E314/21 *Innocency and Truth Justified*, p.41.

38. BL, TT E127/35 *Speciall Passages and Certain Informations from Severall Places*, 15–22 Nov. 1642, p.126.

39. BL, TT E242/33 *A Perfect Declaration of the Barbarous and Cruell Passages Committed by Prince Robert, the Cavaliers and others in His Majesty's Army*, unpag.

40. Cobbett, *State Trials*, p.1391. HMC, *Ormonde*, p.381. Gwyn, *Memoirs*, p.46. Bodl., Ashmole MS 830, ff.292–3; Carte MS 76, f.3.

41. Thomas May, *A Breviary of the History of the Parliament of England*, in Francis Maseres, *Select Tracts relating to the Civil Wars in England, in the Reign of Charles the First*, I, London: 1813, p.57. Rushworth, *Historical Collections* Part 3 1642–1644, Vol II, 1659, p.59.

42. Nugent, *Memorials of John Hampden*, p.326.

43. HMC, *Portland MSS*, III, pp.100–1.

44. LJ, V, p.443.

45. BL, TT E127/15, *A true and perfect relation of the chief passages in Middlesex*, pp.126–7. Bodl., Carte MS 76, f.3.

46. Bodl., Carte MS 76, f.3, dated 16 Nov. [1642].

47. BL, TT E73 *God In the Mount or a Continuation of England's Parliamentary Chronicle*, pp.206–16.

48. BL, TT E127/15, *A true and perfect relation of the chief passages in Middlesex*. C.V. Wedgwood, 'The Chief Passages in Middlesex', *Middlesex Local History Council Bulletin*, 14, (1962), p.1.

49. BL, TT E127/12 *Speciall Passages and Certain Information from Severall Places*, 8–15 Nov. 1642, p.119.

50. HMC, *Portland MSS*, III, pp.100–1. Robert Codrington, *The Life and Death of the Illustrious Earl of Essex*, 1646, p.22. BL, TT E73 *God In the Mount or a Continuation of England's Parliamentary Chronicle*, pp.206–16.

51. May, *History of the Parliament of England*, p.57.

52. Emmanuel de Bois's company of firelocks consisted of sixty-six soldiers, two officers and seven inferior officers; TNA, SP28/131, pt 2. BL, TT E314/21, *Innocency and Truth Justified*, p.40.

53. *CSP Ven.*, 1642–1643, p.201.

54. *A True and Perfect Relation of the Barbarous and Cruell Passages of the Kings Army at Old Brainceford*, 1642; quoted in Chippendale, *Battle of Brentford*.

55. Nehemiah Wallington, *Historical Notices*, 1869 edn, II, p.120.

56. Mary Anne Everett Green (ed), *Diary of John Rous, incumbent of Santon Downham, Suffolk, from 1625 to 1642*, Camden Soc., LXVI, 1856, p.129, quoted in C.V. Wedgwood, *The King's War 1641–1647*, London: Collins 1958, p.142.

57. GL, MS 10464A, f.41. BL, TT E314/21 *Innocency and Truth Justified*, p.41.

58. Daniel Lysons, *The Environs of London*, IV, 1796, p.199. Clarendon, *History*, II, p.395.

59. Chippendale, *Battle of Brentford*, p.16.

60. *CSPD*, 1654, p.351.

61. HMC, *Portland MSS*, III, pp.100–1.

62. Cornwall RO, DDT 1609/1.

63. BL, TT E127/35, *Speciall Passages and Certain Informations from Severall Places*, 15–22 Nov. 1642, p.126.

64. TNA, SP28/141B, pt 3, Account Book of Cornelius Holland and Robert Jenner Esquire... from 2 November 1642 to the last day of May 1643, p.10. The cost of re-clothing them was estimated at £600. TNA, SP28/4, f.16.

65. BL, TT E314/21, *Innocency and Truth Justified*, p.65. Pauline Gregg, *Free-born John. A Biography of John Lilburne*, London: Dent 1961, pp.101–3.

66. TNA, SP28/4, f.122, shows William Burles, who had been a captain in Holles's regiment, receiving money to pay Skippon's regiment in early December 1642.
67. SBTLA, DR98/1704 Accounts of Sr Edw: Peyto, 1642–1643, unfol., 18 Nov. 1642.
68. Roy, *ROP*, I, p.61.
69. Cited in H.L. Blackmore, *The Armouries of the Tower of London: I Ordnance*, London: HMSO 1976, p.228.
70. Robert Codrington, *The Life and Death of the Illustrious Earl of Essex*, 1646, p.22.
71. Bodl., Ashmole MS 830, ff.292-3. Rushworth, *Historical Collections*, II, p.61.
72. BL, TT E73/4 John Vicars, *God in the Mount or a Continuation of England's Parliamentary Chronicle*, pp.206–16.
73. Young, *Edgehill*, p.274.
74. W.D. Macray (ed), *Letters and papers of Patrick Ruthven, Earl of Forth and Brentford, and of his family: A.D. 1615–A.D. 1662*, London: Nichols 1868, pp.84–7. David Lloyd, *Memoires of the Lives, Actions, Sufferings and Deaths...*, 1668, p.674.
75. Bodl., Ashmole MS 830, ff.292-3.
76. BL, TT E127/21 *Certaine Speciall and Remarkable Passages*, 12–18 Nov. 1642, unpag.
77. 'The Journal of Prince Rupert's Marches', *English Historical Review*, XIII (1898), p.731, also refers to the 'Kingstone boats blowne up' on 12 November 1642.
78. TNA, SP28/262, f.146.
79. Gwyn, *Memoirs*, p.47.
80. BL, TT E127/24 *A Declaration and Manifestation of the Proceedings of both Armies*, p.3.
81. BL, TT E127/12 *Speciall Passages and Certain Information from Severall Places*, 8–15 Nov. 1642, p.120. Sir Richard Bulstrode in Young, *Edgehill*, p.261.
82. *CSPVen*, 1642–1643, p.201. Clarendon, *History*, II, p.395.

7. Turning the Tide at Turnham Green

 1. John Rushworth, *Historical Collections*, The Third Part, II, p.59. Thomas May, *A Breviary of the Parliament of England*, in Francis Maseres, *Select Tracts relating to the Civil Wars in England, in the Reign of Charles the First*, I, London: 1813, p.57.
 2. BL, TT E314/21 John Lilburne, *Innocency and Truth Justified*, 1645, p.40. Young, *Edgehill*, p.101–2. Rushworth, *Historical Collections*, The Third Part, II, p.59.
 3. TNA, SP28/141B pt 3 Account book of Cornelius Holland and Robert Jenner Esquire. Yonge, *Diary of Proceedings*, p.111.
 4. LJ, V, p.442. CJ, II, p.846.
 5. CJ, II, p.846.
 6. E.S. De Beer (ed), *The Diary of John Evelyn*, Oxford: OUP 1959, p.45.
 7. Clarendon, *History*, II, pp.395–6.
 8. BL, TT E314/21 *Innocency and Truth Justified*, p.40.
 9. Rushworth, *Historical Collections*, The Third Part, II, p.59. May, *A Breviary of the Parliament of England*, p.58. Not until the following week was a bridge of boats constructed at Putney.
10. CJ, II, p.846.
11. Lawson Nagel, "A Great Bouncing at Every Man's Door': The Struggle for London's Militia in 1642', in Stephen Porter (ed), *London and the Civil War*, Basingstoke: Macmillan 1996, p.85. *CSPVen*, 1642–1643, p.202.
12. Rushworth, *Historical Collections*, The Third Part, II, p.59. May, *A Breviary of the Parliament of England*, p.57.
13. BL, Add MS 40,883, f.49r.
14. James Sutherland (ed), Lucy Hutchinson, *Memoirs of the Life of Colonel Hutchinson*, Oxford: OUP 1973, p.60. Norman Tucker (ed), *The Military Memoirs of John Gwyn*, in Peter Young and Norman Tucker (eds), *Military Memoirs: The Civil War*, London: Longman, Green 1967, p.46.
15. HMC, *Portland, 14th report*, app II, p.101.

16. TNA, SP28/2B f.466; /3A ff.152,178; /4, f.122; /263, f.240; /143 unfol., Capt Vernon's accounts for 11, 12 and 16 Nov. 1642.

17. Yonge, *Diary of Proceedings*, p.139. TNA, SP28/131, pt 2.

18. TNA, SP28/262 ff.434, 467; /263 f.216; the two identified regiments of seamen were under the command of Colonels Peter Andrews and Elias Jordan. Bodl., MS Tanner 64, ff.83, 87.

19. J.S. Clarke, *Life of James II*, 1816, I, p.19.

20. TNA, SP28/136, pt56.

21. BL, TT E127/21, *A Continuation of Certaine speciall and remarkable Passages*, 12–18 Nov. 1642, unpag.

22. Bodl., MS Don c.184, f.29.

23. R. Malcolm Smuts, 'Rich, Henry, first earl of Holland (*bap.* 1590, *d.* 1649)', ODNB.

24. C.V. Wedgwood, *The King's Peace, 1637–1641*, London: Collins 1955, pp.251–2, 264–5. Mark Charles Fissel, *The Bishops' Wars: Charles I's campaigns against Scotland, 1638–1640*, Cambridge: CUP 1994, pp.85–6.

25. Yonge, *Diary of Proceedings*, p.113. Clarendon, *History*, II, p.396.

26. *CSPVen, 1642–1643*, p.198.

27. Ruth Spalding (ed), *The Diary of Bulstrode Whitelocke, 1605–1675*, Oxford: OUP 1990, pp.139–40. BL, Add. MS 37,343, f.260 (Whitelock, Annals, Vol.III).

28. LJ, V, p.443.

29. Young, *Edgehill*, p.275.

30. *CSPVen, 1642–1643*, pp.182, 188.

31. HMC, *Ormonde*, II, new series, p.381.

32. Bodl., MS Rawlinson, D715.

33. Information kindly supplied by Shirley Seaton based on a plan by Alfred James Roberts of 1853, Hammersmith Archives, DC/ED/16, Map no.6444, file no.18,832.

34. VCH, *Middlesex*, VII, p.63.

35. VCH, *Middlesex*, VII, p.59.

36. Warwick, *Memoires*, p.233. Maurice Exwood and H.L. Lohmann (eds), *The Journal of William Schellinks' Travels in England 1661–1663*, Camden Soc., 5th series, I, 1993, p.81.

37. *Military Memoirs of John Gwyn*, p.47.

38. *Military Memoirs of John Gwyn*, p.47.

39. SBTLA, DR98/1704 Accounts of Sr Edw: Peyto, 1642–1643, unfol., 18 Nov. 1642.

40. TNA, SP 28/131, pt2.

41. The royalists' frontage at Edgehill was c.2,400m. Scott et al, *Edgehill*, pp.195–6.

42. BL, TT E127/21 *A Continuation of Certaine speciall and remarkable Passages*, 12–18 Nov.1642, unpag.

43. *Military Memoirs of John Gwyn*, p.47.

44. *Diary of Bulstrode Whitelocke*, p.140. Bodl., MS Don.c.184, f.29r.

45. Yonge, *Diary of Proceedings*, p.113. *Diary of Bulstrode Whitelocke*, p.140. C.H. Firth (ed), *The Memoirs of Edmund Ludlow*, Vol I, Oxford: OUP 1894, p.47.

46. Andrew J. Hopper, 'Meyrick, Sir John (*C.*1600–1659)', ODNB. CJ, II, p.853.

47. HMC, *Ormonde*, II, p.381.

48. *Diary of Bulstrode Whitelocke*, p.140.

49. Bodl., Ashmole MS 830, f.293.

50. BL, TT E127/35 *Speciall Passages*, 15–22 Nov.1642, p.126.

51. LJ, V, p.451.

52. He had also unsuccessfully contested the seat of East Grinstead at the elections to the Short Parliament; Judith M. Maltby (ed), *The Short Parliament (1640) Diary of Sir Thomas Aston*, Camden Soc., 4th series, 35, 1988, pp.46–7.

53. Clarendon, *History*, II, p.397. LJ, V, pp.443, 444. Warwick, *Memoires*, p.232.

54. HMC, *Twelfth Report, Coke MSS*, p.326.

55. R.N. Dore (ed), *The Letter Books of Sir William Brereton*, vol.I, Record Soc. of Lancashire and Cheshire, CXXIII, 1984, p.260.

56. *Diary of Bulstrode Whitelocke*, p.140.

57. LJ, V, p.443.

58. BL, TT E127/24 *A Declaration*, p.3.

59. BL, TT E127/15, *A true and perfect relation of the chief passages in Middlesex*.

60. Scott, et al., *Edgehill*, pp.81–2.

61. BL, TT E127/21, *A Continuation of Certaine speciall and remarkable Passages*, 12–18 Nov. 1642, unpag.; E127/35, *Speciall Passages*, 15–22 Nov. 1642, p.126. Clarendon, *History*, II, p.396. HMC, *Portland*, *14th report*, app II, p.101; *Twelfth Report*, p.326.

62. HMC, *Portland*, *14th report*, app II, p.101.

63. BL, TT E127/15, *A true and perfect relation of the chief passages in Middlesex*.

64. *Diary of Bulstrode Whitelocke*, p.140.

65. Yonge, *Diary of Proceedings*, p.113.

66. HMC, *Portland*, *14th report*, app II, p.101.

67. John Vicars, *Parliamentary Chronicle*, I, p.216, cited in C.H. Firth, *Cromwell's Army*, London: Greenhill 1992, p.214. *Diary of Bulstrode Whitelocke*, p.141. BL, TT E127/8, *A Exact and True Relation of the Battell Fought on Saturday last at Acton*, 14 Nov. 1642, p.8; E127/21, *A Continuation of Certaine speciall and remarkable Passages*, 12–18 Nov. 1642, unpag.

68. Yonge, *Diary of Proceedings*, p.119.

69. *CSPD*, 1641–43, p.408.

70. Warwick, *Memoires*, p.233. *Diary of Bulstrode Whitelocke*, p.141.

71. John Gutch, *Collectanea Curiosa*, II, Oxford: 1781, p.430.

72. BL, TT E242/9 *England's Memorable Accidents*, 14–21 Nov. 1642, p.82.

73. HMC, *Ormonde*, II, pp.381–2.

74. HMC, *Portland*, *14th report*, app II, p.101.

75. Spalding (ed), *Diary of Bulstrode Whitelocke*, p.141. Rushworth, *Historical Collections*, The Third Part, II, p.60.

76. Bodl., Ashmole MS 830, f.293.

77. BL, Add MS 62,084B, f.11.

78. London University Library, *A True Discovery of a Woman's Wickednesse*, 19 Nov. 1642. BL, TT E127/21 *A Continuation of Certaine speciall and remarkable Passages*, 12–18 Nov. 1642, unpag.

79. HMC, *Portland*, *14th report*, app II, p.101.

80. 'The Journal of Prince Rupert's Marches, 5 Sept. 1442 to 4 July 1646', *English Historical Review*, XIII (1898), p.731.

81. Rushworth, *Historical Collections*, The Third Part, II, pp.59, 60. Young, *Edgehill*, p.261.

82. *CSP Ven*, 1642–1643, p.202.

83. BL, TT E127/26 *The English Intelligencer*, 12–18 Nov. 1642, p.3. Bodl., MS Don. c.184, f.29r.

8. The Aftermath

1. Clarendon, History, II, p.397. John Gutch, *Collectanea Curiosa*, II, 1781, p.430. 'The Journal of Prince Rupert's Marches, 5 Sept. 1642 to 4 July 1646', *English Historical Review*, XIII (1898), p.731.

2. Yonge, *Diary of Proceedings*, p.123.

3. Robert Codrington, *The Life and Death of the Illustrious Earl of Essex*, 1646, p.23. Yonge, *Diary of Proceedings*, p.136.

4. TNA, SP28/177, 178, 179, 180, all unfol. GL, MS16,967/4, p.386. Ironmongers' Company Court Book, 1629–46.

5. Roy, *ROP*, pp.12, 359.

6. CJ, II, pp.852, 865, 895.

7. BL, TT E127/35 *Speciall Passages and Certain Informations from Severall Places*, 15–22 Nov. 1642.

8. BL, TT E127/49 *The True proceedings of both armies from 12–24 November*, 24 Nov. 1642.

9. BL, TT E314/21 John Lilburne, *Innocency and Truth Justified*, 1645, p.40.

10. Yonge, p.119. BL, TT E127/49 *The True proceedings of both armies from 12–24 November*, 24 Nov. 1642.

11. Glenn Foard, *Naseby: The Decisive Campaign*, Whitstable: Pryor 1995, pp.288–9. For an explanation of that incident, see C.V. Wedgwood, *The King's War, 1641–1647*, London: Collins 1958, pp.455, 670 n.59.

12. BL, TT E244/9 *England's Memorable Accidents*, 5–12 Dec. 1642, p.111; E244/11 *A Continuation of Certaine Speciall and Remarkable Passages*, 12–15 Dec. 1642, pp.5–6; E244/15 *A Perfect Diurnall of the Passages in Parliament*, 12–19 Dec. 1642, unpag.; E244/16 *England's Memorable Accidents*, 12–19 Dec. 1642, p.116; E245/8 *Marlborowe's Miseries, or, England turned Ireland*, 1643.

13. 'A Relation of the Taking of Ciceter', reprinted in John Washbourn (ed), *Bibliotheca Gloucestrensis*, Gloucester: 1825, p.184.

14. Bodl., MS.Don.c.184, f.129. Yonge, *Diary of Proceedings*, p.136.

15. Codrington, *Earl of Essex*, p.23. BL, TT, E127/12 *Speciall Passages*, 8–15 Nov. 1642, p.121. TNA, SP28/131; SP28/262 f.114; SP16/492 f.48. Young, *Edgehill*, p.102.

16. CJ, II, p.850.

17. BL, TT E127/28 *True Newes out of Herefordshire, containing A brief Relation of the great affright and Hubub... in and about the City of London*, 1642, p.7.

18. LJ, V, p.461.

19. *CSPVen., 1642–1643*, pp.202–3, 205.

20. A.C. Wood (ed), *Memorials of the Holles Family, 1493–1656, by Gervase Holles*, Camden Soc., 3rd series, LV, 1937, p.187.

21. TNA, SP28/4, ff.243, 364. Clarendon, *History*, II, p.402.

22. Yonge, *Diary of Proceedings*, p.177.

23. Yonge, *Diary of Proceedings*, p.115.

24. Clarendon, *History*, II, p.389.

25. LJ, V, pp.448–9.

26. LJ, V, pp.448–9.

27. LJ, V, pp.451–2.

28. LJ, V, pp.451–2. Clarendon, *History*, II, pp.397–9.

29. LJ, V, p.452.

30. The letter is printed in, Patrick Morrah, *Prince Rupert of the Rhine*, London: Constable 1976, p.83.

31. Theodor Meron, *Henry's Wars and Shakespeare's Laws: Perspectives on the Law of War in the Later Middle Ages*, Oxford: Clarendon Press 1993, pp.131–2, 141.

32. Clarendon, *History*, III, p.187.

33. LJ, V, p.454.

34. BL, Harl. 6851, f.114. C.H. Firth (ed), Margaret, Duchess of Newcastle, *The Life of William Cavendish Duke of Newcastle*, London: Routledge 1906, p.x. We owe these references to the kindness of Dr Ian Roy. Ian Gentles, 'Parliamentary Politics and the Politics of the Street: The London Peace Campaigns of 1642–3', *Parliamentary History*, 26 (2007), 153.

35. BL, Harl.164, f.99r-v. We owe this reference to the kindness of Dr Stephen Roberts.

36. S.R. Gardiner, *History of the Great Civil War*, vol.I, Moreton-in-Marsh: Windrush 1987, pp.61–2. Yonge, *Diary of Proceedings*, pp.127–34, 154–5.

37. BL, TT E127/6 *An Extract of Severall Letters which came by the last Post*, 1642, pp.2, 4–6; E127/10 *Exceeding Joyfull Newes out of Surrey*, 1642, pp.3, 5; E127/12 *Speciall Passages*, 8–15 Nov. 1642, pp.120–1.

38. BL, TT, E128/35 *His Majesties Declaration To all His Loving Subjects of his True Intentions in advancing lately to Brainceford*, 1642, p.8.

39. LJ, V, pp.463–4.

40. HMC, *Twelfth Report*, p.326.

41. Bodl., MS Tanner 64, f.109.

42. LJ, V p.504.

43. Yonge, *Diary of Proceedings*, p.125.

44. *CSPVen.*, *1642–1643*, p.207.

45. Yonge, *Diary of Proceedings*, pp.112, 114, 117, 119, 126. CJ, II, pp.848–9, 861, 871.

46. Yonge, *Diary of Proceedings*, p.163.

47. Gardiner, *Great Civil War*, I, pp.64–5.

48. Yonge, *Diary of Proceedings*, p.151.

49. BL, Add.MS 40,883, ff.45v,61r.

50. Charles Trice Martin (ed), *Minutes of Parliament of the Middle Temple, II, 1603–1649*, London: Butterworth 1904, p.928.

51. Yonge, *Diary of Proceedings*, pp.151, 165.

52. Clarendon, *History*, II, p.409.

53. LJ, V, p.457. Ian Roy, 'The Royalist Council of War, 1642–6', *Bulletin of the Institute of Historical Research*, XXXV (1962), p.157. J.F. Larkin (ed), *Stuart Royal Proclamations Volume II: Royal Proclamations of King Charles I 1625–1646*, Oxford: OUP 1983, nos 372, 434.

54. CJ, II, pp.871–2. LJ, V, p.457.

55. *CSPVen.*, *1642–43*, p.235.

56. Yonge, *Diary of Proceedings*, pp.180, 181–2, 186, 223. CJ, II, pp.883, 884. LJ, V, p.524.

9. THE SIGNIFICANCE OF LONDON'S DEFENCE

1. Bodl., MS Don.c.184, f.29r.

2. BL, TT E127/21 *A Continuation of Certaine speciall and remarkable Passages from both Houses of Parliament*, 12–18 Nov. 1642, unpag.

3. James Sutherland (ed), Lucy Hutchinson, *Memoirs of the Life of Colonel Hutchinson*, Oxford: OUP 1973, p.60.

4. Ruth Spalding (ed), *The diary of Bulstrode Whitelocke, 1605–1675*, Oxford: OUP 1990, p.141.

5. John Adair, *A Life of John Hampden The Patriot (1594–1643)*, London: Thorogood 2003, p.203.

6. Andrew J. Hopper, 'Meyrick, Sir John (*C.*1600–1659)', ODNB. Stephen Porter, 'Dalbier, John (d.1648)', ODNB.

7. R. Malcolm Smuts, 'Rich, Henry, first earl of Holland', ODNB.

8. Andrew Clark, *The Life and Times of Anthony Wood, antiquary, of Oxford, 1632–1695, described by Himself*, I, Oxford Historical Soc. 1891, p.71.

9. LJ, V, p.461.

10. J.S. Clarke (ed), *Life of James II*, 1816, I, p.19. Clarendon, *History*, II, p.396.

11. Norman Tucker (ed), *The Military Memoirs of John Gwyn*, in Peter Young and Norman Tucker (eds), *Military Memoirs: The Civil War*, London: Longman, Green 1967, p.47.

12. Clarendon, *History*, II, p.390.

13. Ian Roy, "This Proud Unthankefull City': A Cavalier View of London in the Civil War', in Stephen Porter (ed), *London and the Civil War*, Basingstoke: Macmillan 1996, pp.156–70.

14. Cited in, Richard Ollard, *Clarendon and his Friends*, Oxford: OUP 1988, p.81.

15. For the example of the Netherlands, with the contrasting reactions of the Stadholder and the States-General, see, Pieter Geyl, *Orange and Stuart, 1641–1672*, London: Orion 2001, pp.13–19.

16. Keith Roberts, 'Citizen Soldiers: The Military Power of the City of London', in Porter (ed), *London and the Civil War*, pp.102–3.

17. Mary Anne Everett Green (ed), *Diary of John Rous, incumbent of Santon Downham, Suffolk, from 1625 to 1642*, Camden Soc., LXVI, 1856, p.129.

18. Samuel Rawson Gardiner (ed), *The Constitutional Documents of the Puritan Revolution, 1625–1660*, 3rd edn, Oxford: Clarendon Press 1906, p.372. C.V. Wedgwood, *The Trial of Charles I*, London: Collins 1964, p.130.

19. Philip Warwick, *Memoires of the Reign of King Charles I*, 1701, p.232. *Dictionary of National Biography*, sub Sir Philip Warwick, 1609–1683.

20. Sir William Dugdale, *A Short View of the Late Troubles in England*, Oxford: 1681, pp.111–12.

21. Robert Codrington, *The Life and Death of the Illustrious Earl of Essex*, 1646, p.22. A.G.H. Backrack and R.G. Collmer (eds), Lodewijck Huygens, *The English Journal 1651–1652*, Leiden: Leiden University Press, 1982, p.109.

22. James T. Boulton (ed), Daniel Defoe, *Memoirs of a Cavalier*, Oxford: OUP 1991, pp.xxi–xxiii, 171–5. Blair Worden, *Roundhead Reputations. The English Civil Wars and the Passions of Posterity*, London: Allen Lane 2001), pp.11, 44.

23. A.B. Worden (ed), Edmund Ludlow, *A Voyce from the Watch Tower*, Camden Soc., fourth series, 21, 1978, p.131.

24. Philip Warner, *Famous Battles of the Midlands*, London: Osprey 1973, p.94. English Heritage, Battlefields Panel, Minutes of the meeting held on 16 March 2005, para 5.2.

25. Samuel R. Gardiner, *History of the Great Civil War 1642–1649*, I, Moreton-in-Marsh: Windrush Press 1987, p.60.

26. Austin Woolrych, *Battles of the English Civil War*, London: Batsford 1961, pp.16–19, and *Britain in Revolution 1625–1660*, Oxford: OUP 2002, pp.240–1. Charles Carlton, *Going to the Wars. The Experience of the British Civil Wars, 1638–1651*, London: Routledge 1992, p.118. The fullest account is by C.V. Wedgwood, 'The Chief Passages in Middlesex', *Middlesex Local History Council Bulletin* 14 (1962), 1–7. See also, Ivan Roots, *The Great Rebellion 1642–1660*, London: Batsford 1966, p.74.

27. W.P.W. Phillimore and W.H. Whitear (eds), *Historical Collections relating to Chiswick*, London: Phillimore 1897, p.72. Warwick Draper, *Chiswick*, London: Philip Allan 1932; new edn, Anne Bingley and Hounslow Leisure Services 1973, pp.67–8.

28. Charles Duke Yonge (ed), Horace Walpole, *Letters of Horace Walpole*, II, London: Fisher Unwin 1890, p.403. Fred Turner, *History and Antiquities of Brentford*, Brentford: Walter Pearce 1922, pp.68–9. Neil Chippendale, *The Battle of Brentford*, Leigh-on-Sea: Partisan Press 1991.

29. C.V. Wedgwood, 'The Strategy of the Great Civil War', in *History and Hope: Essays on History and the English Civil War*, New York: Dutton 1989, pp.122–3.

30. *Brentford Advertiser*, quoted by Alan Godfrey, *Kew, Gunnersbury & Old Brentford 1894*, London sheet 84, Old Ordnance Survey Maps, Gateshead, 1991. Harold P. Clunn, *The Face of London: The Record of a Century's Change and Development*, London: Simpkin Marshall 1932, p.430.

31. Underground trains first used the station in 1877. Information kindly supplied by Caroline Warhurst at the London Transport Museum.

32. VCH, *Middlesex*, vol.VII, pp.56–61, 63–4.

Bibliography

Adair, John, *Cheriton 1644. The Campaign and the Battle*, Kineton: Roundwood Press 1970

Adair, John, *A Life of John Hampden. The Patriot (1594–1643)*, London: Thorogood 2003

Ashton, Robert, *The City and the Court, 1603–1642*, Cambridge: CUP 1979

Ashton, Robert, 'Insurgency, Counter-Insurgency and Inaction: Three Phases in the Role of the City in the Great Rebellion', in Stephen Porter (ed), *London and the Civil War*, Basingstoke: Macmillan 1996

Backrack, A.G.H. and Collmer, R.G. (eds), Lodewijck Huygens, *The English Journal 1651–1652*, Leiden: Leiden University Press 1982

Beaumont, William (ed), *A Discourse on the Warr in Lancashire*, Chetham Soc., old series, 62, 1864

Beckett, Ian, *Buckinghamshire in the Civil War*, Aylesbury: Buckinghamshire County Museum 2004

Beier, A.L., 'Engine of manufacture: the trades of London', in A.L. Beier and R. Finlay (eds), *London 1500–1700: The making of the metropolis*, London, Longmans 1986

Besly, Edward, *Coins and Medals of the English Civil War*, London: Seaby 1990

Blackmore, H.L., *The Armouries of the Tower of London: I Ordnance*, London: HMSO 1976

Bond, Shelagh (ed), *The Chamber Order Book of Worcester, 1602–1650*, Worcestershire Historical Soc., new series, 8, 1974

Boulton, James T. (ed), Daniel Defoe, *Memoirs of a Cavalier*, Oxford: OUP 1991

Brenner, Robert, *Merchants and Revolution: Commercial Change, Political Conflict, and London's Overseas Traders, 1550–1653*, Cambridge: CUP 1993

Breslow, Marvin Arthur, *A Mirror of England. English Puritan Views of Foreign Nations, 1618–1640*, Cambridge, Mass.: Harvard University Press 1970

Brissenden, Alan (ed), Thomas Middleton, *A Chaste Maid in Cheapside*, London: A&C Black 1968

Broxap, Ernest, *The Great Civil War in Lancashire 1642–51*, Manchester: Manchester University Press 1973

Carlton, Charles, *Going to the Wars. The Experience of the British Civil Wars, 1638–1651*, London: Routledge 1992

Chippendale, Neil, *The Battle of Brentford*, Leigh-on-Sea: Partisan Press 1991

Clark, Andrew, *The Life and Times of Anthony Wood, antiquary, of Oxford, 1632–1695, described by Himself*, Oxford Historical Soc. 1891

Clarke, J.S., *Life of James II*, 1816

Clunn, Harold, P., *The Face of London: The Record of a Century's Change and Development*, London: Simpkin Marshall 1932

Cobbett, William, *Complete Collection of State Trials*, 1809

Crankshaw, David J., 'Community, City and Nation, 1540–1714', in Derek Keene, Arthur Burns and Andrew Saint (eds), *St Paul's: The Cathedral Church of London 604–2004*, New Haven & London: Yale University Press 2004

Cressy, David, *England on Edge*, Oxford: OUP 2006

Davies, Godfrey, 'The Battle of Edgehill', *English Historical Review*, 36 (1921)

Davies, Godfrey, 'The Parliamentary Army under the Earl of Essex, 1642–45', *English Historical Review*, 49 (1934)

Day, Jon, *Gloucester and Newbury 1643: The Turning Point of the Civil War*, Barnsley: Pen & Sword 2007

De Beer, E.S. (ed), *The Diary of John Evelyn*, Oxford: OUP 1959

Dore, R.N., *The Civil Wars in Cheshire*, Chester: Cheshire Community Council 1966

Dore, R.N. (ed), *The Letter Books of Sir William Brereton*, vol.I, Record Soc. of Lancashire and Cheshire, CXXIII, 1984

Draper, Warwick, *Chiswick*, London: Philip Allan 1932; new edn, Anne Bingley and Hounslow Leisure Services 1973

Dugdale, Sir William, *A Short View of the Late Troubles in England*, Oxford: 1681

Edwards, Peter, *Dealing in Death: The Arms Trade and the British Civil Wars, 1638–52*, Stroud: Sutton 2000

Exwood, Maurice, and Lohmann, H.L. (eds), *The Journal of William Schellinks' Travels in England 1661–1663*, Camden Soc., 5th series, I, 1993

Firth, C.H. (ed), *The Memoirs of Edmund Ludlow*, 2 vols, Oxford: OUP 1894

Firth, C.H. (ed), Margaret, Duchess of Newcastle, *The Life of William Cavendish Duke of Newcastle*, London: Routledge 1906

Firth, C.H., *Cromwell's Army*, London: Greenhill Books 1992

Fisher, F.J., *London and the English Economy, 1500–1700*, London: Hambledon Press 1990

Fissel, Mark Charles, *The Bishops' Wars. Charles I's campaigns against Scotland 1638–1640*, Cambridge: CUP 1994

Fletcher, Anthony, *The Outbreak of the English Civil War*, London: Edward Arnold 1981

Foard, Glenn, *Naseby: The Decisive Campaign*, Whitstable: Pryor 1995

Gardiner Samuel Rawson, *The Constitutional Documents of the Puritan Revolution 1625–1660*, 3rd edn, Oxford: Clarendon Press 1906

Gardiner, S.R., *History of the Great Civil War*, Moreton-in-Marsh: Windrush 1987

Gentles, Ian, 'Parliamentary Politics and the Politics of the Street: The London Peace Campaigns of 1642–3', *Parliamentary History*, 26 (2007)

Geyl, Pieter, *Orange and Stuart, 1641–1672*, London: Orion 2001

Green, Mary Anne Everett (ed), *Diary of John Rous, incumbent of Santon Downham, Suffolk, from 1625 to 1642*, Camden Soc., LXVI, 1856

Gregg, Pauline, *Free-born John. A Biography of John Lilburne*, London: Dent 1961

Groos, G.W. (ed), *The Diary of Baron Waldstein. A Traveller in Elizabethan England*, London: Thames & Hudson 1981

Gutch, John, *Collectanea Curiosa*, II, Oxford: 1781

Harland, John, *The Lancashire Lieutenancy under the Tudors and Stuarts*, Chetham Soc., old series, 49, 1859

Havran, Martin J., *Caroline Courtier. The Life of Lord Cottington*, London: Macmillan 1973

Hey, David (ed), Richard Gough, *The History of Myddle*, Harmondsworth: Penguin 1981

Hobson, M.G., and Salter, H.E. (eds), *Oxford Council Acts 1626–1665*, Oxford Historical Soc., 1933

Holles, Gervase, *Memorials of the Holles family 1493–1656*, Camden Soc., 3rd series, vol.55, 1937

Hopper, Andrew J., 'Meyrick, Sir John (*c.*1600–1659)', *Oxford Dictionary of National Biography*, 2004

Huehns, G. (ed), *Clarendon: Selections from The History of the Rebellion and The Life by Himself*, Oxford: OUP 1978

Hughes, Ann, 'Feilding, Basil, second earl of Denbigh (*c.*1608–1675)', *Oxford Dictionary of National Biography*, 2004

Hutton, Ronald, *The Royalist War Effort 1642–1646*, London: Longman 1982

Inwood, Stephen, *A History of London*, London: Macmillan 1998

Johnson, George (ed), *The Fairfax Correspondence*, London: Richard Bentley 1848

Knowles, James (ed), *The Roaring Girl and other City Comedies*, Oxford, OUP 2001

Larkin, J.F. (ed), *Stuart Royal Proclamations Volume II: Royal Proclamations of King Charles I 1625–1646*, Oxford: OUP 1983

Lawrence, Anne, *Parliamentary Army Chaplains 1642–1651*, Woodbridge, Royal Historical Soc. 1990

Lindley, Keith, 'London's Citizenry in the English Revolution', in R.C. Richardson (ed), *Town and Countryside in the English Revolution*, Manchester: Manchester University Press 1992

Long, C.R. and Roy, Ian (eds), *Richard Symonds's Diary of the Marches of the Royal Army*, Cambridge: CUP, 1997

Lysons, Daniel, *The Environs of London*, IV, 1796

Macray, W.D. (ed), *Letters and papers of Patrick Ruthven, Earl of Forth and Brentford, and of his family: A.D. 1615–A.D. 1662*, London: Nichols 1868

Macray, W.D. (ed), Clarendon, Edward, Earl of, *The History of the Rebellion and Civil Wars in England*, Oxford: Clarendon Press 1888

Maltby, Judith M. (ed), *The Short Parliament (1640) Diary of Sir Thomas Aston*, Camden Soc., 4th series, 35, 1988

Manning, Brian, *The English People and the English Revolution*, 2nd edn, London: Bookmarks 1991

Markham, Clements, *The Life of the Great Lord Fairfax*, London: Macmillan 1870

Martin, Charles Trice (ed), *Minutes of Parliament of the Middle Temple, II, 1603–1649*, London: Butterworth 1904

May, Thomas, *A Breviary of the History of the Parliament of England*, in Francis Maseres, *Select Tracts relating to the Civil Wars in England, in the Reign of Charles the First*, I, London: 1813

Morrah, Patrick, *Prince Rupert of the Rhine*, London: Constable 1976

Meron, Theodor, *Henry's Wars and Shakespeare's Laws: Perspectives on the Law of War in the Later Middle Ages*, Oxford: Clarendon Press 1993

Morrill, J.S., *The Revolt of the Provinces*, London: Allen & Unwin 1976

Nagel, Lawson, The Militia of London, 1641–1649, Ph.D. thesis, King's College, University of London 1982

Nagel, Lawson, "A Great Bouncing at Every Man's Door': The Struggle for London's Militia in 1642', in Stephen Porter (ed), *London and the Civil War*, Basingstoke: Macmillan 1996

Newman, Peter, *Royalist Officers in England and Wales, 1642–1660*, New York: Garland 1981

Nicholl, Charles, *The Lodger: Shakespeare on Silver Street*, London: Allen Lane 2007

Nugent, Lord, *Memorials of John Hampden: His Party and his Times*, London: Chapman & Hall 1880

Ollard, Richard, *Clarendon and his Friends*, Oxford: OUP 1988

Ollard, Richard (ed), *Clarendon's Four Portraits*, London: Hamish Hamilton 1989

Peachey, Stuart, *The battle of Powick Bridge, 1642*, Bristol: Stuart 1993

Peachey, Stuart, *The Edgehill Campaign and the Letters of Nehemiah Wharton*, Leigh-on-Sea: Partisan Press 1997

Peacock, Edward, *The Army Lists of the Roundheads and Cavaliers*, London: John Camden Hotton 1874, reprinted 1983

Pearl, Valerie, *London and the Outbreak of the Puritan Revolution*, Oxford: OUP 1961

Phillimore, W.P.W., and Whitear, W.H. (eds), *Historical Collections relating to Chiswick*, London: Phillimore 1897

Phillips, William, 'Ottley Papers' *Trans Shropshire Archaeological Soc.*, 2nd series, VII (1895)

Porter, Stephen (ed), *London and the Civil War*, Basingstoke: Macmillan 1996

Porter, Stephen, 'Dalbier, John (d.1648)', *Oxford Dictionary of National Biography*, 2004

Raikes, G.A. (ed), *The Ancient Vellum Book of the Honourable Artillery Company*, London: Bentley, 1890

Reid, Stuart, 'Ruthven, Patrick, earl of Forth and earl of Brentford, (d.1651)', *Oxford Dictionary of National Biography*, 2004

Roberts, Keith, 'Citizen Soldiers: The Military Power of the City of London', in Stephen Porter (ed), *London and the Civil War*, Basingstoke: Macmillan 1996

Roberts, Keith, 'Battle Plans: The Practical Use of Battlefield Plans in the English Civil War', *Cromwelliana* (1997)

Roots, Ivan, *The Great Rebellion 1642–1660*, London: Batsford 1966

Roy, Ian, 'The Royalist Council of War, 1642–6', *Bulletin of the Institute of Historical Research*, XXXV (1962)

Roy, Ian (ed), *The Royalist Ordnance Papers, 1642–1646*, Oxfordshire Record Soc., vols 43, 49, 1964, 1975

Roy, Ian, 'The City of Oxford 1640–1660' in R.C. Richardson (ed), *Town and Countryside in the English Revolution*, Manchester: Manchester University Press 1992

Roy, Ian, 'This Proud Unthankefull City': A Cavalier View of London in the Civil War', in Stephen Porter (ed), *London and the Civil War*, Basingstoke: Macmillan 1996

Roy, Ian, 'George Digby, Royalist intrigue and the collapse of the cause', in Ian Gentles, John Morrill and Blair Worden (eds), *Soldiers, writers and statesmen of the English Revolution*, Cambridge: CUP 1998

Roy, Ian, and Reinhart, Dietrich, 'Oxford and the Civil Wars' in Nicholas Tyacke (ed),*The History of the University of Oxford, Volume IV Seventeenth-Century Oxford*, Oxford: Clarendon Press 1997

Russell, Conrad, 'The First Army Plot of 1641', *Trans Royal Historical Soc.*, 5th series, 38 (1988)

Rylands, W. Harry (ed), *Visitation of Buckinghamshire, 1634*, Harleian Soc., vol.58, 1909

Scott, Christopher L., Turton, Alan, and von Arnim, Eric Gruber, *Edgehill: The Battle Reinterpreted*, Barnsley: Pen & Sword 2004

Sheppard, Francis, *London: A History*, Oxford: OUP 1998

Slingsby, Sir Henry, *Memoirs Written During the Great Civil War*, Edinburgh: Constable 1806

Smith, David L., 'Philip Herbert, first earl of Montgomery and fourth earl of Pembroke (1584–1650)', *Oxford Dictionary of National Biography*, 2004

Smurthwaite, David, *The Complete Guide to the Battlefields of Britain*, London: Michael Joseph 1984

Smuts, R. Malcolm, 'Rich, Henry, first earl of Holland (*bap.* 1590, *d.* 1649)', *Oxford Dictionary of National Biography*, 2004

Snow, Vernon, *Essex the Rebel. The life of Robert Devereux, the Third Earl of Essex, 1591–1646*, Lincoln, Ne: University of Nebraska Press 1970

Spalding, Ruth (ed), *The diary of Bulstrode Whitelocke, 1605–1675*, Oxford: OUP 1990

Styles, Philip, 'The City of Worcester during the Civil Wars, 1640–60', in Philip Styles, *Studies in Seventeenth Century West Midlands History*, Kineton: Roundwood Press 1978

Sutherland, James (ed), Lucy Hutchinson, *Memoirs of the Life of Colonel Hutchinson*, Oxford: OUP 1973

Tennant, Philip, *Edgehill and Beyond*, Stroud: Sutton 1992

Thirsk, Joan (ed), *The Agrarian History of England and Wales*, Volume IV 1500–1640, Cambridge: CUP 1967

Thompson, Christopher (ed), *Walter Yonge's diary of proceedings in the House of Commons: 1642–1645, Vol. 1, 19th September 1642–7th March 1643*, Wivenhoe: Orchard Press 1986

Thomson, George Malcolm, *Warrior Prince. The Life of Prince Rupert of the Rhine*, London: Secker & Warburg 1976

Tönnies, Ferdinand (ed), Thomas Hobbes, *Behemoth or The Long Parliament*, London: Simkin, Marshall 1889

Tucker, Norman (ed), *The Military Memoirs of John Gwyn*, in Peter Young and Norman Tucker (eds), *Military Memoirs: The Civil War*, London: Longman, Green 1967

Turner, Fred, *History and Antiquities of Brentford*, Brentford: Walter Pearce 1922

Turton, Alan, *Chief Strength of the Army*, Leigh on Sea: Partisan Press undated

Wanklyn, M.D.G., and Young, P., 'A King in Search of Soldiers: Charles I in 1642. A Rejoinder', *Historical Journal*, 24 (1981)

Warner, Philip, *Famous Battles of the Midlands*, London: Osprey 1973

Warwick, Philip, *Memoires of the Reign of King Charles I*, 1701

Washbourn, John (ed), *Bibliotheca Gloucestrensis*, Gloucester: 1825

Webb, John, *Memorials of the Civil War in Herefordshire*, London: Longmans 1879

Wedgwood, C.V., *The King's Peace, 1637–1641*, London: Collins 1955

Wedgwood, C.V., *The King's War 1641–1647*, London: Collins 1958

Wedgwood, C.V., 'The Chief Passages in Middlesex', *Middlesex Local History Council Bulletin*, 14, (1962)

Wedgwood, C.V., *The Trial of Charles I*, London: Collins 1964

Wedgwood, C.V., *History and Hope: Essays on History and the English Civil War*, New York: Dutton 1989

Wicks, Alan (ed), *Bellum Civille*, Leigh-on-Sea: Partisan Press 1988

Wood, A.C. (ed), *Memorials of the Holles Family, 1493–1656, by Gervase Holles*, Camden Soc., 3rd series, LV, 1937

Wood, Andy, 'The Civil War Allegiances of the Miners of the Derbyshire 'Peak Country'', *Historical Journal*, 40 (1997)

Woolrych, Austin, *Battles of the English Civil War*, London: Batsford 1961

Woolrych, Austin, *Britain in Revolution 1625–1660*, Oxford: OUP 2002

Worden, A.B. (ed), Edmund Ludlow, *A Voyce from the Watch Tower*, Camden Soc., fourth series, 21, 1978

Worden, Blair, *Roundhead Reputations. The English Civil Wars and the Passions of Posterity*, London: Allen Lane 2001

Yonge, Charles Duke (ed), *Horace Walpole, Letters of Horace Walpole*, II, London: Fisher Unwin 1890

Young, Peter, *Edgehill 1642: The Campaign and the Battle*, Moreton-in-Marsh: Windrush 1998

List of Illustrations

10. The king levied an army during the summer of 1642 and on 22 August the royal standard was raised on the castle hill at Nottingham in windy conditions, but inauspiciously blew down that night. The raising of the standard was taken to mark the beginning of hostilities against parliament. The scene was depicted by George Cattermole, c.1865. © Simon Marsh.

11. Prince Rupert was Charles I's nephew, son of his sister Elizabeth and her husband Frederick V, Elector Palatine and briefly King of Bohemia. Rupert was vilified by the London press as a rapacious soldier who would bring the dreadful and destructive practices of the Thirty Years War into England. He commanded the royalist cavalry during the campaign which culminated in the battle at Turnham Green. © Simon Marsh.

12. Robert Devereux, 3rd Earl of Essex, by William Faithorne, 1643. He was appointed by parliament as its Lord General and commanded its army in the campaign during the autumn of 1642. Criticized for being a cautious commander, he nevertheless kept his army together after the battle of Edgehill and returned to London, achieving his objective of securing the capital's safety by successfully halting the royalist advance at the battle of Turnham Green. © Simon Marsh.

13. Robert Rich, 2nd Earl of Warwick, was appointed Lord High Admiral in March 1642 and at the outbreak of the Civil War secured the navy's adherence to parliament. He commanded the army raised to defend London during the autumn of 1642 and was one of the parliamentarian commanders at the battle of Turnham Green on 13 November, before relinquishing his command to the Earl of Essex. © Simon Marsh.

14. Philip Skippon was an experienced officer who had fought in the wars in the Low Countries. In 1639 he was appointed Captain-Leader of the Society of the Artillery Garden and in early 1642 as Sergeant Major General of the trained bands. He was responsible for organizing London's defences and commanded the trained bands at the battle of Turnham Green. Skippon was subsequently appointed as Essex's senior infantry commander. © Simon Marsh.

15. A section of Wenceslaus Hollar's 'Long View' of London from Bankside, drawn in 1647. St Paul's Cathedral dominates the skyline, with densely packed houses crowded between it and the Thames. In the foreground is the palace of the Bishops of Winchester, which was commandeered by parliament in 1642, as a prison for those suspected of supporting the king, as they attempted to secure London from subversive activities. © Jonathan Reeve JR1221b67pxvii 16001650.

16. New Palace Yard, with Westminster Hall to the left, behind which was the chamber of the House of Commons, and Whitehall Palace beyond, drawn by Wenceslaus Hollar in 1647. The yard is crowded with the coaches of the aristocracy and gentry in that part of the capital which was the focus of English politics and the centre of government. © Jonathan Reeve JR1220b67plit 16001650.

17. George, Lord Digby, after Van Dyck. Digby served as a colonel of horse at Edgehill and may have joined the royal army with reinforcements on 9 November as it advanced on London. He succeeded Lord Falkland as Secretary of State and reverted to a political role, becoming an anathema to the military commanders. © Simon Marsh.

18. Westminster from the river. After the Battle of Edgehill, Prince Rupert proposed a swift march by a mounted section of the royal army to capture Westminster, with its three key buildings that are prominent in Hollar's view: the Parliament House, Westminster Hall and St Peter's Abbey. © Jonathan Reeve JR1088b1opi116 16001650 and © JR1222b67plB 16001650.

19. Charles I on campaign, dictating instructions to Sir Edward Walker, Secretary at War, artist unknown. Walker, appointed in September 1642, accompanied the king on most of his campaigns. © Simon Marsh.

20. The first fortifications around London were erected in October and November 1642. Mount Mill was built on the north side of the City, as a circular fort with an outer line of defence consisting of angled bastions. According to an observer who walked the line of the fortifications during the spring of 1643, it was one of the first forts to

be built in the previous autumn. The windmill which gave it its name stood within the fort. © Simon Marsh.

21. Lucius Cary, 2nd Viscount Falkland, was appointed one of the two Secretaries of State by Charles I in January 1642 and accompanied the king during the campaign in the autumn of that year. He was responsible for drafting the declarations issued by the king before and after the battles at Brentford and Turnham Green. He was killed fighting with the king's cavalry at Newbury in September 1643. © Simon Marsh.

22. This contemporary depiction of the Battle of Nördlingen, fought by the French/ Swedish and Imperial armies in 1645, shows the almost chaotic scenes around the wagon train during a battle. TNA, MR 1/484 © Simon Marsh.

23. Robert Bertie, 1st Earl of Lindsey, had a long military career and was appointed Lord General of the royal army. After a disagreement with Prince Rupert concerning the battle formation that the army should adopt, he chose to fight with at the head of his regiment at the battle of Edgehill and was killed. © Simon Marsh.

24. The battle of Lens between the French and Spanish armies in 1648, with the field artillery placed between of the blocks of infantry, which consisted of musketeers and pikemen. The parliamentarian field artillery at Edgehill was deployed in a similar fashion. TNA, MR 1/486 © Simon Marsh.

25. The Savoy Palace was built in 1245 by Peter, Earl of Savoy and Richmond. In 1505 it was rebuilt and endowed by Henry VII as a hospital for poor people. When parliament urgently required a hospital for soldiers wounded at the Battle of Edgehill in October 1642, its investigations showed that the Savoy had 150 beds but only two residents, and so it was selected as Parliament's military hospital. It was probably used to treat some of the casualties from the battle of Brentford. © Jonathan Reeve JR1125b67pxlixT 16001650.

26. Richard Browne was a Londoner who was appointed captain of a troop of horse to be raised in the city in 1642. He rose though the ranks of the parliamentarian armies and was appointed Major General in 1644. Royalist writers who were sarcastic of the background of those Londoners who achieved prominence in parliament's service sneeringly described him as a 'woodmonger'. Yet Browne was knighted by Charles II at the Restoration, in May 1660, and was lord mayor in 1660–1. © Simon Marsh.

27. Plan of the western approaches to London. On reaching Colnbrook, the royalist high command decided against an advance on London along the most northern route via Uxbridge and Acton. Instead, they gathered the royal army at Hounslow Heath and moved along the Great West Road through Brentford. © Simon Marsh.

28. Windsor Castle was secured by parliamentarian forces at the beginning of the Civil War and its garrison refused to surrender when summoned by Prince Rupert. The royalists were compelled to leave it in parliamentarian hands in their rear as they marched on towards London. Charles I proposed it as a possible place where negotiations between the two sides could be held. The perspective view is by Wenceslaus Hollar. © Jonathan Reeve JR1189b67plixB 16001650.

29. Brentford is depicted on Moses Glover's plan of Isleworth Hundred of 1635. The viewpoint is from the town, looking west. Syon House can be seen on the riverside on the left of the view. Sir Richard Wynn's house is marked on the road beyond Brayneford End and before the cross-roads. Fighting there was the first engagement of the battle of Brentford. © Collection of the Duke of Northumberland.

30. Sir Richard Wynn's House, described as Little Syon House. Wynn was a courtier who held offices in the households of Charles I and Henrietta Maria. He was elected an MP for Liverpool in the Long Parliament, but did not join the king's army or support his cause. His property in Middlesex came to him through his wife Anne, daughter and co-heir of Sir Francis Darcy of Isleworth. © London Metropolitan Archives.

31. Syon House was the seat of the Earl of Northumberland, a supporter of parliament and one of the commissioners sent to negotiate with the king in November 1642. The house was captured by the royalists during their attack on Brentford and sustained

some damage in the fighting and during attacks on parliamentarian barges on the river. © Simon Marsh

32. The fifteenth-century tower of St Lawrence's church, Brentford. This is shown, topped by a spire, on Moses Glover's plan, close to the River Brent. It gave the parliamentarian defenders a vantage point, but that was of no help on the morning of the royalist attack because of the thick fog that hung over the area. © Simon Marsh.

33. John Hassall's painting of 1928 shows royalist cavalry charging across Brentford Bridge to attack an improvised parliamentarian barricade at the end of the street which ran through the town. In fact, the engagement there was between the infantry of both sides and the royalist cavalry were not engaged in that phase of the battle. © Author's collection.

34. John Lilburne fought at Brentford, where he was captured and taken to Oxford as a prisoner. He was condemned to death and reprieved only after strenuous efforts by his wife Elizabeth and parliament's threat that its forces would execute royalist prisoners in retaliation. Contemporary usages of war were clear, but it took cases such as Lilburne's for them to be adapted to the fighting in the Civil War. © Simon Marsh.

35. This account records payments to 20 officers and more than 300 soldiers of Denzil Holles's and Lord Brooke's regiments 'that were taken prisoners and stript att Brentford'. TNA, SP28/141B © Simon Marsh.

36. The open space covered by Turnham Green, Acton Green and Chiswick common field, superimposed on John Rocque's plan of 1746. Acton is at the north of the map and Chiswick is close to the River Thames. Enclosures had been created since the battle, 104 years earlier. TNA, MR1/675 © Simon Marsh.

37. The notional disposition of the two armies at Turnham Green superimposed on a twentieth-century plan, redrawn by Malcolm Dickson. © Stephen Porter.

38. In this interpretation of the battle of Turnham Green by John Hassall, painted in 1928, royalist cavalry have broken into the ranks of the parliamentarian pikemen and musketeers. In fact, the two armies did not engage in any fighting at close quarters in the way which Hassall portrays and forays by the royalist horsemen were not successful in luring the parliamentarian foot into combat. © Author's collection.

39. The allegations of barbarous practices that were directed at Prince Rupert during the campaign of 1642 continued throughout the Civil War. Here he is shown, with his dog 'Boy', prancing on horseback and firing his pistol, with Birmingham in flames in the background. Roughly eighty houses in the town were burned and some of its citizens killed when his forces captured it, less than five months after the sack of Brentford. © Simon Marsh.

40. Although the royalist march on London was halted at Turnham Green in November 1642 and the military threat receded, work on London's fortifications was continued in 1643, with more forts constructed and a continuous line of earthworks thrown up by the enthusiastic citizens. George Vertue's plan was first published in 1739 and is not entirely accurate in its depiction of the line of the defences. © Stephen Porter.

41. The campaign that culminated at Turnham Green demonstrated that the royalist armies would be unable to capture London, and so an armed uprising to seize the city was planned. This was focused around the MP and poet Edmund Waller, assisted by Nathaniel Tompkins and Richard Challoner. The plot was uncovered. Waller got away, but Tompkins and Challoner were tried and executed, in Fetter Lane. The scene on the scaffold was depicted by the Victorian painter J. Quartley. © Jonathan Reeve JR1224b40p91 16001650.

42. The memorial to the 1642 battle of Brentford was first erected in 1909 through the efforts of a local historian, Montague Sharpe, though not in its current location. It commemorates two other battles at Brentford, supposedly an opposed crossing of the Thames by Julius Caesar in 54BC and King Edmund Ironside's defeat of Cnut in 1016. Until the establishment of a battlefield trail in 2007 by the Battlefields Trust, this was the only acknowledgement of the battle in the town. © Simon Marsh.

43. Muskets being fired by a reenactor group. © Simon Marsh.

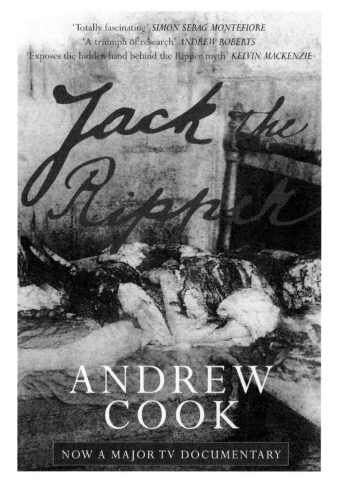

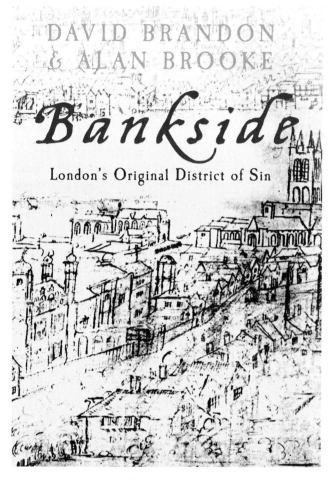

Also available from Amberley Publishing

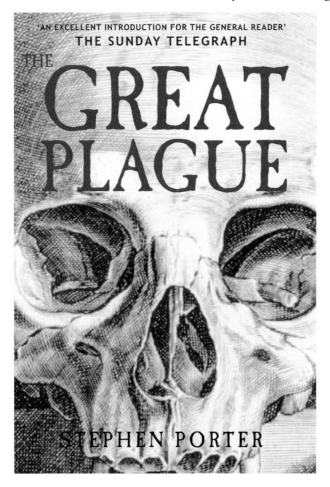

'An excellent introduction for the general reader'
THE SUNDAY TELEGRAPH

The bubonic plague epidemic which struck England in 1665-6 was responsible for the deaths of almost a third of London's population. Its sheer scale was overwhelming and it was well-recorded, featuring in the works of Pepys and Defoe and described in terrible detail in the contemporary Bills of Mortality. Stephen Porter describes the disease and how people at the time thought it was caused. He gives details of the treatments available (such as they were) and evokes its impact on the country. We will probably never know the reasons for the disappearance of the bubonic plague from England after 1665. What is clear is the fascination the subject still holds.

£12.99 Paperback
61 illustrations
192 pages
978-1-84868-087-6

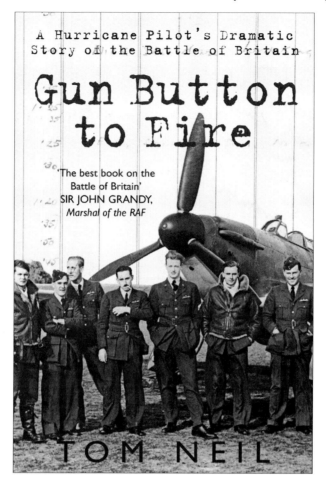

Index